SIX MONTHS TO LIVE?
I DON'T THINK SO!

Judi's Journals

Judi Seall

To Mick Collins
with my very best wishes
Judi Seall

ARTHUR H. STOCKWELL LTD
Torrs Park, Ilfracombe, Devon, EX34 8BA
Established 1898
www.ahstockwell.co.uk

British Library Cataloguing-in-Publication Data.
A catalogue record for this book is available
from the British Library.

ISBN 978-0-7223-4653-2
Printed in Great Britain by
Arthur H. Stockwell Ltd
Torrs Park   Ilfracombe
Devon EX34 8BA

DEDICATION

These journals are dedicated to the memory of:

Paul Manchip
Bryan Frost
Gary Dennis
June Mullen
Danny de Meuleneare
Joss Cleeve
Tony Phipps

My love and thanks to
my very best friend,
St Bridget

CAST LIST

Sam	My husband
Bridget	My best friend and surrogate sister
Sue C.	A very special friend
Peter	Bridget's husband and a very dear friend
Tom and Louise	Bridget's daughter and her husband
Wendy	My sister
Sue and Joe	My sister and her partner
Thalia	My best friend and surrogate sister
Linda and Joss	Good friends
Lucy	Friend and creator of 'Buddies'
Roz	Acquaintance
Jane	Acquaintance
Pam	Friend from New Zealand
Lesley and Ian	Very special friends
Charles	Acquaintance
Sarah	Very good friend and neighbour
Danny, Els and Bram	My special Belgium family
Carol	Friend
Michael	Very good friend
Bob and Deborah	Friends
Lazlo	Sam's really good friend
Hugh	Always my best friend ever
Dangerous	Obviously Dangerous Brian
Amy	My very good friend and hairdresser
John and Jenny	Friends
Nick and Dale	The gamekeeper and his wife, really good friends
Lynette	Flat-coat friend
Janet and Maurice	My cousin and her husband
Ian	My nephew
Claire and Paul	My lovely niece and her husband
Graham Cox	Good friend

Clive and Sheila	Acquaintances
Brenda	Flat-coat friend
Debbi	Indianna's other mummy
Terry	Vicar
Duncan	A and D chairman
Rusty	My chemo nurse
Chris	Friend
Jonny	Sir Jonny
Angela	Good friend
Neil	My nephew
Shirley and Stuart	Friends
Alana and Brian	Friends
Steph	Friend
Glenis	Good friend
Bettina	My 'Buddies' friend

PROLOGUE

Faced with writing this prologue and revisiting my journals has been difficult and emotional. Obviously I had put all the information in my journals at the very back of my mind and reading letters from consultants, psychologists and nurses from almost a decade ago was a huge and shocking jolt to my memory.

Diagnosed with Stage 3 non-small cell cancer, a 5.2-mm tumour in my right lung in July 2006.

With my then duties as CLA Gundog chairman at the end of July for the Game Fair, and with thousands of people 'under my umbrella', I was totally committed and just did not have time to meet with my oncologist until the latter part of August.

I did, however, with dear Bridget's help, manage to fit in MRI scans, CT scans, a lung biopsy and endless appointments before the Game Fair.

I finally met with my oncologist, instantly dubbed Captain Chemo, and any future reference to him will be just that or CC throughout.

He instantly had my attention before I could back-pedal too far and hesitate to agree to the chemo. I was told without the chemo I would be lucky to live six months – if I had the chemo then perhaps twelve to eighteen months of good-quality life – scary.

I had the chemo – it's all in here – followed by six and a half weeks of radical radiotherapy. In January 2009 after a PET scan showed mediastinal disease in my lymph nodes – I refused more chemo.

My first journal was intended to be just one for my family and friends to read after my death. That, however, did not happen, so I continued to write until 2010 and then I was surrounded, consumed, with the deaths of the people I loved and the journals came to an end.

The following pages have been meticulously typed by Jane – no mean feat reading someone else's handwriting and typing at the same time. There are no chapters, some dates, each journal given its own place.

I hope my journals, my thoughts, my treatment, my reminiscing will be of help to others who perhaps find if difficult speaking about it, to take up pen and paper and just write it all down!

Fast-forward to 2015, what have I done in those extra life years? I jumped out of a plane to raise money for The Rowans Hospice, I moved house and now live in a bungalow – phew, no more stairs – I went to Tom and Lou's wedding. I was still around to see my great nephew at just a few days old. Sam and I had a wedding blessing on our twenty-fifth anniversary – who would have thought that? I had a big party on my seventieth birthday.

My quality of life has changed, my outlook on life has changed and even after two years of appointments with my psychologist, I still wonder why and how I am still here.

I haven't been able to drive for four years and I cannot walk unaided, nerve endings are my nemesis. However, I have wonderful friends and family who drive me – mostly to the dentist – but that is another story.

I believe I owe it all to fresh air and three litres of water a day . . . . . . and the medication.

Judi Seall

JOURNAL 1

12TH JULY 2006 – 4TH JANUARY 2007

THE FIRST SIX MONTHS

12th July 2006 – I went to the Doctor's today! Just had not been feeling too great and thought perhaps it was stress-related with the lead-up to the Game Fair. Also, have been coughing up some blood, which is somewhat disconcerting. Doctor recommended blood tests and X-rays.

17th July – Had blood tests.

19th July – Went for chest X-ray and was slightly concerned when the radiographer asked to see me again for a further X-ray. I asked how long it would take for the results to reach my GP and was relieved to hear that it would take two weeks so I didn't need to make another appointment with my GP until after the Game Fair – fantastic!

20th July – The following day! Received a phone call from the nearest hospital asking me to make an appointment as a matter of some urgency for a scan. Impossible before the Game Fair so have an appointment for 1st August.

21st July – Saw my GP before surgery started. He informed me there was a large unidentified mass in my right lung with a high risk of being cancer! Immediate reaction was that Sam must not know! I needed him to start his new job at Avington as it was important to me that he was settled. We had to go and meet all the staff at Avington that evening and I could not help thinking that with all the talk of the future I would not be there.

22nd July – I told my dear friend Bridget, who I know will be strong for me, and for the first time I felt really emotional but my priorities remained the same. Sam must not know until I know a bit more and he is settled at Avington.

In the evening I went to my cousin's fiftieth wedding anniversary. Wendy, Sue and myself were bridesmaids. It was a really enjoyable evening and I was momentarily distracted. However, on the way home I did wonder if I would ever see them again and it made me feel rather subdued.

23rd July – Sam's last day at Meon Springs and I was home alone all day. I started fretting a little about the dogs and who could home them for me. Would I be able to do the shooting season? Would I be rushed into hospital?

24th July – Decidedly chipper today and spent all day at Broadlands as the run up to the Game Fair gets ever closer, so I didn't dwell on my future as there was no time.

25th July – Last minute 'at home' preparations before moving on-site tomorrow and I really do want to know the prognosis now. In a strange sort of way I feel lucky to be able to have the opportunity to put everything in order before I die. Had a long talk with Jan at the Beauty Clinic (had a spray tan!). She used to be a sister on a respiratory ward and was very knowledgeable on lung cancer and explained quite a lot to me. Actually it was good to talk to her as she is not related or particularly close and I did not feel emotional at all. She said I could go and talk to her anytime after I had been to see the consultant on 1st August and I think I would like to do that.

26th July – On-site by 9 a.m. and will stay here now until Monday 31st. Hopefully I will be so busy I won't have time to dwell on the future – or lack of it! I am quite resigned to it now and just hope everything doesn't happen too quickly as I need some time to sort things out.

Too hot! Have not had much time to reflect on what will be. I had an hour of peace before everything started 'kicking off'. PA systems in the wrong place, tents and people arriving etc. Tomorrow will be worse and the only thoughts I have are just being very aware that this could very well be my last CLA Game Fair and probably the very last time I shall see some of these people, some of whom are good friends. I shall try not to think about it and hopefully enjoy a little of what I've worked for over the past twelve months. Onwards and upwards.

27th July – My first night sleeping in the caravan and I have to say my years under canvas in the Girl Guides are long gone. I can't see me taking this up as a hobby and joining the Caravan Club! Massive thunderstorm right overhead and fitful sleep, waking with a blinding headache. Onwards and upwards.

28th July – The Anglo/Euro Challenge, followed by a barbeque at Gundog control had to be the longest, hottest day ever. Consequently a very brief entry to my diary as exhaustion set in. Plus, dogs dying from heat exhaustion and people collapsing made it a very stressy day.

29th July – The international competition got under way amidst the usual noise from the teams, who are so full of their own importance it is hard to believe. Managed to 'escape' for an hour. Then I was persuaded to go off site with a few of the team for a Chinese. I really didn't want to go, but I washed my hair and went and really enjoyed it. They were right, it did me so much good to forget everything and disappear for a while.

30th July – The last day and I already feel pretty emotional. The end of the two-day competition, get the presentation over, debrief and thank-you gifts to the 'team' and then let's see how I feel! Tuesday getting ever closer and it is now on my mind, but you know I reckon they have made a mistake and it's absolutely nothing to worry about – yeah, right! Presentation ran like clockwork, we all drank champagne until quite late and I guess that's it – over!

31st July – Clear up, pack car, go home – exhausted and wait for tomorrow's appointment and see what that brings.

It is 1.15 p.m. on Sunday 6th August and this is the very first time I have sat down with little time for myself since arriving back from the Game Fair p.m. on Monday 31st, so this week has been a complete roller coaster and this next entry will be a combination of all subsequent days.

I cannot believe just how good it feels to sit here with my feet up – ON MY OWN – luxury, at least for a minute.

Monday afternoon – I arrived home with the car jam-packed full and I did attempt to unpack some of it. Sam was here and helped me get the main things in. The dogs were mental and absolutely delighted to see me. Sorted quite a bit out, but by 5 p.m. I was completely knackered so I had a bath. What luxury after a week of cold showers in the caravan, then to sit in a proper chair and put my feet up, then my own bed – bliss!

Tuesday – The dreaded appointment with the consultant. I had built myself up for this totally thinking that I would get some answers and perhaps thinking of talking to Sam about it. How wrong could I be? Picked Bridget up and then we drove to Louise and Tom's, left the car there and got a taxi to the hospital to avoid the horrendous parking situation. Waited an hour then saw a nurse who weighed me, took some details and tested my lung functions. Back to the waiting room and another half-hour before finally seeing the consultant. Answers – no way. Scary – yes! Saw the X-ray plus one that was taken in October 2005. On that one there was absolutely no sign of the 'growth', so in nine months this has appeared. He talked a lot of jargon, Bridget took notes then he sent me for blood tests and made an appointment for me to have a CT scan on Thursday, which was forty-eight hours away – how scary was that? Suddenly remembered Pam was coming to stay so we dashed round the supermarket on the way. Oh yes, momentarily forgot that Sam started his new job today so had to keep upbeat and motivated for him, but he was fine and when he arrived home he had really enjoyed the job. It's so important that he settles there.

Wednesday – I spent the day washing, getting a room ready for Pam, unpacking the rest of the car and generally trying to organise the dogs etc., while I arranged to disappear again on Friday morning for the CT scan! They have been so good, what with me being away for a week at the Game Fair and then constantly leaving them again for wretched hospital appointments. I so want to go privately, but the consultant does not advise it as the appointments would not be so quick.

Thursday – Drove to Bridget's then she drove to yet another hospital – St Mary's – for the CT scan. It is seriously hard to believe that this has actually happened in the past three weeks. Had to drink a pint of something really disgusting before the scan, but it was over quite quickly and I was home by lunchtime. Quick turnaround and picked up Pam from Petersfield Station.

Been home one hour and just sat down and the consultant that I had seen on Tuesday PHONED to say he had the results of the scan – from four hours ago! Still had no answers but I now have to go into Queen Alexandra Hospital on Tuesday for a general anaesthetic and a 'guided CT biopsy'(?) Followed by another appointment with him on Friday where I hope to know what is going on because I am really beginning to get stressed about not knowing and keeping it all from Sam.

Had a fairly quiet evening with Pam, which was nice and we discussed what I would do if the news was bad etc. Actually it was good to talk with Pam as she was completely unemotional and straightforward to talk to.

Friday morning – Pam took some of the dogs for a walk and I started to write my thank-you letters – what a pain! Lunchtime Paula came and picked us up and we met Danny, Els and Bram in The George for lunch, which was a nice distraction. Went to bed early – absolutely shattered – my body is complaining, but I still push to my absolute limits.

Saturday – Pam got up early and went to Avington with Sam. I did a few chores here, cleaned out the chickens etc., and then I took Hamish and Fletcher and went to collect Pam from Avington before she asked too many questions!

Sunday – Pam took the dogs out for me again and I finished off writing my thank-you letters. Just need to write my report and I can, hopefully, put the Game Fair to bed. Pam decided to go back to Carol's. She flies back to New Zealand on Wednesday, so I ran her to Petersfield Station – I wonder if I will see her again. We made plans for Blenheim 2008 – will I make it? I think, although I am being quite philosophical about this, if I am to be completely honest, I really don't believe it's happening and that next Friday I will be told it's a virus!

Monday – I generally caught up and actually did the ironing and mundane chores. First day I have had to myself for ages.

Tuesday – The dreaded lung biopsy, which was not the walk in the park I thought it would be. Had a long talk with the consultant, who did not beat about the bush and referred to the problem as 'The Tumour', and explained that the biopsy was not to find out whether it was cancer but to establish what type! Stark reality, huh? I am so worried about telling Sam, I know what he is like and I just don't need him going to pieces. Amazingly, while I was in recovery I chatted to a woman for ages and it turned out that she was a Presbyterian priest – how spooky is that! She was so nice and I would like to talk to her again. I know where her little church is – Court Lane – so I really think I may try and pay her a visit. Had a long chat with Bridget on the way home and

I have asked her to be there when I tell Sam, so, hopefully, she and Pete will come up on Saturday evening with fish and chips or something and I will tell him then.

Wednesday – Have taken to my bed – completely unheard of, but I feel really grim. Didn't sleep well as I could not get comfortable where the biopsy was done, incredibly sore for such a small area and now I am coughing up blood. I guess 'The Tumour' is annoyed at having needles thrust in it. Have decided to give 'The Tumour' a name, but haven't come up with one yet, not quite the same as naming puppies! Talking of which, I am really glad that I decided not to breed any more – just imagine if I had the added worry of a litter of puppies! What about ET? Sounds good to me – will think about it and confirm later.

Sam is out doing the dogs and I am in bed! I so, so need him to be strong about this and I need him to continue at Avington. Not sure how I feel about Friday and the long-awaited prognosis! Whatever happens, having been fast-tracked for the last three weeks I want to take a deep breath and really think about things and consider my options. The NHS have really moved fast on this, but I would like to be transferred to BUPA once I get the prognosis, just couldn't bear to have to go into Queen Alexandra's Hospital. That's not snobbery; it's just that to cope with all this I need to feel happy about where I am.

Just gone back to the beginning of this – 12th July 2006 – less than a month ago! With the Game Fair in between – absolutely unbelievable.

Thursday, 10th August – Time flies when you are having fun – not! Feel OK today although still a bit sore. I have done the dogs and a few chores and much better really. Tomorrow should know the full SP and plan to tell Sam on Saturday evening. Don't want to tell him tomorrow as I am out judging for Paula all day Saturday and he will be home alone and brooding. Best to wait until I get back on Saturday and then Bridget can come up and be here when I tell him! So – that's the decision! Michael picking me up on Saturday, which is good as I don't really want to drive and will probably be knackered by the time I get home and will be quite nervous as I am planning on telling Sam then.

Friday – Today the reality has set in and I know I have Grade 3 terminal cancer. It has spread from my lungs to my lymph nodes around my chest, it is inoperable and chemotherapy will lengthen my life. I still have no clear answers on life expectancy or my options without chemotherapy and now have asked to be transferred to BUPA together with a week's breathing space to get my head around this. Have also decided that I will tell Sam this evening as I cannot leave it any longer. Told Sue this afternoon and she was reasonably stoic about the whole thing and I now wonder how the hell I will tell Wendy. Dreading telling Sam, but have spoken with Lazlo today and asked him to come and see him while I am out judging tomorrow.

Saturday, 2.15 a.m. – Told Sam and now can't sleep, worried about everything now. Worried about the impact this is going to have on everything and everybody, worried that I am not going to have enough time to do everything, worried about the dogs, field trials, picking-up, my head is all over the place. I am going to die and Sam will not be able to cope. I am thinking of refusing the chemo and staying well as long as I can, do as much as I can and then, when everything is sorted, choosing my time. Hope I have the courage. Must try and sleep, judging tomorrow. Feel like shit and hope I can get through the day.

Judging. Michael picked me up at 8.30 a.m. and it was nice not to have to drive. Sam seems pretty OK this morning, although I think he is in shock. Actually had a nice day judging. I enjoyed it, but at the end I asked all the committee to stay behind and I told them the 'news' and said it was imperative they find a replacement for me asap, although my intention, with luck, was to see this shooting season out.

All in all an incredibly emotional weekend and I really don't want to cry any more, at least for a day or two.

Bridget and Pete brought fish and chips over for supper, which was brilliant – haven't had fish and chips for years! They went home early as I was completely knackered and emotionally drained and went straight to bed.

Sunday – Waiting for Bob to come and look at the Subaru. He said they would be here at 9 a.m. and it's already 10 a.m. with absolutely no sign of them – ugh! I really, really hate it when people are late! Phoned John and Jenny as I really didn't want them to hear it second hand as once the Gundog jungle drums start beating it will spread like wildfire – bit like cancer really! Well, the upside is I won't get any more wrinkles than I have already, I won't end up in a home for the elderly and I can organise my own funeral!

It's Sue and Joe's party today, but I really don't think I can face it. Ian, Claire etc., will all be there and I really do not want to break down again. Sue phoned to say she has told Wendy. I feel guilty about not telling her myself, but I hope she will understand I just couldn't face the emotion. I will try and ring her later in the week. Fed up waiting for Bob, so going to take the dogs out now – sod it!

Monday – Why am I so exhausted? I can hardly put one foot in front of the other. I just hope I have told everyone I want to tell and I will just leave the jungle drums to do the rest. Thalia came round and the phone keeps ringing, but I am so tired! Haven't got my appointment through yet. I wonder how long I have got left. I hope there is enough time to sort everything out beforehand. I am seriously thinking of not having chemo, but how will I tell everyone? They will all want me to give it a go, but it's my body and I don't want it filled with poisons. Daft isn't it? – cancerous tumours OK, but I won't have chemicals.

Tuesday – Going to Lucy's for supper. Been at home all day, nothing much else, did housework and one or two chores. Took Kate and Fletch to vet for boosters and that's about it. Feel OK today.

Wednesday – Strange kind of day really with nothing to say about it – Wednesday just happened! Bob and Deborah came over and Dangerous stopped by for a chat – he was really sweet.

Thursday – Paula and Sue came and we stuffed and stamped 400 envelopes ready for the trials. They were brilliant. It took us two hours, but if I do it on my own it takes a week! Went to the pub afterwards and then I dashed into Petersfield to collect Rhea from the vet. She had a couple of lumps removed, but she's fine.

Having had a pretty good couple of days I'm feeling somewhat emotional tonight. Firstly, Jane phoned – she had heard 'the news' and I was a bit upset. Flowers arrived from Pam in NZ. Wendy phoned – that was a difficult one, but not as bad as I thought it would be. Sam came home and showed me a card he got from Charles, whom he had obviously been talking to. I hope Sam is OK. He seems quite strong, but I don't think he is; I think he is putting a brave face on things for my sake.

I have an unidentified back pain, like a dull ache quite high up and not a bone-type pain, so I can only assume it is my lungs. Perhaps this is the start of it? Still no appointment from the oncologist. If I don't hear anything tomorrow I will ring. My own fault really for calling a halt to the proceedings, I guess.

Friday – Really felt unwell all day today, nagging pack pain, pins and needles in my right arm and general feeling of being unwell. Rang to see when I was supposed to see the BUPA consultant and when he rang me back he told me he was going on holiday for two weeks, but if I didn't want to wait that long he could see me next Tuesday. NO, I don't want to wait that long – I want some answers and actually I really don't feel that anyone has actually told me anything positive. Because I've been sitting around all day, I have been thinking about it all day and now feel worse and have convinced myself that there is no way I will be well enough to do the shooting season or the trials. Worried also that I am going to die so quickly I won't have time to organise everything. Worried about Sam as I think he needs more time to adjust.

Tuesday is Bridget's birthday! How can I possibly expect her to come to the hospital with me on her birthday? Shit, shit, shit. E-mailed Els, and Paula said she was worried about me. Lynette phoned, Moa has had nine pups: seven dogs and two bitches. I would have had a boy but no way now! Shit, I am so angry today. I know I smoke, but so do thousands of other people who probably smoke more than me. Although I have also worked in a bar and a betting office. Pissed off today. PLUS bloody power cut from 6 p.m. to 9 p.m. so missed the *BB* final – bollocks.

Saturday – Really energised today! Went shopping, cleaned out the chucks, picked blackberries with Sam, made blackberry whisky for field trials. Will pay for this tomorrow. That's how it goes – one good day, knackered the next. Called in to see Nick and had a chat. Sue told Janet and Maurice, so spoke to Jan for about thirty minutes. I do find that I am the one comforting other people! How strange is that? Got my first BUPA appointment through with Captain Chemo next Tuesday and I want some straight answers. I know I shall get upset again, but I need to know what's what. Still determined not to have the chemo. We shall see. Phoned Roz to see if she could sort me out a cleaner. I know I shall need one pretty soon and if it's a choice I would rather use my energy picking up than hoovering.

Sunday – Felt OK a.m. then had the most excruciating pain in my back that seemed to take over my whole body and quite took my breath away. Had to stop everything and sit down. I have no idea what this pain is, it is not normal back pain and just takes over. It still lingers four hours afterwards, but not as debilitating.

Sam home again today and started pulling the ivy down at the front of the house, which drove me absolutely mad as it will now turn brown and look a complete and utter mess, as did the conservatory when he did the same to that. I do worry about how the hell he would manage without me! I really don't think he could cope! When we had the power cut the other day he didn't even know how to reset the bloody microwave! He doesn't know how to light the Rayburn and what would I get to eat if it was left to him? He said today that he hoped I would still be here in ten years' time and at the time I was quite touched – but just cannot help wondering if he would mean that if I were an invalid. Or am I being completely unreasonable?

Monday, 21st August – Appointment with my GP at 9.30 a.m. Had quite a long chat and told him I was quite concerned that Sam seemed to be withdrawing and not saying much and he said to tell him he could talk to him. Had hair done p.m. – all cut off! Just an impulse thing, but quite like it now I have had it done.

Tuesday, 22nd August – Bridget's birthday and my first appointment with the oncologist, Captain Chemo, at BUPA. Bottom line – and it's not easy to comprehend – without chemo I would deteriorate quickly and could be talking about months; with chemo (if it works) perhaps two years! I can't take it in; thought I could, but I can't. Can't believe I may not get though this shooting season – I bloody will – I will give these dogs one last season even if I just do the mornings. *Please* let me do this season, let me do Windsor, let me make sure Sam is OK.

Wednesday, 23rd August – Vet with Rhea and took Hamish for his booster. I wish I could find somewhere for Flinn. Seriously depressed today. Didn't sleep much last night, so obviously tired. I still cannot believe that I am going to deteriorate so rapidly and I would so, so like to opt out of chemo and take my chances and do the shooting season. It just seems so unfair; I just want to give the dogs (and me) this one more season. I always said I would retire after the two days at Windsor – why can't I do that?

Sam is very quiet. I am going to have a chat with him at the weekend. He must not bottle things up; he must tell me what he wants. I still have my stash of sleeping tablets and I always said if I were diagnosed with anything terminal I would make my own decision as to when and where. But – would I have the courage? How ill would I get before I made up my mind? It's quite tempting to just give in to this. I am very aware that something is going on inside my body that is alien and making me feel so tired.

This is not the first day of the rest of my life – I'm dying – that's the first time I've said that. I've just watched a programme that I recorded called *Angela's Dying Wish* and it was about a woman who was diagnosed with breast cancer and died within four and a half months. That's how quickly it happens. I'll admit that I now feel extremely frightened for the first time. With those statistics I would be lucky to make Christmas if I don't have chemo. But even if I do have chemo it may not work and there is a chance it won't work. I need to talk to someone before I crack up.

Thursday – Much better today, not as depressed. Took the dogs up to Butser Hill for a walk then started cleaning! Obsessively! Bridget came over and we talked through the chemo prospect and I know I have been absolutely against it, but it looks as though I am going to agree to give it a go. Thalia came over and left a chocolate cake on the doorstep. I am supposed to be meeting her and Linda tomorrow for shopping, but I am going to ring her and see if we can do a pub lunch instead. I just can't face trawling round the shops when it would be pointless buying anything! I should have rung her today, but I get too tired in the evenings and usually go to bed at 8.30!

Bridget has taken my dining-room curtains to be dry-cleaned. They were absolutely disgusting! She was so ashamed of them she made excuses at the counter! Have so much clearing-out before I die I think I should make a list and prioritise. Also, I should alter my will. I need to make some alterations, plus I need to sort out my funeral at some stage and perhaps I should think about paying for it now.

Phone rang several times this evening. Didn't answer it. Janet left a message, also Lesley. Will ring them both tomorrow – too tired for phone calls.

Friday – Didn't go and meet Thalia and Linda, but made arrangements to meet up for lunch next week. Took the dogs to Butser Hill again this morning – beautiful weather, could almost touch the IOW. Cleaning again – windows, floors, furniture etc. Still loads more to do. Was completely knackered by 12 noon so sat down for an hour then started again.

Bad back pain today and a cough plus a strange pain mid chest, almost like heartburn. Although I have never had heartburn, I guess that's what it's like.

The gardener's here today, BT phoned, Lesley, Bridget and some idiot about field trials. Hamish seems to be settling in and sleeping on the bed – there's a surprise!

Have had to sit down – this is when I know there is something wrong with me. Normally I would keep going and push myself to the absolute limit, but I can't do that any more. My chest feels tight, back hurts and I feel completely exhausted. SHIT!

Saturday – Next appointment with Captain Chemo 12th September and chemo the following week if I decide to go ahead. You know, I won't ask, "Why me?" I know why – smoking! Is there anything I wish I had done and haven't? God, yes! Parachute jump, seeing the primates. What have I achieved? Dunno, not much. Have I enjoyed my life? Bits of it – I regret loads of it. Sam has been home all day and I asked him to talk to me and he said he couldn't as he had not got his head around it yet. I can't handle that. I'm here on my own most of the time and it would be a comfort to know that when he is here we can have a discussion about it. The worst thing he can do is bury his head in the sand, but it looks as though that is the way it is going to go. I can't worry about Sam all the time; I need him to support me.

Sunday – Sam home again today. I was supposed to go to Edenbridge, but that all fell through. Chap was supposed to come for Subaru, but he didn't arrive! Cleaning all morning. Took the dogs to Butser Hill and the world and his wife were up there plus every breed of dog imaginable. Fletch fell in love with a boxer called Alice! Spoke to Hugh this evening and did not get emotional at all, helps to have a couple of oceans as buffers. Sam said he would clean the windows, but he didn't. Started worrying about my soul! Having always been restless, a worrier and forward-planner, I would like to be completely at rest when I die, but I have this vision of wandering around the universe and not settling. What a terrible thought. Of course, there may not be an afterlife!

Bank Holiday Monday – I was just thinking back and I know this would upset a lot of people, but I really cannot remember a time in my life when I have been truly happy. Not that complete happiness you see in people. Bridget and Pete have it and Sue and Joe have it, but I have never had it. I always seem to be searching for something and that's what is worrying about my soul because I don't think I will ever be at rest. Janet and Maurice have it.

Took the dogs to Butser again – went really early and there was no one there. Great, they just ran and ran.

Feel really tired today. Have done some of the ironing and fully intended cleaning upstairs, but just cannot face it. Thalia rang; having lunch with her and Linda on Friday. She wanted to go to Alresford, but I really couldn't be bothered – how dreadful is that? I persuaded her to meet me at The George instead.

On my mind all the time today. I guess I need something to distract my thoughts from my death!

Spoke with Graham today. I knew there was something wrong with his e-mail and I am right. Haven't heard from him since the Game Fair and I wanted to tell him myself before the Gundog jungle drums got to him.

Tuesday – Feel like shit today, breathless, tired etc. Wendy came round. Without appearing horrible I just find constant visitors a bit wearing. Why have they come? Is it because they think I will look different? Because I don't. I just wish someone would come and offer some practical help like clearing a cupboard instead of just visiting when I feel I have to entertain them and make them drinks.

Good news – Louise came and she has agreed to come and do the cleaning. Yes! Yes! She is a lovely girl and it will be so convenient with her living on the estate. Bridget has collected my curtains, bless her. She is an absolute star and I don't know what I would do without her. Took the dogs to Butser again this morning and there was absolutely no one else there. Got home at 8.15.

Wednesday, 30th August – Woke up exhausted. Slept from 9 p.m. to 6 a.m. – that's nine hours. I can't believe how tired I feel. Not to worry – onwards and upwards. Off to Butser Hill again, will write more later – possibly!

Bonus thought for the day – I won't ever have to move from Orchard Cottage now!

31st August – Mother's birthday. I just wish that when I thought of her I didn't feel so much resentment and I still blame her for making me what I am. She really was a bully when I was a child and I blame her for making me so quick-tempered then and so rebellious. I'm sure now it was just me attention- or even affection-seeking – dunno – all I remember is her shouting and hitting and the copper stick. Then as an old woman she turned into a really pathetic person and I remembered how strong she was when I was a child. You know, I really hate how I feel about her. I know I shouldn't feel like this, but I have to be honest; I can't lie and say how much I loved her and how much I miss her, because I just don't.

Drove to Thursley to meet Sue C. for a dog walk in the heather and began to regret the arrangement when I was held up at Hindhead for thirty minutes with four fretting dogs in the back and the temperature rising! However, once there we had a lovely walk and went to the pub for lunch afterwards, which was good. Knackered now so going to wash my hair and have a sit-down.

Friday – One thing to report – sold the Subaru! Yes! Yes! Had lunch with Thalia and Linda, which was nice, and did Butser with the dogs – backache, but apart from that I'm fine!

Saturday, 2nd September – Seems longer than that since 12th July, but it's not even two months! A and D (Arun and Downland) competitive training day and barbeque today. Went to help Paula.

Sarah drove me, thank goodness! It was a great day, but it made me realise just how fragile my life is at the moment because, although I hadn't really done that much all day apart from write a few certificates and drink red wine, I was completely exhausted when I got home and was in bed at 8 p.m. It has actually made me really concerned about the two-day trial at Windsor Great Park because that will be walking up and not easy, so I am now a bit scared about that, plus all my optimism about the shooting season and field trials has taken a bit of a slump – not forgetting that on top of all this I will be on chemo cycles by then and obviously will feel worse than I do now!

Sunday – Quiet day. Busy morning, but have done absolutely nothing all afternoon! Still exhausted from yesterday. Sam kept insisting that I rest, but was quite happy for me to get his lunch, hoover, make his sandwiches for tomorrow, do the washing and clean the conservatory! Perhaps that's a bit unfair – he did do the dogs for me, but he has got to realise there are numerous other chores to be done on a daily basis and he has to be able to work the washing machine etc. He hasn't got a bloody clue and can't even reprogram the microwave when we have a power cut.

Actually – last week was pretty hectic and that has probably not helped. Looking at next week, it is much quieter and I am not dashing around all over the place, so perhaps I can rest up a bit and feel better.

Monday – Nothing to write really. Felt great today and have done loads of cleaning, cooking etc.

Tuesday – Didn't sleep last night and had a rough day today. My chest feels really tight, but I still managed a hike round Butser Hill with the dogs! Clive and Sheila came round and brought me a chair for the garden that Clive had made – really kind. Wonder if I shall be here to sit in it next year. Really feel washed out today – serves me right for doing so much yesterday. This is driving me MAD. I need to get on and do things and I bloody well can't do it any more. Tell you what, I won't be able to handle this, but I do have an option. I will give the chemo a go, but if it doesn't work and the outlook is bleak and I feel my quality of life is shit, then I will use the option. Negative thoughts today.

Wednesday – Full of energy today, gardening and cooking. I will pay for this tomorrow. Butser Hill is becoming a regular routine now and the dogs are getting really fit. Saw Nick and Dale and the baby today and Nick said I could walk the dogs there, but I think my dogs would range just a bit too far and I prefer to go to Butser, where they can really let off steam. Feel OK, no tight chest – nothing. Not even too tired today, but not looking forward to the chemo starting.

Thursday – Still feel great, full of energy – Butser, made cakes, cleaned all kitchen cupboards – have they made a mistake? I'm sure there is nothing wrong with me, I feel absolutely fine. However, what will I be like when I start chemo? This is what I mean – why start chemo and make myself feel ill when I feel OK at the moment? I shall try one cycle and if I can't carry on my life as normal, I will not carry on with chemo.

Friday – Too tired to write anything today really. Have been really busy all day. Took Fletch and Cracker to visit the inmates at Westbury p.m. Sue and Joe came etc., etc., etc. Feel absolutely fine. Phoned Wendy and hope she isn't upset, but I don't want people rushing around to visit me when they don't normally. Why don't they come when I am really ill? Why don't they take me out for dinner? Being bitchy now – obviously overtired! Knew I shouldn't have written anything today.

Saturday, 9th September – This week finally caught up with me! I did, however, walk the dogs, go to Morrisons, get all the goody-bag ingredients, clean the car and clean the chickens out before I completely collapsed in the chair and fell asleep! I seem to have a new penfriend – Brenda is having chemo and has already had five cycles and seems to be coping with it and now writes to me daily! Actually, it is quite interesting to read how she reacts. No two people are the same and no two chemos are the same, but it does rather help to know someone else is in a similar situation.

Sunday – Went to country sports day at Tichborne with Sarah.

Monday – I'm home alone and busy, but feel knackered today. Seeing Captain Chemo tomorrow – dreading it as I guess he will want to get the bloody chemo sorted out – shit! I am scared about the chemo. At the moment I feel OK, not 100% but probably more OK than dozens of other people. I can still do everything – walking, cooking, housework, gardening etc. Now, if I have this bloody chemo is that all going to change? Am I going to be getting something that is going to make me feel ill? Is it worth it? Why don't I just carry on the way I am until I start feeling ill? And then . . .?

Tuesday – Consultant Day – 5.15 p.m. and just got back from seeing Captain Chemo, who has left me in no doubt that I am going to die! However, he still maintains without chemo six months or less, and with chemo two years or more. I just cannot believe he is talking about me! I look OK, feel OK, but apparently that is what happens – that is why it is called the silent killer! So – chemo starts next Tuesday and in the meantime I have to have a kidney function test as this determines the mix for the chemo, but he anticipates mine will be OK. Oh, great – my kidneys will be OK if nothing else. Blood tests on a weekly basis plus X-rays of my chest at the beginning followed by constant monitoring to see if ET has shrunk! Apart from all that, today has been OK.

Wednesday – Today I am depressed. Ninety-five per cent of the time I am pretty focused, upbeat and OK – today is a five per cent off day. Feel sorry for myself – why me? Life full of disasters. Couldn't I just end my life without all this? I must have been really bad to deserve this. Don't remember a particularly happy childhood – my mother was a bully. Two failed marriages, early hysterectomy, hip replacement – enough is enough. But no, whoever deals the cards out there hasn't finished with me. Could easily give up today!

Thursday – I got through a night out yesterday, but had to put on quite an act. In reality, though, I could not wait to get home and go to bed. I woke this morning feeling just as desperately unhappy, but forced myself to go to Butser Hill with the dogs. Didn't want to go to Hayling Island and was relieved when it pissed with rain and I had a reason to cancel. Anyway – fickle as ever – decided to go and we really had a good time. Dogs really enjoyed it and are now knackered – me too. Don't really feel too great still, but keep onwards and upwards. I hate having cancer and I hate the fact that I am going to die! Bollocks – bollocks – shit.

Friday – Had a really sweet letter from Nick which made me cry. He is such a nice guy and was a huge help to me all through the Game Fair. Still really depressed and anxious about the chemotherapy – I so do not want to have it. Had a long chat with Paula about it this morning.

Cancelled supper at Thalia's tomorrow – so antisocial, I know, but I just cannot face putting on a brave face for another evening as this week I am having one of my least brave times.

I do try and count my blessings – as I write this I am in my bedroom, the sun is shining and there are cows and calves – and a bloody great bull – outside my window. I can hear the pheasants, the birds are singing and I guess I could be stuck in a flat somewhere in the middle of a town. If I hadn't met Sam I would never have experienced shooting, field trials, judging or gundogs. I have been to some fantastic places and met some amazing people through this sport and I wouldn't have missed it for the world. I know I never wanted to move here, but I am happy I did now and I wouldn't want to end my days anywhere else.

Saturday – Didn't really have time to write anything as Bridget and Louise came over and we had a massive clearout day so

I'm too knackered to write. However, at 3 a.m. this morning (Sunday) something really weird happened! I don't normally take any notice of dreams or strange thoughts in the night, but this woke me up with a start and I can remember every detail vividly. My mother – yes, my mother – rode past the end of my bed very slowly on her bike. I know it sounds crazy, but I can still see her now and it's 10 a.m. on Sunday, I'm fully awake and have been out with the dogs. She rode past the end of my bed on her bike, basket in front, wearing her red coat and I think I shall never forget the facial expression. It wasn't a smiley, wavy, hello kind of thing; it was a sideways glance with a knowing look. That's about it. How weird is that! Is she waiting for me like some kind of preying mantis, or perhaps I'm just overtired? I don't think so. I really saw it and I am not a fanciful person.

Monday – Home all day. Didn't do much as I knew I was going to Buddies. Enjoyed it – kids were great. Home at 9 p.m. and bed.

Tuesday – BLOODY CHEMO DAY – how do I feel? Like shit. Venturing into the unknown and will take this with me to record events and how I feel. Got up at 6 a.m., took dogs on Butser, got Sam's lunch, made sure his supper was prepared, and cleaned the toilet and conservatory – will I be able to do that tomorrow?

Arrived at BUPA – Bridget brought enough food for an army – I did tell her food would probably be supplied, but you know what she's like! First to X-ray then up to my room – within five minutes. Coffee arrived and the lunch menu! Hey ho – like I will want lunch – although my friend would probably eat it! Blood test next. Nothing to do now for an hour or so – guess I may watch some television as Bridget has stolen my magazine that I bought especially on the way here. Ordered ice cream for lunch – sounds about right. I know this sounds completely selfish, and I do love Bridget dearly, but I would quite like to be on my own and have completely made my mind up that if I feel OK after this I will come on my own next week – definitely. Totally bored waiting now and none too happy!

Escaped to the garden, but they discovered I had gone and knocked on the window – shit. Got back to the room and the mixture of chemo had arrived and a very large trolley and drip thing and it all looks rather ominous. Here we go then – this is it! However, on the plus side, have told him I can't do the third cycle as I'm in Windsor for the two-day stage and he (Captain Chemo) says that is OK, so that's sorted then – hoo-bloody-ray!

That's it – first one over. Going home – watch this space; got my next four appointments.

Wednesday, 1 a.m. – Can't sleep, just so very emotional and can't stop crying. No one said this would be a side effect unless I am just so emotionally drained it's not true. My mind is working overtime thinking of planning my funeral, my head is completely spinning. Frightened to have a drink or eat anything in case I throw up. Poor dogs, will they get a walk on Butser tomorrow? Pain in my chest – fucking poison in my body. I'm not doing this any more. I was horrible to Bridget yesterday – I hope she realises I don't mean it! Just my way of coping with things, I guess. Trying to read this book by Lance Armstrong. Michael (my vet) lent it to me and said it was inspirational. Dunno really, he seems a bit up his own ass actually (not Michael – Lance Armstrong), but I'll give it a whirl, perhaps I'm judging him too soon! PLEASE LET ME SLEEP.

2 a.m. – Still awake! Got up, made peppermint tea, had a banana – hope I don't throw it up. I thought I would just crash out today and have a good sleep and sink into oblivion, but it hasn't happened. Still thinking about a service – not in church, but in the open air with the countryside I love all around – you don't have to be in church to worship and the countryside is the Creation all around us, not crammed into a tiny little church when God's country is all around and the air is fresh. Hope I can organise (my favourite word) it and perhaps my ashes can be made into cartridges or clays so that people can enjoy sending me off with a bang. I so want to go to sleep, but can feel this bloody stuff going through my veins and all round my body. My feet and legs are tingling and I have double vision. But the bonus – I seem to have stopped crying! Have pains all down my right arm. Not sure if I am supposed to get that. Have come home with all sorts of anti-sickness medication and a thermometer! If my temperature rises to 37.5 I have to call the hospital immediately and be taken in as it is life-threatening! At the moment that would be a blessing!

6.30 a.m. – What a night. Just got up and fed the dogs and feel as though I have been run over by a steamroller. Beautiful day – now am I going to be a hero and take the dogs to Butser or am I going to be sensible, go back to bed and hope the dogs will understand? You figure it out.

Thursday, 21st September – Second night without sleeping – raging headache and I have got up now and am just trying to get myself together to do the dogs. My face is bright red and swollen, my eyes are puffy, my head aches, I'm constipated – and I'm never constipated – my ears are buzzing, all my joints ache and I feel sick, but apart from that I feel fine! I cannot believe I am putting myself through this and if you asked me this morning if I am going to carry on with it then my answer would be NO.

9.30 a.m. – Just had to phone the hospital to see what headache tablets I can take and they also said I can take a sleeping tablet tonight, so I will, thank God. Bridget is going to get me some shopping – what a star she is. Still very emotional, spoken to Sue C. this morning and was tearful. Duncan phoned and I almost didn't answer the phone, but actually it was OK and managed a conversation without bursting into tears. Perhaps I will feel better later; haven't even got the energy to do my shopping online today – unbelievable.

Bridget went and got my shopping – she is such a star. Came back laden with painkillers, figs, pure yoghurts, laxatives – everything I need to hopefully make me go! She is really the most caring, thoughtful friend anyone could wish for.

Still feel grotty, but I am going to take a sleeping tablet tonight.

Done some shopping online – wore me out. PLEASE LET ME FEEL BETTER TOMORROW. PLEASE LET ME SLEEP. PLEASE LET ME GO TO THE LOO.

Friday – Slept for five hours, tried to go to the loo and it is now really hurting. Took the tablets Bridget brought me, but nothing has happened and I don't feel better. How much longer? I thought I would bounce back after a couple of days. One thing is for sure, I am not taking any more of these anti-sickness tablets. I think I would rather throw up! Actually, I don't have a headache – yet – this morning. Fed up with all this moaning and would like to write something positive, but it's not happening.

Saturday and Sunday – Too awful to write anything much. Thank God for Bridget and Tom and Louise. Had to get emergency services Saturday morning as I am so weak. Still not eating, still being sick and almost unrecognisable when I look in the mirror. Don't want anyone to visit me.

Monday – Started off wobbly, but actually improved as the day wore on. Bridget came and brought shopping. Had flowers from Sam's sister, actually washed the dogs' bedding and have it out on the line, which was a huge step for mankind as I haven't been able to lift my head for three days. Rusty phoned from BUPA – ice cubes and ice lollies – why hadn't anyone thought of that before? Brilliant anti-sickness cure although slightly too late in discovering to add to my shopping requirements with Bridget, but Carol next door had a friend coming for lunch whom she has diverted to Clanfield to purchase ice lollies. (NB, I have eaten three today!) Wendy came at lunchtime just as Bridget was trying to tempt me to eat a fish finger (or two). Anyway, to summarise the eating of the aforementioned fish fingers – Judi, one; Bridget, three; Wendy, three; and Katy (the dog), one! Amy (my hairdresser for twelve years) came p.m. with flowers and tears! Gave me a hairdo while I still have some and we have decided to shave it off if it starts falling out and put henna patterns into my scalp.

Dreading tomorrow – back there again, which does seem

rather a shame as I just started to feel OK and now they are going to start on me again. No headache or sickness today and I ate two more fish fingers and a slice of toast at teatime – big deal, huh? Have obviously cancelled picking-up on Wednesday – shit. Cancelled Buddies this evening – shit. Will I get there next week? Will I get to Macmillan Day on Friday? YES.

Tuesday, 7 a.m. – So I thought by staying awake all day yesterday and not going to bed until 8.30 p.m. and taking a sleeping pill I would sleep until at least dawn. Wrong – out for the count until 1.30 a.m. and then that was it. Up – a quarter of a cup of tea and half a digestive. Planning my funeral, deciding to write my own service – what? Yes, that's what I decided. Started another book of notes regarding the funeral and I guess I won't rest until it is sorted.

Plus – I am completely terrified about today and how I am going to feel again tomorrow and the thought of Bridget being away for a few days and losing her as my security blanket is a bit worrying. However, if I feel as bad as I did this week, at least I get one week without any treatment at all, so that's got to be a bonus and at least after today I can say I have completed the first cycle. Sam home today and tomorrow, so that's the dogs sorted, thank goodness.

9 p.m. – Well, I've done it – that's the first cycle over with, Day 1 and Day 8, so I just wait for the after-effects now. Haven't slept today, but have eaten a sandwich and a poached egg so hopefully that will stay put.

I have my supply of ice lollies ready in the freezer, plus sick wristbands, anti-sickness pills, anti-sickness suppositories, anti-constipation medicine, anti-constipation suppositories, oh yes, and a week's supply of antibiotics as my immune system is now so shot to pieces that I am really susceptible to disease and have to take my temperature on a daily basis for the next ten days! Bridget has been a star again (now dubbed my comfort blanket) and I am optimistic that I can control the symptoms over the next few days.

Sam has fitted a new battery to the car and it is ready to rumble. Tomorrow? Nah. Although if I feel OK I may just pop round at lunchtime. Let's see and let's hope that on Monday I will be there for real.

No good – *can't sleep*. Want to slip into oblivion for a few hours, but it won't happen and I'm not tearful. Got a few ginger biscuits, so will munch and write for a while.

How do you confront your own death? If I am going to die, and I am, do I want to confront it clawing and fighting or in a peaceful surrender? Am I content with my life and what I have done, or not? Basically not as I have launched myself and others around me into one traumatic experience after the other. I do believe, however, that I do hold certain beliefs and although my upbringing had organised religion growing up from my mother, Sunday school on Sunday mornings and church in the afternoon, my father was a complete atheist, so although I prayed a lot then I don't pray now. I have developed a certain mistrust of organised religion.

Having said all that, I do feel I have a capacity to be a spiritual person and hold some spiritual beliefs. If there is a spiritual God at the end of my days standing in judgement over me, I hope He doesn't say, "But you are not a Christian, so you are not going to heaven." If that happens, not only will I have been unfulfilled in life, but also in death.

Do I believe in the doctors and nurses? I believe they do everything in their power to save lives no matter what the outcome. That is belief in science, not God. Belief is one of the most valiant and long-lived human characteristics. To believe when we all know nothing can cure the briefness of life and that there is no remedy for our basic mortality, that is a form of bravery. So I have to continue this in the belief that science and not faith in God will pull me though this. Without belief we would live every day with nothing but overwhelming gloom. I know why people fear cancer; it is because it is a slow inevitable death, it is the very cynicism and loss of spirit. So I will believe.

Chemo has a cumulative effect, it fills your body with the deadliest toxins which proceed to attack not only the cancer cells but also the immune system and healthy cells. It destroys red corpuscles. I feel as though my veins are being scoured out. I know that unless the tumour (ET) and all the surrounding cells have shrunk by at least a small amount this is not going to work. Had I mentioned there is only a thirty per cent chance of reduction anyway?

Wednesday, 12.45 a.m. – Computer on – will sort out paperwork for field-trial training day. Can't sleep so no point lying here getting super-frustrated. Done all e-mails and Hawstead info – would really like three more entries just to make a decent day of it. Sleep just isn't going to happen, which will make tomorrow even more exhausting. You can feel the toxins going round the body. My body keeps tingling and just when I think it will stop it goes into spasms, so sleep is a no. Have done some work on PC, but finding it difficult to focus so will have to give up as I shall end up making all sorts of mistakes.

Got up at 6 a.m. Fed dogs then went back to bed. Phoned surgery to get some stronger sleeping tablets and my GP delivered them by hand along with his new registrar. They stayed for a half-hour chat to see how I was getting along – I was really touched.

Then, at 1.30 p.m., I decided to go and say hello to all on the shoot! Put the dogs in the car then stayed on the shoot for the afternoon. I didn't do much, but the dogs had a great time and we are now all knackered. Will pay for it tomorrow, I guess.

Haven't been sick and have eaten soup, toast, and watercress and feta salad. Have all the medications now for any eventuality, I hope, and feel more prepared for any side effects I get this week, but fingers crossed I will not feel as ill as I did last week as I would not like to lose track of time again.

Thursday, 4.30 a.m. – Took the stronger sleeping tablet at 9.30 p.m. and slipped into oblivion until 3.30 a.m. – so that was six hours. Desperately tried to go back to sleep, but as soon as I am even semi-conscious my mind starts working overtime. I gave up at 4 a.m. and made a cup or tea, so will just try and write a little, take some medication and hopefully drift off for another hour or so.

I am still reading the Lance Armstrong book that Michael lent me, but was disturbed by a few pages written about a female friend of his that had been diagnosed with lung cancer. Diagnosed in January, inoperable, chemo didn't work, she died in March. That hadn't even occurred to me before; could I really die that quickly? That is too quick. I need to organise everything. You know, I am sure that once I have everything sorted and I can tick all the boxes, I will be able to accept everything then. I must do a filing box for Sam with everything clearly labelled about banks, bills, pin numbers etc. and, of course, my funeral and my dogs. At this rate even Gary the guinea pig is going to outlive me and I never dreamt for a minute that Nymph and Rhea would outlive me.

9 p.m. – Just come to bed and have quickly looked back at my entry last Thursday as I have lost all track of time and just wanted to see if this week is better, and it is. I have eaten properly today, felt tired (but that's OK), but have actually been very busy! Washing, cleaned Gary out, did dogs. I know it's not much, but each thing at this stage is an achievement and I am beginning to accept the fact that I am ill and cannot do what I normally do. Thalia came – with flowers, prawns and salad. Bridget came with ginger tablets and liquorice and Sue C. came with sunflowers! But I didn't get to see her, she just crept in and out again and I just saw the tail end of her car going out of the drive. So, to summarise, this is a big improvement on last week, but the downside is that I will have to go through it all again on 10th October. Plan for tomorrow is to drive to Petersfield (Bridget as minder), go to the pet shop, have a cup of tea then come home. I should really be at Buddies Macmillan Day, but not allowed to subject my non-immune system to all those germs.

Still feel quite let down by the BUPA lack of aftercare and may even think about changing back to the NHS if it weren't for Bridget. They just come in and attach the bloody drip and you don't see anyone again until it is time to go home. Very disillusioned with them actually. What if it doesn't work and the chemo has no effect on ET? I could be dead in six months! So much to do, so little time.

Friday, 3.36 a.m. – Slept for five and a half hours – not bad and I may, with a bit of luck, doze off again for a while. Decided it's not much use trying to work on the computer at this hour because in the cold light of day anything I have done is just not good enough.

Jane is coming to take Fletch for a run tomorrow and my huge aim is to feel well all weekend and turn up for picking-up for the whole day on Monday. Must try and catch up with some phone calls over the weekend as it is looking as though this is going to be the best week of the twenty-one-day cycle.

6 a.m. – Sleep didn't happen again – getting up. This has definitely been my best day since the dreadful Day 1, when I was given some of the most toxic substances known to man, poisons that ravaged my body. I feel poisoned.

Cleaned the kennels, changed bedding, all washed, dried and away, cleared another two drawers out and did some paperwork. Drove to Petersfield (Bridget with me), did some shopping, came home, did dogs and got supper. Now knackered, but I'm absolutely OK. Eaten well and want to pick up on Monday. Fletch had a good time with Jane and her two dogs on Butser and I have quite made my mind up that if I feel as good as this tomorrow morning I am going to take the dogs up there myself. I have decided I must take advantage of every good day I have and push myself to the limits. If I don't do that I will never get through this. I dread 10th October – the next big whammy – and I know I may just as well draw a line through the following week.

Saturday, 6 a.m. – Actually slept rather well! Woke at my usual 2.30 a.m. and went to the loo then thought that was it and I wouldn't get back to sleep, but I did and had it not been for the most horrendous thunderstorm at 5 a.m. I think I would have slept on. Got up, though, as I knew the dogs would be completely beside themselves, but they are OK now so I have made a cup of tea and come back for an hour. Still plan on going to Butser today and I intend sorting out the field-trial training day this weekend so that, whatever happens at the next chemo session, everything will be ready.

I don't feel like the same person any more because I am now very aware that I have cancer and not only is this disease present in my body, but it also takes over my mind. Will it teach me anything? Will it be the first thing people think of when they see me? Will it be the big story or just an item mentioned now and again? People say how brave such and such a person is in their fight against cancer – I don't look at it as a fight against cancer. I don't believe that is what I am doing. I believe I am learning to live with the fact that I do have cancer. I'm not fighting it; I am just trying to keep it at bay for a while. I think it has always been there, just waiting and lurking for the opportunity to grow and it tries to do just that without making you aware of it – that's why it is called the silent killer. I think every single one of us has cancer cells just waiting around inside for their opportunity. I also think that a very high percentage of us die from something totally different without the dreaded cancer ever rearing its ugly head. It's the remaining percentage that gets it regardless of age and creed. If you are going to get it I think the cell was inside you at birth. Disregard smoking, drinking, black coffee etc., etc., etc., all those things they tell you contribute to cancer. Not very believable in babies, children and non-smoking, clean-living Catholics, is it?

I hope cancer forces me to develop a plan for living and just aim for smaller goals on a daily basis. I hope it teaches me how to cope with losing and face the fact that I cannot manage without help and to ask for it when I need it. Obviously feeling very profound this morning; probably the pouring rain beating on the bedroom window has sent me into some kind of hypnotic state!

Sunday – Actually I had quite a good day yesterday, although I now regret doing quite so much. Trouble with me is I never know when to stop. Achieved my goal of walking the dogs on Butser – they were wild and Fletcher and Flinn just took off! I knew they would always come back. Did most of the paperwork for the training day, which was good but only highlighted the fact that I have to get my ass in gear and sort the open out now. I just want it to be normal and I don't want to let anyone down. First day yesterday when I was home alone all day and fully able to cope – that's more like it. Did some washing, cooking etc. Bridget is away now until Thursday, but I hope she has a good time, very jealous of Monkey World and wish I could go with them. Still planning on picking up tomorrow, but will be sensible about it and will have a word with Chris and tell him I have no intention of being a hero and will just do what I can manage. Have developed another side effect from the poison – mouth ulcers and the corners of my mouth are cracked and sore – very attractive.

8.30 p.m. – Had a really busy day. Car is ready for picking-up tomorrow although the weather forecast is still shit. I'm still going although if it is really bad and I don't feel great I won't be a hero, I will come home.

Cleaned out chucks and Gary the guinea pig and tidied up my dog-food shed as I have a delivery on Tuesday. Made a cake. It's like I'm preparing for a siege or something, but I am so aware that my next bout of chemo will put me out of action for another week and I want to be prepared this time.

Sue and Joe came and brought chocolates from Spain, perfume and ice lollies. I have a vast selection in the freezer now and am pretty much addicted to at least two a day. Amy texted and she is coming to give me a blow-dry at 4 p.m. tomorrow – looking forward to that!

Monday, 4 a.m. – Can't sleep. I think if I'm honest I am a bit nervous about picking up today. Stupid really, something that is just so much part of my life and I'm nervous. I think I am just worried about my body and its capabilities. I really want to do the whole day as I thought I would take Fletch, Katy and Tess this morning then come back at lunchtime and leave them behind and take Flinn and Nymph with me. We'll see.

9 p.m. – Did the whole day – it pissed with rain non-stop and I got through three coats and three pairs of gloves. Brought Katy, Fletch and Tess home and left them with jackets on at home and took Nymph, Rhea and Flinn back p.m. for one drive. Very tired and bad-tempered and, in fact, not sure that I haven't got a temperature, but I'm not going to take it! Hopefully I will get a good night's sleep and feel OK tomorrow. I did enjoy being there and seeing everyone – it was great.

Another hospital appointment tomorrow – kidney function test, which involves a radioactive injection and three blood tests spread over six hours – whoopee doo! So looking forward to it!

Tuesday, 3rd October, 6.30 a.m. – Just made a cup of tea, fed the dogs and come back to bed. No apparent after-effects from being out in the rain all day yesterday and I slept quite well. Now washing and drying everything ready for Friday – I'm going again!

Not looking forward to the kidney function test much today and the injection of radioactivity! Poignant thought for today because although I am not consciously thinking about dying of cancer every waking moment, I quite obviously am. Quite a contradiction, but it is the first thing that springs to mind as soon as I open my eyes. The one good thing about knowing you are going to die is just that. There is no uncertainty. I won't have a stroke and be debilitated that way; I won't have a heart attack and end up not functioning; I won't get Parkinson's or Alzheimer's; I won't end up in a care home having my nappies changed waiting for God. So in a very positive way I hope I get another couple of years. I would like to go to Blenheim with Paula in July 2008 and I'm actually wondering if I could possibly organise some kind of holiday with Sam before I die, but I would need someone to move in here – Wendy? He is seventy in March – perhaps we could go somewhere with John and Jenny? Just a thought – then I could die. But first things first, let's get the shooting season over first.

9 p.m. – Very stressful day. Sue dropped me off at the hospital, met Wendy there and the day was horrendous and I had been quite enjoying this week! Arms bruised with injections, blood tests, needles – it is becoming increasingly difficult for them to find a good vein to draw blood from.

During the two-hour wait between blood tests Wendy and I found the Macmillan day centre – what an amazing place. Quiet, restful, charming people, but again reality hit me. The charity I had helped fundraise for was now going to be part of my future. Having picked up (and read) some of their information leaflets the harsh reality of my death has hit me fair and square between the eyes again today and consequently (once more) this evening I am emotional and depressed.

Good news today, though – Claire phoned Wendy when we got home to tell her the news that she was going to be induced to have her baby at 10 a.m. on Sunday. So this time next week I should be a great-aunt and I am happy that I shall be around for a while to see the new baby at least start to grow up.

Wednesday, 4 a.m. – Made a cup of tea and came back to bed. One of those nights when it just keeps playing on my mind. Cannot believe that I could be eligible for a Disability Living Allowance and a Carer's Allowance. Would Bridget be prepared (or physically fit enough) to take that on? Would Pete be eligible for that if he left work? Could Bridget cope with us both?

Sue C. coming today and we are going to take the dogs to Butser and then go for lunch – fat chips at the Thomas Lord. Then I have made a doctor's appointment for 3.30 p.m. and want to make absolutely sure that I have enough medication to see me over the next cycle. Sue will cheer me up and make me snap out of it, that's for sure.

Spoke with Annette last night and hopefully have persuaded her to do the training day and then with a bit of luck persuade her to stay for another year just until the A and D has got used to losing me and the complete reshuffle that will inevitably follow.

I have really started to become bad-tempered with the people that care about me and I honestly don't mean it. One minute I'm OK and the next I am snapping at someone, then I end up by thanking for help and apologising for being hateful at the same time. I can only put it down to hating the fact that I am losing control of my life.

I have decided to get a box – a pretty one – and start to leave things in it for people to read when I have gone. Is it too early to start doing that sort of thing? Still haven't sorted the funeral arrangements or contacted my solicitor about my will. Must do that. Had a really nice walk on Butser with Sue and Surrey dogs then we went for lunch at The George – really nice to see her.

9 p.m. – Feel knackered and emotional. Very strange visit to the surgery. I was told on arrival to go straight through as my GP had left a message to tell me to go straight in. Always have to wait, normally. I would have liked normally! She wanted to tell me how shocked and sorry she was to hear about the diagnosis and I really didn't want any sympathy. She picked the phone up while I was there and told the pharmacist to put a flu jab in the fridge with my name on it as soon as they arrived. I told her that I had come to get some medication as backup to cover any eventuality after chemo next week. I gave her a list of what I wanted and she just typed it up – have just looked at the prescription again and it's repeated for three months so she obviously anticipates I will be here that long at least. She then told me not to come to the surgery again as there were too many germs and anything I needed they would bring to me. I was not allowed to sit in reception to wait for my prescription; the pharmacist brought it in for me. ANYONE WOULD THINK I WAS FUCKING DYING! I know she was trying to be kind, but that visit made me think I probably only have a couple of weeks left. No one could ask for nicer doctors, I really like them both, but today I didn't feel normal and I want to feel normal. Tried to phone the Petersfield Cancer Support Group – went through to answerphone so left a message, but no one has called back. Tried to contact Age Concern as I want to know about their funeral plan – same thing, answerphone.

Bridget is back tomorrow – don't tell her, but I've really missed her!

Thursday, 5 a.m. – Splitting headache so a cup of tea (still don't want coffee) and some ginger nuts(?), which I don't normally like, and some headache tablets were called for. The dogs are getting quite used to me wandering about in the middle of the night and don't rush up any more, just stay in their beds, which is good. I have a few priorities on my mind – I must get my funeral organised, see the vicar, make sure it is all OK with Bill re Mascombe and I'm going to ask Carol to do the catering! I must get all these trials completely ready to rumble and I am contemplating asking Pauline to take all the phone calls, changing runs etc. I must write all my letters and leave them in a box. I must sort out individual gifts and box them as well. Then if I have time, sort the rest of my clothes, artwork etc. out. Plus, must do a little filing box for Sam with everything ready. My GP has put me in panic mode and made me wonder just how long I have left now.

Staying fairly quietly at home today and I have A and D meeting tonight and I will be knackered, and I'm picking up again tomorrow so will really try and rest as much as possible today. Sarah picking me up, but also Duncan phoned and offered me a lift, Michael phoned and offered me a lift and also Sue – really sweet.

Wrote to my solicitor today to sort out changing my will, so I can tick that box. Also started writing my letters and putting them in a box. Plus, phoned and requested funeral plan to be sent and also getting Disability Living Allowance information pack sent so have ticked a few boxes today. Phoned Petersfield Cancer Support Group (again) and left another message, but they still haven't got back to me. Phoned Macmillan centre and left a message and they still haven't got back to me – hmmm! Perhaps

Bridget and I can drop in there one day – might be easier than constantly phoning.

Friday, 6.30 a.m. – Meeting went OK, but completely wiped me out. Had one glass of red wine and have woken with the headache from hell. Have fed dogs and made tea, so will just stay in bed until I feel a bit better as the plan was to go picking up! Have made the lads a chocolate cake. I have been voted up as chairwoman when I throw in the towel for field trials. I tried to explain that I may not even make the AGM, but they weren't having it so I'll just run with it and see what happens.

Made it picking up and the weather was horrendous, but I am glad I went. Jane was there and it was good to see her – hadn't seen her in ages. All dogs went – Katy, Fletch and Tess a.m., Flinn, Nymph and Rhea p.m. Claire phoned, excited and scared about Sunday – hope it all goes well for her. Great-Aunt Judith – wow!

Saturday – Hopefully a quiet day. I need to tidy the car up from yesterday and go to the post office and perhaps sort out all the stuff for the training day on the 21st. I will organise the cremation and get Bill's permission for an outside service at Mascombe, and once I have filled in the form for the funeral plan that will be another job sorted.

Dreading next Tuesday and asking Captain bloody Chemo if I can postpone the next cycle and I guess what I am dreading is his answer and then the ongoing realisation that I will not make Windsor. My thoughts on that at the moment are perhaps Pauline would go up on the Sunday, stay at the hotel on Sunday night and start the trial off on Monday, and perhaps Sarah could pick me up and take me there on Monday. I've got to have some kind of backup plan. Must see if someone can run those signs up to Windsor for me before the trial and I must phone John to see if I can perhaps take a vehicle round with me, which I know is quite unorthodox but hopefully Her Majesty won't mind. At least it won't be the turquoise ornament as John is taking me up there.

4.30 p.m. – Actually done far too much today. Cleaned car, washed dog beds, cooking, paperwork and I definitely feel frazzled. Just taken temperature and it is high, but I'm not going to tell anyone but just hope it drops if I rest. I have another side effect and the only way I can describe it is nappy rash – my bum feels as though it is on fire! Let's just hope it's the badness coming out. Good news: spoke to Pauline and she is definitely going to take over as field-trial secretary at the end of the season. I am so pleased, she will be great.

Sunday – Going to attempt not to do so much today although my intention is to take the dogs to Butser early. Bridget is coming after church and then, although I have quite a few trial phone calls to make and a little paperwork and washing, I intend having a rest this p.m., so we shall see how that pans out. Claire's baby is being induced today – keep fingers crossed.

I'm trying to get everything sorted before next Tuesday's chemo so that I'm not fretting about things, but there is so much to do that I won't be able to. I hate being ill, I cannot accept it. Ninety per cent of the time it is such a surreal feeling as I carry on doing normal things, but then that ten per cent when I have to ask for help, when I know I cannot go out for an evening without getting completely drained, when I do everything in slow motion, when I have to sit on the bed to do a simple chore like changing the sheets. I know that I am gradually going to die and I really do wish that people wouldn't say, "Well, you never know, you will probably outlive all of us." I won't – I just know I won't. I'm sure Sam hasn't accepted it although he does do the most extraordinary caring things these days. He won't manage without me and I am quite worried about him. I just wish he would have a conversation with me about the funeral etc., but he won't so I am going to have to do it and just leave everything ready for him.

8 p.m. – Still no baby – Wendy has phoned a couple of times, but at 6.30 p.m. there had just been a couple of twinges. Very tired, so bed at 8 p.m. Done loads today.

Monday, 9th October, 6 a.m. – Have fed dogs and checked messages. Nothing from Wendy about Claire yet. Bet it has been a long night for Claire and Paul. Should hear something today. Going to go into Petersfield today, but won't tell Bridget or she will insist on driving over and coming with me and there really is no need.

Must also speak to Bridget to arrange a visit with the vicar to get this service in place and make sure it is OK to have it in a field.

It's Louise's birthday on Thursday and I have given Bridget the Jerusalem cross and chain that I bought in Jerusalem to give to her. Have decided to do that at Christmas, give each family member a piece of my jewellery. That will give me some pleasure to know that I have actually chosen something for them.

Tomorrow looms ever closer – please don't let it be as bad as the last time.

CLAIRE HAS HAD A BABY BOY and tonight that is all that matters. God Bless them and I hope Claire, Paul and the baby have long and happy lives.

Tuesday, 10th – Chemo day! Still don't know how much the baby boy weighed and not sure what he will be called, but I think it will be Will or Henry – personally, I like Henry.

I'm going to be positive today and keep on top of this bloody chemo. Will start taking the laxative as soon as I get home tonight and will keep up the sick pills. If it turns out OK then I will have the third cycle before Windsor.

Sorted out my funeral plan yesterday and also made arrangements with Bill for Mascombe and Carol for the catering. Plus have almost finished alterations to my will. I am in a position to actually give various items to people, especially my jewellery, as I intend giving some away for Christmas presents. Have chosen my hymns etc.

Why can't I just die and leave all this for other people to arrange? I just can't, I need to do this. I need to know that Sam will have everything done for him and that all the decisions are mine. Control freak until the end, I guess. Lynette keeps surprising me with her concern. She phoned last night and was talking for half an hour or more, she even offered to come and get Fletcher and Katy and take them home with her, groom them and then take them back. So very thoughtful, but out of the question. I may phone her later this week to see when she could fit them in and I feel sure Sue C. would take me over, then we could have some lunch and go and collect them.

Wednesday, 2.45 a.m. – Slept from 9 p.m., so that is five hours. Thunderstorm woke me up and now I am fretting about the dogs. Yesterday's chemo was just as awful, but I was not so stressed and it all went smoothly this time without me throwing any major tantrums. Had my X-ray and was scanned to see if ET (the tumour) had shrunk as that is what everyone is aiming for. Frankly as far as I was concerned there wasn't a shit's worth of difference, but Captain Chemo convinced Bridget that it didn't come as far over one of my ribs as it had. Bridget then, in turn, convinced Sue, who called in to see us, and also Sam when we got home. So they are all convinced it's working and obviously want me to carry on. I think I might take them along to the vet next time I go and we can have a good look at them then.

Claire still in hospital, but there are no problems and the baby is perfectly normal and to be called William Paul, so that's his name, and he weighed 7 lb 9 oz and was born at nine minutes past seven on 9th October. I really hope I am going to see them both soon.

Just looked back at this time three weeks ago. I was emotional and really upset all night after the first chemo so, as I am feeling very calm about not sleeping, I think it is looking more positive this time. Let's hope so. Bridget was an absolute star again yesterday and brings everything in her vast handbag – a bit like Mary Poppins. Yesterday she had sweets (a selection), Quavers, ginger biscuits and apples just in case I fancied anything – bless. It was good that Sue called in; it made the time go quicker and gave Bridget someone else to talk to. She may come next week as well.

Thursday – Just checked on the entry I made on the same day of the first cycle where I had not slept, raging headache etc. Somewhat of an improvement, I think. Let's hope so and then I can get on track for Windsor. I have no headache (yet), slept reasonably well (hoorah for the sleeping tablets), woke at 3 a.m. then did manage to doze until 5.30 a.m. so that's the best yet. Then I have to take a tablet without food, wait half an hour then get up, feed the dogs, make a cup of tea with some biscuits and take the two tablets I have to take with food. As food is a bit of a problem at the moment, I find two ginger biscuits – dunked, of course – are about all I can manage. These are the tablets that make my face bright red and my eyes all puffy – very attractive. Then I have to take 20 ml of liquid to attempt to relieve the constipation caused by the anti-sickness pills and my steroids have been doubled to counteract the sickness. Haven't finished yet! Then I have to stick a suppository up my bum – also for anti-sickness – and I have another one of those mid morning for another reason – to help with the constipation which is caused by the chemo. Just thought I would share all that with you and this is the person that used to take a cod liver oil tablet, evening primrose oil and a vitamin C – a few Nurofen painkillers here and there if the joints were playing up.

This house is beginning to look like a bloody pharmacy and it is slightly reminiscent of my parents, who always seemed to have boxes and packets of medication packed to the rafters in their bedroom. Pills for this, potions for that. Well, I find it extremely irritating (well I would) to try and remember what time and what tablet. I guess as long as I don't eat one of the ones I am supposed to shove up my bum I will be OK-ish!

Bridget will be here today. I didn't see her yesterday as Sam was here all day, so she had the whole day off! She is absolutely the very best friend anyone could have and I really don't deserve her. She has so many health issues of her own and is in constant pain and there is also the constant worry concerning Pete's Parkinson's, which worsens by the day. Now when she is thinking of moving she will need help herself and I just hope I am fit enough to help her. Sam thinks she is just the best person in the world and so do I.

Haven't heard how young William Paul is today. I didn't phone yesterday, but I will call today. Thought I might get him some Premium Bonds. Think I will go on the hill with the dogs this morning. As soon as Sam disappears down the road I'll be up and back before anyone can blink. The dogs need to go, they haven't been since Monday.

Friday, 6 a.m. – Had to get up to go to the loo – thank you, God. Feeling a bit more positive that I shall make it to Windsor now if I improve like this. Did absolutely far too much yesterday, so I'm completely wiped out and overtired; consequently did not sleep as well, but I did manage a few hours!

Claire called me yesterday before I had a chance to call her and they had a few problems with Just William on his first night at home, which basically boiled down to the fact that the poor child was starving and Claire's milk wasn't coming – all sorted now so hopefully plain sailing from now on. Great-Aunt Susan obviously visited (before me – bitch) and took a lovely photo of him and sent it to me on my phone. Plan is that Wendy is going to pick me up on Sunday, then Bridget and we can go and see him then. Bridget arrived yesterday with soup, something for Sam's supper, juice for me in her 'Mary Poppins' sack. Sometimes I fully expect her to arrive on the doorstep under an open umbrella, dropping from the sky! I absolutely love her and no one could have a more loyal, caring friend and I'm sure I don't deserve her.

Paula came and took everything I had prepared for the training day at Hawstead Farm including the signs, so all I have to worry about are the cakes and all my paperwork. Hopefully Sarah will be able to give me a lift. Wendy called at the same time to update me on the news of William Paul, but I already knew! So all these visitors at once kind of wore me out a bit, but it was really lovely to see them.

Finished altering my will and sorted out a filing system for Sam and it is all in one place now so he really cannot go wrong.

Funeral is all sorted now and I just need to write down what I would like for the order of service and that should be it. Sam has no idea about it and he won't discuss it with me, but Bridget has told him I should be allowed to do what I want and he must go along with it. Actually I'm a bit pissed off that I won't be there now – well, I suppose I will be in a way. Must tell Sue C. about Paula's plans for the terrier wreath. It was bad enough when she wanted my Daubery boots, but now she wants a large flower wreath with the word 'Terrier' depicted. That's because I always say she is just like my little terrier.

Think it may be a bit hectic today. Lou is coming to do the cleaning and Sue and Joe are coming to do the garden! Better get up to Butser then into Waitrose before anyone realises I've been out.

Saturday, 5 a.m. – Really bad night. Went to bed at 8 p.m. and slept until 2 a.m. and that was it. Completely my own fault, I just don't seem to get the hang of this rest thing and 'don't be a hero' thing. I just cannot sit and do nothing and when the sun is shining I can't go to bed. Anyway, having been to Butser with the dogs, which was OK and not too tiring, I then drove to Petersfield, paid credit card, did some shopping, walked round to the pet shop, carried that back to the car, then did Waitrose, and it all takes me twice as long as it used to. Came home thinking I wouldn't be discovered and Louise had come in early to do the cleaning! Unpacked car, put it all away, washed the dog beds and cleaned Gary the guinea pig out. Louise went home. I sat down for an hour then Sue arrived to do the garden! By the time Sam came home I was too tired to eat, speak or watch television, so came to bed!

Bridget rang to see if I wanted any shopping and I did not dare tell her I had been and got some! Shouldn't really drive while I am on these tablets – why do I do it? I am so fed up with feeling ill. This is not me; it must be another person. I cannot bear not being in control of my own life and really do not feel I am mentally able to just continue to deteriorate until I become so dependent on other people it will be intolerable.

Know what? I will not get to that stage; I will try and find out about voluntary euthanasia in Switzerland or something.

On a lighter note – I have been! That's a weight off my mind because that was a huge problem after the first cycle. The liquid stuff I have to take to make this happen is absolutely vile – slimy and vile – but if that's the price to pay for a number two then so be it.

Claire and Paul still struggling to get into a new routine with young William. I am going to see him tomorrow. Didn't realise they didn't have a dishwasher; may ask Sue if she wants to go halves on one for them.

Let's hope today improves – hope so as this time in three weeks I should be going to Windsor. Must make a mental note to STOP MOANING! THINK POSITIVE! You haven't thrown up for days! You can do it! Picking up on Monday – absolutely. Hawstead on Saturday – without a doubt. Chemo on Tuesday, though – shit, shit, shit. Bridget keeps telling me about my language, can't help it, just get angry.

Living here there are some of my very favourite sounds. When I am lying in bed I have the sound of the pheasants going up to roost in the early evening, the owls at dusk and again in the early morning, the birds in the morning, badgers and foxes. I am so very glad I have spent all these years in the country, no traffic sounds or fumes. It is a long time now since I lived on the outskirts of a town and I thank God I don't live in one now. Today at 6.47 a.m. the birds are twittering, although nowhere near as deafening as in the spring and summer; you can't sleep through the dawn chorus then. The cattle are outside my bedroom window munching on the grass (and probably the hedge). Not quite light yet so no partridges or pheasants are down from the roost yet, but there will be soon. Rabbits everywhere this morning; the little copse must be full of their burrows. No deer out there today, but it is quite normal to see them. Just heard the first 'cock' and they will be out and about soon.

Sunday, 6 a.m. – Sam is going fishing with Lazlo today and I have just made him a cup of tea. I am supposed to be driving to Bridget's house to pick her up to go and see William, but I think that may have been cocked up slightly and she may have to come here and get me instead. Because I don't think I dare drive that far! Took a 7.5-mg sleeping tablet at 8.30 p.m. last night – slept until 12.30 a.m., got frustrated with waking up and took another one so now I feel as though I am on another planet. Not supposed to leave until 10 a.m., so I will see how I feel then. My not-sleeping routine is really beginning to get me down; I can't even nod off in the chair any more! Did loads of work for Windsor on the PC yesterday, hosed out kennels, did some gardening, but still no sleep.

Bridget and Louise came round bearing gifts and nibbles as usual. Louise was really pleased with her Jerusalem necklace that I gave her for her birthday; glad I decided to do that. If she had received it when I was dead I would never have known that she was pleased with it. Pam phoned from NZ. It was great to hear from her and we had a long chat. She was wearing her Meon Springs T-shirt in a store and someone asked her if she worked at a fishery! Wish she lived closer.

This ET, this tumour – strange that I don't cough or cough up blood or anything, don't you think? It just stays there invading my body, quietly killing me and I just don't know it's there. Well, that's not strictly true; having the poisonous chemo certainly makes me very aware that something dreadful is happening to me and when I look in the mirror and see how drained and old I look, it is very scary. My skin is like paper, like an eighty-year-old's. Sometimes I find it difficult to get about; other times I am quite perky. I cannot come to terms with being unable to rush here, there and everywhere any more. The slightest added exertion (like driving to Waitrose) is a huge task.

Planning on taking the dogs picking up tomorrow, but if I am too exhausted by lunchtime I will come home. Bonus point, I couldn't even contemplate picking-up on the Monday following the first chemo. Not going to take any sick pills today – why not? Because they make me feel bloody sick!

Monday, 6 a.m. – Blinding migraine in the night and I now fully accept that I cannot drive very far. Bridget and I went to see William yesterday and I insisted on driving as it wasn't too far, but it was obviously too much for me. I also did a bit of shopping at Morrisons and just a little gardening in the afternoon and I was wiped out. I cannot believe how weak I am and I am now seriously worried about Windsor. Even if I get there and manage to get through the days, I won't be able to stay up and eat with the judges I will be so exhausted. I planned on picking up today, but that is looking doubtful at the moment. My head aches, I am shivering, my hands are shaking and I have mouth ulcers. Apart from that I feel great!

William is absolutely gorgeous – the image of Paul and they are so proud of him. Still having problems with him at night, but they have cracked the daytime routine and everything is calm and serene during the day. I held him for ages. So very pleased that I am still around to be a part of this huge occasion. They are going to make amazing parents and I am very proud to be Great-Aunt Judith (GAJ for short). Really cheered me up to see them so happy.

I haven't said this to anyone, but I don't think this chemo is working! I am getting worse not better. Every little task is an effort and I can see how easy it would be just to slide down that slippery slope of despair and non-existence. I guess I am fortunate to have the stimulation of the dogs, which forces me to do things – walks, wash beds, feeds etc. I also have the added motivation of the shooting season and the trials. I do confess, though, much as I have planned and looked forward to Windsor, I shall be so very, very glad when it is over and out of the way. I did say I was going to stop moaning, but actually it isn't moaning. I can't say a lot of these things out loud and it does help to write it all down. I feel as though I have said it then and it makes me feel better.

Sam's (bless him) quote of the week:

ME: Just look at me, I cannot believe this is what I have come to.
SAM: Don't keep putting yourself down – you are run-down.

RUN-DOWN? I feel as though I have been run over by a steamroller! Does he really understand that I am truly dying? Is he really thinking that I may get better? Because I won't and that's not me being defeatist; I am being realistic, we just don't know how long. Scares me how it's going to happen. Did have some thoughts about voluntary euthanasia in Switzerland (I know, I watch too much television).

Tuesday, 4.40 a.m. – Went picking up yesterday! In the morning I was absolutely frozen (no immune system). Everyone was walking round in shirt sleeves and I looked like the Michelin man! I had a T-shirt, roll-neck, one pull-on fleece, one zip fleece and a thick deer-hunter coat, a scarf, gloves and my hood up! However, the mist did eventually clear and the sun came out and I managed to shed a layer or two. Thoroughly enjoyed the day even though I struggled to walk on occasions and this morning my hips are quite painful, but as it is a chemo day I'm sure I will forget about the hips quite soon! Katy, Fletch and Tess had a great morning and then I swapped over and gave Flinn, Nymph and Rhea a run out in the afternoon. Poor little Rhea really isn't up to it any more, but she enjoyed her run out. She struggles now and would never do more than one drive. Nymph isn't much better, but she's a tough old bird (bit like me), so she keeps going but I can't see either of them out on the pheasant drives. Flinn improves every time I take him out and I am really glad I didn't let him go. If Sam had just given him a bit more time he would be a great dog. He doesn't bark at people any more and I actually like taking him. If only I could get over this problem of him bringing the birds back when there are other dogs around. I am actually feeling quite confident that I could rehome him with the right person now. So, all in all, had a good day. Then as an added extra Amy came and did my hair for me on her way home from work. I have got some great friends. Amy is not just my hairdresser, she is also a friend now.

Rent-a-crowd is coming to chemo today! Bridget, Sue and Thalia are coming. That should make the time go quickly –

wonder what Bridget will have in the Mary Poppins bag this week?

Wednesday, 18th October, 4.30 a.m. – Had second cycle of chemo, but yesterday actually wasn't all about me and the chemo for a change. The day started off badly with Bridget ringing to say she had really hurt her bad shoulder, the one she is in constant pain with anyway, and that she would be unable to drive to chemo. So much wrapped up in myself I have started to forget about other people. Pete (bless him) offered to drive us there and drop us off in Havant (at Waitrose), then we got a taxi to BUPA and Louise (bless) came and collected us straight from work p.m. so that was sorted. Bridget should have been resting; I guess she did most of the afternoon, but she still looked drawn and in pain. Honestly, the three of us in the car, Pete with Parkinson's, Bridget unable to move her head and me with terminal lung cancer – put us all together and you would get a good one!

Before all of this I get a text message from Sue (my sister, who had planned on being rent-a-crowd for BUPA) to say she wouldn't be able to come today as she was in hospital with a suspected bleed on her brain! That threw me into a complete state of panic and I had to be satisfied with a couple of texts she sent me from her hospital bed. Basically, she has been suffering with mega headaches for eight days with pain relief having no effect. They wanted to do a CT scan on her brain, followed by a lumbar puncture to see what was going on. Finally got hold of Joe's mobile and spoke with him, and she had been in there since Monday night and not yesterday a.m. as I had assumed. I texted Wendy to let her know what I knew and then Sue phoned me at BUPA to put me in the picture. At 3.30 p.m. she had been in there twenty-four hours, but still no tests done. The only consolation there is that had it been life-threatening they would have moved a bit faster. Last message I got was 8 p.m. last night and they were keeping her in again last night.

My support group are dropping like flies! Only Bridget and myself at BUPA, and then Thalia came for a couple of hours after the dentist – it was good to see her. Had a message from Claire and Paul. When I saw them on Sunday I mentioned that they could do with a dishwasher and that Auntie Sue and I would buy them one if they could fit it in. I think they are quite keen! Paul has already chosen one and sent me details and price and they have a plumber coming in today to see if it is feasible. Claire tells me that Paul (bless him) isn't the best at DIY. Very willing, but the end result can be disastrous. So I suggested they took professional advice (price is going up!).

So, on with today. I have promised to take it easy today as I am home alone and it's the day after chemo, but I am more concerned about my sick friend and sister.

6.30 a.m. – Just taken Sam a cup of tea and made myself some toast. Forgot to mention that I had quite a long chat with Liz yesterday – one of my nurses at BUPA. Funny thing is although I fully accept that I have terminal cancer, and whatever happens I will not be cured, I cannot accept the uncertainty of not knowing when. I don't think I am afraid to die; I just want to know what happens next. When will it happen? She just tells me that everyone is different, but the reality is that I could go though this chemo shit and it may not work so I will still die within the next six months. Then of course I could defy all the odds and go on for another few years. Apparently if I get pain then I get pain relief. The most likely scenario is that I won't be able to breathe so will then be hitched up to bloody oxygen! Me – that walks miles and always on the run – I don't think I could face that. I always said that if I was diagnosed with anything terminal I would take my entire stash of sleeping tablets. Now there are quite a lot of factors still in favour of that idea and I really think that once I had set everything in order I could do it. I think although it would be a huge shock for everyone it would at least save them having to suffer and watch me suffer. The only thing that worries me, and this is going to sound stupid, is *my soul*. If I commit suicide it is a sin in the eyes of the law and the Church, so what would happen to my soul? Having always been such a restless person, just imagine if there truly is a life hereafter and my soul is unable to go one way or the other and finally settle and I end up in limbo for eternity. Never discussed this with anyone before, but I think I would like to go and meet that lady who was a vicar when I was in St Mary's Hospital – I may see if Bridget is up for that.

Thursday, 4.30 a.m. – Slept for three hours, then another two and a half, then tried to doze but finally gave up and made a cup of tea. Been persisting with rain and gales all night so not sure if we shall make Butser this morning. Would like to as the dogs would settle when I go for my appointment at Macmillan today. Was quite busy all day yesterday. I do try to rest, but I am so hyper all the time it is impossible to sleep during the day; I do at least try and put my feet up for an hour or so.

Sue is still in hospital, CT scan on brain was clear so no brain bleed, thank goodness. Spoke with her last evening and she had a lumbar puncture which was most unpleasant and painful and they were still waiting for the results to come back from Southampton at 7.30 p.m. last night, so she was anticipating another night at Queen Alexandra Hospital! Hope she comes out today and they don't find anything serious. Spoke with Bridget and she felt a bit better today – I am surrounded by sick friends and family!

My draft will came back today and I have checked that over and obviously added a few things I forgot. I also told my solicitor that I had written separate instructions for Sam which were not included in the will. He has advised me to get that signed and witnessed before the will is signed so that it is all legal, so will do.

On a lighter note (not) – constipated again! However, with the amount of medication I have taken plus the unmentionable glycerine bomb I have just shoved up my backside, one would anticipate movement quite drastically in a short time!

Hugh has climbed the Sydney Harbour Bridge for me! With my name on his back! I am doing rather well with my support group so will add Hugh to the list. Masses are said for me regularly in Lesley's church. Bridget and Angela pray daily.

Spoke to my cousin Janet last night, who is a devout spiritualist, and I am on their healing prayer list at church – not sure how far up that list I am, but they had better move me up quick. Spoke to Janet about voluntary euthanasia and told her I would be worried about my soul floating about in limbo. She said that I would come back as another life and finish off the life I was supposed to – great – so I knock it on the head, float around in limbo annoying everyone then reappear in another form and die from lung cancer anyway? Not sure I believe that. Does that mean that all my animals that I have had put to sleep are not in doggy heaven playing with each other, but they are all floating round in limbo? Also, Janet firmly believes that you live several times otherwise what would be the point of it all? You never learn everything first time around so you are recreated again and again. Hmmm! Wonder if you get to choose a lifestyle? I think I would like to come back and be born to a wealthy family in the Highlands with a vast shooting estate, edged with river fishing, a lake to sail on, plenty of animals and loads to paint; then I could become a famous Scottish artist. Yep – go back to my roots, that will do me. Although, with Janet's reasoning, I've probably already done that and been beheaded at some stage so my previous head is hanging around somewhere too. Think I'm getting a tad hysterical, so—

Friday, 20th October, 6 a.m. – Actually was awake at 3.30 a.m. – made a cup of tea and took a second sleeping tablet and slept until 5.45 a.m., and if Fletcher had not barked I think I probably would have slept a bit more! Will ask the doctor if I can have more sleeping tablets, perhaps a lighter dose, to take in the middle of the night. Will see someone today as they left a message yesterday to say my flu jab was ready and needs to be organised, so will phone as soon as they are open.

Took the dogs for a good run on Butser yesterday and didn't get wet at all. Then Bridget and I had to trek all the way down to the Macmillan centre at St Mary's to meet with Maria (the benefits expert), who believes I will be entitled to Disability Living Allowance! Yeah right, let's just run that one up the flagpole and see which way the wind blows.

Completely exhausted last night, which has prompted me to

decide against – yes, that's right – picking up today. I am out all day at the field trial training day on Saturday, which is a huge test and I think I need to be as rested as possible before that. No driving though as Sarah is picking me up and Paula already has most of what we need with her, so that's great. Will compromise and take the dogs for a good stretch on Butser Hill instead. Could have gone to the seaside if the weather had been good, but perhaps next week.

Jan from the beauty clinic rang last night (she used to be an oncology sister at King Edward VII). Really lovely person and knows what she is talking about, so we had a great chat and I made her laugh with the funeral arrangements. Whoever is reading this may wonder at this stage how my sister Sue is faring in hospital with all sorts of horrendous implications from her diagnosis! I am not going to go into any detail – it is too horrible – and it crossed my nephew Ian's line of no go! But if you ever meet Sue, do ask her the story and her conversation with her Indian consultant. I on the other hand am only prepared to say thankfully all tests were clear. No bleeding on the brain, no malfunction in the lumbar-puncture test. Diagnosis – and this is as far as I go – 'thunderclap orgasmic headache'.

Saturday, 6.30 a.m. – Field-trial training day. Having decided that one sleeping tablet just wasn't doing it for me, I discussed it with my GP and she has now prescribed even more. At this moment I have enough to do the job myself, but would have to research on exactly how many I would need to take! However, last night I took a large dose, one at 9 p.m. – slept till 2.30 a.m. – didn't get up and do my usual walkabout, but took another smaller dose and slept until 6 a.m. RESULT! Not certain how I shall function after that today, but hey, who cares – I slept.

Didn't go on the shoot yesterday; decided it would be too much to expect my body to keep going for two days! Did loads of practical things, though. Washed the Frontera and tidied it up for shooting next Wednesday. Did a load more paperwork and had another bonfire. Sam's instruction box is almost ready; wonder how long it will be before he needs to take over the finances etc.

Had my flu jab today – first on the list before all the really old pensioners! Have to have a pneumococcal one as well (that's for pneumonia), but need to check with oncologist when I can have that.

My funeral order of service etc. is all but finished. I just need to sort out the vicar and the music and then I can put it well away and get on with what I have left of my life. I like to be able to tick the boxes and when they are all done I can relax. HOWEVER, all being well, I would rather like to organise something for Sam's seventieth birthday in March. Must give that some thought. PLUS Blenheim in 2008 – I still plan on being there as a guest for the very first time. I'll order a small caravan to be delivered on-site and just enjoy it all for a change. Yep, that's the plan. Feel good this morning and although Michael has organised me a lift round the shoot, if I feel like this I'll walk.

Sunday, 22nd, 4 a.m. – Tablets didn't work! The field trial training day was an absolute huge success and Paula was a complete and utter star. Committee was hugely supportive and all the food was brilliant. The competitors were beside themselves with the day and I also had a good day doing what I do best. Sheila presented me with a large outdoor planter and I was completely overwhelmed! People think I am so tough, but the emotions are just there under the surface and I am hopeless when anyone is nice to me. Keeping my fingers crossed for Windsor; once that is out of the way, Exbury and Bereleigh will be a breeze. Blowing a gale outside and raining, so think I will stay put for another hour or so. Short entry today as it was such a happy day yesterday.

8 p.m. – Sam came home in a really bad mood – all I needed. Been here on my own all day and the least he could have done was pass the time of day with me when he got in. Instead he just said, "You OK?" I said, "No, I'm fed up" and he said, "Me too" and that was it, he just buggered off upstairs. I suppose he is fed up with that job now. I'm going to bed, feel really lonely and depressed.

Monday – I'm not in such a bad mood this morning as I had a relatively good night's sleep – not without the aid of two sleeping tablets, I hasten to add. Don't think the weather helped yesterday, torrential rain and was literally stuck indoors and not able to get out in the fresh air at all apart from a twenty-minute dog walk in the morning. At least when it is dry I am able to get outside and prune a few plants. It makes life bearable, but there is only so much daytime television and drawer clearing-out that I can take. Hoping to get through the village before it is closed for a week so that I can take the dogs out early, so keeping my fingers crossed I don't have to do a ten-mile detour.

No chemo this week! Week off! Whoopee! I don't think I am ill at all; I think they are giving me this chemo to make me ill as some kind of punishment. Then when I stop having it I will just go back to normal!

Have been thinking about painting again this week. Once I have cleared every drawer I need to clear and everything else is organised as I want it to be I think I may pick up the paintbrushes again. Bit out of practice, but hopefully it will be like riding a bike.

Sometimes I wonder about the hand that life deals you. There is nothing you can do with it apart from just get on with it. How would you go about changing the hand you have been dealt or is it all completely mapped out for you from the day you draw your first breath? Could you change it if you wanted to? You know, I don't think you could. I think this is it and you just get on with it. There are obviously ways in which you can improve your life, but fate takes a big hand in the rest of it. Although, having said that, what about medicine? What about transplants? Someone who has been dealt the hand of heart disease now could perhaps change that by having a transplant so that would change the hand they had been dealt. Debatable subject.

Tuesday, 24th October, 4.30 a.m. – The second sleeping tablet didn't work. Having said that I took the large dose at 9.30 p.m. and slept until 3.15 a.m., so almost six hours – took the second one, and nothing. I cannot believe the permanent buzz I am on; it is impossible for me to relax during the day although I do make a conscious effort to sit down for an hour at lunchtime. I am probably doing more now than I was before chemo and steadily ploughing my way through every drawer in the house and having a massive clear-out. I guess the time to worry would be when I start on Sam's room, but even I won't go there! Bathroom cabinet, underwear drawer and T-shirts got the treatment yesterday. Plus, I took the dogs on Butser Hill, then drove into Petersfield; shouldn't really, but there was no one here to stop me. Shopping at Waitrose and then I even went to Clusons to buy myself another coat! Did I need it? Probably not, but do I care? Absolutely not.

Bridget has pulled her shoulder again. I wish she would take more care. How is she supposed to manage me when she isn't well?

Windsor draws ever closer. I am so determined to do it I just hope a) I manage to get the show on the road, b) I manage to stay upright for three days, and c) I don't get too emotional! Although I think if I am going to get emotional at any of them it will be Bereleigh as that is my last one. I must have a word with Pauline as it is necessary to start thinking about dates for next year.

I think my hair is coming out – definitely getting very thin and every time I run my fingers through it handfuls come with it – shit. Perhaps I had better organise that cap with the braids before too long.

Sam was in a much better mood when he came home yesterday ☺; think he was just having a bad day – weren't we all?

Have now finished sorting the filing box for Sam, the funeral, the list of phone numbers to call, the service at All Saints, East Meon, and the order of service; written all the letters, but I now want to sort out my jewellery and that's it. Haven't got around to any clothes-sorting yet – perhaps they would like to do that themselves?

Actually, I felt so well yesterday that I found it really hard to believe there is anything wrong with me. Be interesting to see what (if any) changes there are on the X-ray next week. I don't know about structural changes with ET, but I know something is happening to it. When I used to clear my throat there was blood resulting in ghastly brown phlegm; now if anything it is just very pale, almost white. So dunno what that means.

Wednesday, 4 a.m. – Shall just have to give up with these sleeping tablets. If they are not working they are just one more poison going into my body! MY HAIR IS FALLING OUT! They promised it wouldn't, but I have handfuls of it to prove it. Please just let it be thinning and it's not going to come out in great clumps! Got so depressed yesterday I phoned the Wig Company and ordered the baseball cap with braids. Not quite the same now I'm not ordering it as a joke! I wanted to buy it just as a joke to wear at the trials, but if I haven't got any hair the joke will be kind of lost. I think it is meant for a younger person, but – BOLLOCKS – I won't wear it all the time anyway.

Jane phoned from BUPA. I am going to have a permanent line fitted as they are having so much trouble getting blood from me that I can't bear it any more and my hands and arms are permanently black and blue.

Sam came home from work yesterday with a bloodshot eye, then went to bed without supper. Here we go again – what the hell will I do if he is rushed into hospital again? I shall make him a doctor's appointment and he can go in late. The hours at Avington are worse than Meon Springs.

Petersfield Cancer Support Group rang to ask if I wanted to be on the next 'Living with Cancer' course with Macmillan, but I can't because of chemo. So she is going to put me on the next available one after chemo has finished. Is chemo going to finish? When? I thought this was my life now.

Going picking up today – forecast is appalling, but what the hell, I've got tomorrow to recover. Bridget came – with two carrier bags, Ovaltine, Horlicks, breadsticks, frozen curry for Sam, a pomegranate, fizzy drinks and a toffee apple for Halloween! Amazing. Think I had better get another one of these books before I run out.

Next Tuesday looms every closer – please, please don't let me react badly; I need to be really on good form for Windsor.

WHAT IS SAM GOING TO DO WHEN I DIE? I don't mean initially, because everyone will help him through it. I mean after that when life must go on. Obviously, I will leave everything in order to make things straightforward, but what about life? I should never have done everything. He does nothing inside the house apart from wash a couple of dishes occasionally. No washing, no ironing, no changing sheets, clean towels; he is very bad at changing his clothes. I do all his meals, all his lunch boxes and even when I go away (or used to go away) there were always meals in the freezer and filled rolls for his lunch boxes. I deal with the money, the ordering, the bills; I cut his hair. What in hell's teeth is he going to do? He won't be able to look after the dogs, order the dog food, so I think that perhaps once I know that I am on the way out my dogs must become a priority. If Nymph and Rhea are still around I honestly think I should have them put to sleep. I'm not saying that Sam doesn't love them, but management-wise he does not notice things. He wouldn't notice if they were lame unless it was critically lame; he wouldn't notice if they were drinking too much etc. I may talk to the vet about it. Sue C. will have Tess. I know she has offered to have Nymph as well, but would it be fair to impose such an old dog on her? She would have the heartache then. Cracker will obviously stay with Sam.

Katy, my beloved little Katy who had such a rough start in Ireland and has been so happy here. She has definitely nine or twelve lives at least. Lost and found twice, near death twice, but still here and I always said she wouldn't make old bones as she is such a frail little thing, but frail she is not – I actually think she is as tough as old boots. A home for her will be so difficult. I don't want her to go to a shooting home, she may get lost. I would like her to be someone's special girl for the rest of her life and I just cannot think who it could be. Shirley and Stuart spring to mind, but I don't think they would. I wonder if she would settle with Sue C.? Would she have her?

Fletch. Big, bad, adorable, single-minded softy – Fletch. Still so young. Someone is just waiting for him. I did think of Jane. I know he's not a golden retriever, but she absolutely adores him and he would be completely loved to absolute bits. Plus she could still take him picking up and wouldn't care if he did anything wrong. Next time I see her I will mention it. Obviously, no one is going anywhere until I am dead. If Fletch and Katy come to the funeral they could go after that.

Thursday, 5 a.m. – Slept reasonably well (with the aid of two tablets). I was knackered though as I picked up all day yesterday and did more walking than I have done this season. The last drive nearly killed me and I was so out of breath when I got back to the car I could hardly breathe. Still I did it and all the dogs had a good time – two shifts; took the oldies p.m. with Flinn. Poor Terry lost little Mo and was frantic, but I drove round and found her and it was a great feeling. Shame I never find my own when they go missing. But the look on Terry's face said it all. I had a really nice day and thoroughly enjoyed everyone's company. My only problem is that I have done something to my right arm and it is extremely painful, right up the arm and under the armpit. Probably something really stupid in my weakened state.

Sam came home early and went to the doctor's with his eye, which was really bloodshot, and everyone worried him by telling him it was high blood pressure! Anyway his blood pressure is normal and the eye is just a broken blood vessel.

Danny and Els are arriving at the weekend and I'm not going to be able to spend much time with them. Monday I was going to take them picking up, but I can't as I now have to go to hospital. Tuesday chemo, Wednesday and Thursday rest and then a slight chance I may be able to pick up on Friday.

Friday, 27th, 6.10 a.m. – Had quite a good night's sleep again thanks to the pills. Yesterday I did far too much and I still cannot stop pushing myself to the absolute limits. I didn't walk the dogs as they were all quite tired from the previous day, so first thing I dashed into Petersfield and got some shopping, went to the bank etc. Still can't do a big shop and find it much easier to get all the heavy items online. Cleaned out Gary and the chickens, which I have been meaning to do for ages but the rain recently has made it impossible. Anyway, the chucks are nice and clean now and I will do the dog kennels on Saturday.

I also decided to do some gardening just to really finish myself off! Planted up a new hanging basket and some pansies and finally took the wrapping paper off the present that I had received from the competitors at the training day last Saturday.

My next project, having sorted out my will, funeral and everything else, is to do a living will as I am now worried about being resuscitated, but I'm not quite sure how to go about it. Perhaps I will ring the Macmillan centre – someone there must know what to do. I always said (to myself) that if I were ever diagnosed with something terminal I would finish the job before I got really ill, but I am changing my mind about that. Not that I wouldn't do it and I certainly have enough tablets, but now when I have the opportunity it doesn't seem like the right thing to do. Plus it isn't legal, plus what would happen to my soul, plus I think it would be more upsetting for the family. I am not afraid to die, I'm annoyed to be missing the funeral party. I just hope and pray that when the time comes I am not a complete wreck and that I can die with some dignity. I wish someone would tell me how it happens, the deterioration, pain. Will I still be able to function properly? Walk my dogs?

Start of third cycle on Tuesday and will have an X-ray, so should see if ET has shrunk. If not, Captain Chemo has threatened to change my chemo mixture, which will be an absolute shit thing to do as I guess my body would react violently again and with Windsor next week I can't let that happen.

I shall be extremely glad to get Windsor out of the way. Sad that something I was really looking forward to is now a challenge and something to get over, done and dusted, out of the way. Exbury is my next trial on 20th December, but I know that will not be a problem. Surrounded by friends, support and a shoot that I know and love will not worry me at all. Haven't heard from Ian, but will see him at Christmas and find out then if he is going to be living permanently in Australia as from next year. Don't blame him. What has he got here really? And he does so love Australia. I will have a chat with him at Christmas because I do not want him travelling all the way from Down Under just for my funeral. I would like him to do one of the readings if he is here, but if not then it is not a problem – perhaps Neil would do it.

Picking up today – weather forecast is good – won't tell Sam! If I make it that will be two days this week!

Saturday – I picked up all day yesterday and if I didn't know I had something seriously wrong with me it would be hard to believe. I was pretty tired last night, but actually no more than usual after a shoot day. I walked right up my 'usual hill' at Smokey Hollow – only stopped for breath a couple of times, but that is fairly normal. Katy did her let's go missing in the wood bit and frighten Mum to death, and then I found her completely disorientated so left her in the car for the next drive. Tess worked rather well yesterday. Fletch, the flying flat-coat, had a great day. Swapped dogs at lunchtime and took them up behind Lodge Piece and they completely knackered themselves in the pen. Had to put Rhea in the car; thought she was going to have a heart attack, but they all had Mars Bars to up their sugar level. Had a really enjoyable day with Jane and I took her to the exact spot that I want my ashes to go. She didn't want to go at first, but I think she was pleased that I had shown her. I felt really strong all day yesterday and did quite a bit of walking. We all agree that because I am so physically fit from walking the dogs it is helping me overcome the weakness. Plus I am really trying to eat properly; I even had some food with the beaters yesterday. Should be a fairly quiet day today. I need to get all my things ready for Windsor in case I don't feel too great next week – ugh!

3.30 a.m. – But it's really 4.30 a.m. so I have made a cup of tea. I now have a CD Walkman so when this happens I can plug it in and play something tranquil in the hope that it sends me back to sleep. I am going to try that in a minute – just as soon as I have drunk my tea. Felt good all day yesterday, did loads, washed car and all rugs etc. Got my things ready for Windsor and even packed my bag so that I know it's all ready. Paula is coming today to collect everything and then we will go and meet Danny and Els for a couple of hours. I've got it into my head now that I need to paint my bedroom as the yellow is beginning to get me down. Holding myself back from starting it just at the moment though.

6.15 a.m. – But it's really 7.15 a.m. Had the CD player plugged in and it sent me off to sleep again – brilliant. So thanks, Bridget, for the relaxation CD.

Going to get the dogs out to Butser as soon as Sam has gone! Paula is coming at 10 a.m. to collect all the Windsor equipment and then we are going to meet Danny and Els at their cottage. I can't entertain them this year. I normally have them for supper, but I just can't do it. I hope they go to the shoot tomorrow; they are expected and everyone knows who they are. I shall have to wipe Monday, Tuesday and Wednesday off the calendar and hopefully catch up with them again and take them picking up on Friday all being well. Just quickly will refer back in the journal to see how I was in comparison to the first week. All looked a bit up and down and obviously I had done far too much, but there was a great improvement from the previous session. So if I plan next week very carefully I should be OK. Definitely rest Wednesday and Thursday then perhaps just do the morning picking-up, then off to Windsor on Sunday. Let's do it!

Monday, 30th October – Paula came yesterday with Steph and the baby and collected all the things for Windsor. Then we went down to see Danny and Els at their cottage. The plan was that we were going to go to the pub for lunch, but the longer we sat there the more exhausted I began to feel and I realised I didn't want to do it. Paula then suggested that they all come back to the farm with her and have lunch there, so it was quite a relief when they dropped me off at home and carried on to Paula's. It's actually visitors and visiting others I find a huge strain and I don't know why. I love them all and want to see them and then when I do I can't cope with it. I'm just not the same person any more. We made plans for Blenheim 2008! If I am still alive, we are going to have a caravan delivered to the site with an awning and I am going to share it with Danny and Els, so we shall pay half each. Will I still be alive? You know what, I actually doubt it. Came back yesterday and just kept falling asleep. I ended up going to bed at 7.30 p.m., slept until 2 a.m., took another pill and slept until 4.30 a.m., so all in all not too bad.

Have to go to the hospital today to have a permanent line put in as it is becoming such a problem to find a vein, so an extra trip today then bloody chemo tomorrow. Amy is coming this evening to do my hair, so it is going to be a long day. Hopefully I will have the energy to take the dogs out before going to the hospital.

Sam came home last night and informed me that he didn't fancy the curry I had cooked for his tea and I got really annoyed. Does he realise how much effort goes into cooking his meals? If he really didn't want it why didn't he just throw it away and pretend he had eaten it? So – because he didn't fancy that he didn't have a meal! Why didn't he make himself cheese and biscuits? Toast? Anything? No, because it wasn't prepared for him he didn't eat. I AM GOING TO DIE. I WON'T BE HERE TO DO IT. WHAT IS HE GOING TO DO?

I want to paint this bedroom as the colour is really beginning to get me down. Why on earth did I paint it yellow? I am going to attempt to do it myself. I definitely won't be able to do the ceiling, but hopefully someone will do it for me. If I have to spend quite a bit of time in here I can't stand this colour. Can I fix it? Of course I can!

Tuesday, 31st October – Halloween. Took dogs to Butser yesterday then off to BUPA to have my 'picc' put in, which is a permanent line into the vein to avoid all that bruising and poking around every time they want to take blood or give me chemo! I wasn't aware that it would be so complicated! Actually had to go to the operating theatre. Very dramatic and also quite painful! Quite interesting to watch on the screen as you see it going into the vein and then up your arm then head off over your chest area and end up just above your heart. I thought it would be just a little hole with a cork in that they took off when they needed to. How naïve – how wrong – it's quite long with a kind of butterfly clip on the end and has to be folded back and covered with a dressing which must not get wet and must not get any germs in it. Hopefully it has been the right thing to do. Apparently when it settles down (blood everywhere at the moment and oozing through the dressing; good job I'm back in today for them to sort it out!) you don't even realise it is there and I have also been advised to invest in several rolls of cling film to wrap over my arm to avoid it getting wet (a bit like a turkey)! Met some fellow cancer patients yesterday for the first time. They were just so jolly (and both rather fat) that they almost got on my nerves! Both had lost their hair and one was wearing a very bad wig, and the other lady who had been having chemo for three years was just bald. The wig lady had breast cancer and good chances of recovery. The non-wig lady had secondaries everywhere, hence the constant repeats of chemo. Don't know how I would feel in that position, but she was very upbeat and chirpy – made me feel rather ashamed of having my 'black days' occasionally, but I expect she does too.

Big chemo for me today, but I think there may be a little bit of good news. I haven't told Sam yet as I don't want to get his hopes up, but when I saw my X-ray yesterday I was pretty sure that ET had shrunk! Need to hear it from Captain Chemo before I broadcast it, but in my absolutely non-professional opinion I think it has got a bit smaller.

The other bit of good news – VERY GOOD NEWS FOR ME – is that Amy came to do my hair last night and completely wiped away my fears of losing my hair! Although it is coming out in handfuls it is just thinning and probably due to the chemo, but she assured me that when your hair falls out through chemo it happens very quickly, within the first two weeks. Plus, it doesn't just come out in handfuls, it comes out in huge clumps. So, fingers crossed, the hair won't go, so that has cheered me up somewhat.

It is hugely important that I don't allow this dose to take over this week. I know I must rest tomorrow, but then I really do have to be completely upbeat about everything and just build up all my strength and go for it at Windsor. John is picking me up at 5.30 p.m. on Sunday then I have to keep really strong and well until Monday afternoon – no, that's wrong, Tuesday afternoon – and I will do it.

Wednesday, 1st November, 5.45 a.m. – Had an appalling day at chemo yesterday and also an appalling night. It just went on and on. We didn't get home until 7 p.m., so it was an exhaustingly long, stressful day. Rent-a-crowd didn't even work as Carol and Glenis came, but I was so stressed because my machine kept breaking down, making the whole poisonous experience even worse and more long-winded than ever. It was nice to see Carol after all this time. She is looking relaxed and happy after her many holidays this year. Still don't think she can be that happy and she seems to be a bit of a lost soul spending so much of her time away from home. I won't moan about everything, but this entry will be much shorter than usual. I just hope that this is not an omen and I am going to react badly this time. I will rest as much as possible today hopefully.

There is a bit of positive news! ET has shrunk by approximately one centimetre. That's good news. I now definitely will have to carry on for another four cycles of chemo plus additional CT scans in between, plus I have to go every week and have my line flushed out. However, I think we can safely say that I will live longer than six months. Captain Chemo won't commit himself and this is the answer he gave me to the question "How long?" – "Possibly two years, could be more, could be less." Pretty non-committal at this stage, but who can blame him? Still the same answer to "Will it cure me?" – "No."

It goes by now without saying that Bridget was again an absolute star. She has the patience of a saint with me and puts up with all my tantrums. I do love her to bits and could in no way manage without her. Sam was stressed when we got home – too much going on. Danny and Els arrived with flowers for me, Tony delivered the dog food, Louise arrived to clean the house and Chris arrived to collect his dog food. Sam was so busy he didn't have time to eat his lunch and when we got home he didn't know where to look for a light bulb! Just as well I have a bit of extra time to train him a bit better.

Thursday, 2nd November, 5 a.m. – I am on those wretched tablets that double the insomnia for three days so was prepared for a bad night – even the music didn't work!

Had a pretty restful day yesterday and didn't go over the top rushing about. Sam was here anyway so didn't get the opportunity to dash off in the car with the dogs, but hopefully I will today and then go picking up tomorrow as long as I am not throwing up! Everyone has been fantastic with Danny and Els and it has really taken the strain off me. They were at QE Park yesterday then training with Sue C. p.m. then pub in the evening. Paula is taking them somewhere today and then I will take them picking up tomorrow then they go home on Saturday. It has been an unfortunate week for them to visit really, but I think it has all worked out well and they have enjoyed themselves.

Showed Sam how to poach eggs yesterday – well, it's a start, but I'm not sure we shall ever get to the shepherd's-pie stage. I reckon he will live off anything anyone cooks him and he can put it in the microwave and reheat it. Then when he goes to the supermarket he will get frozen meals and live off those. I actually never thought I would die before him as he is so much older than me, so I didn't think I would have to worry about him.

We actually had a discussion yesterday about what would happen to him when I die. I suggested he stay here for as long as possible especially as Nymph and Rhea are still here. I think he would like somewhere smaller on the estate, but I can't think of anywhere. It may be a good idea at a later stage to put him on the council list individually and see what comes up. I also suggested a lodger when he said he wouldn't want to rattle round here on his own. I think a lodger might work especially if they got on and were like-minded.

Told Paula that ET had shrunk, so she is really excited about Blenheim 2008 now as she thinks I will still be here! Good news from the practice nurse: she is trained to flush out my line, so that will save me having to go back to BUPA on my week off to have it done. It has to be flushed and kept scrupulously clean so on chemo days they will do it and change the dressing, but on the one week out of three that I don't have chemo it will be so much better with our nurse coming here to do it for me. I have to bring everything that she needs home with me, so even more medication, dressings etc., etc. but I am so thankful she is going to do it. Just gives a break from going to the hospital.

Captain Chemo is threatening radiotherapy after I finish six cycles of chemo in January! This has to happen on a daily basis – how the hell am I going to do that with the dogs etc.? I think he is talking four to six weeks and it would have to happen at St Mary's – imagine the parking fees for that! Fifty pounds a week at least, which I will find hard enough to manage. How the hell do people really afford these fees? People visiting terminally ill patients for months? Children? The mind boggles really. At least I don't normally have to pay to park at BUPA. Anyway, I haven't agreed to do that yet. He would have to put up a pretty good case FOR if I am going to agree.

Friday, 3rd November, 5 a.m. – Bad night, not feeling great but hopefully still going to go on the shoot. Just did too much yesterday and completely exhausted myself, so was in bed by 8 p.m. Slept until 1.30 a.m. and that was it. Washing, cakes, cleaned windows, dogs on Butser, Bridget visiting, endless phone calls – too much. I hate being like this. Everyone is so pleased that the tumour has shrunk, but I hope they don't get too excited. I'm pleased, of course I am, but I am also realistic and realise there is a long way to go and so much more to go through before I can anticipate anything more than eighteen months. All I can aim for at the moment is the end of the shooting season, a barge trip hopefully in March for Sam's seventieth birthday and Blenheim in July 2008 and if I achieve that then that is a milestone.

Danny and Els go home tomorrow and I am glad that everyone has rallied around and kept them amused for me because I sure couldn't have done it. Hopefully a couple of hours on the shoot with them will placate them and they'll be happy that we have spent a couple of hours together. It's a shame they didn't come in a week's time when I will have improved from this latest intrusion into my body.

Big frost outside this morning. I have already been down and fed the dogs, so will have to de-ice the car before I do anything else, but I will make it this morning even if I don't stay all day. Then if I keep it fairly quiet tomorrow and tootle off to Windsor late afternoon, I'll just keep my fingers crossed that I make it through the two days. It would be rather nice if someone waved a magic wand and told me I didn't have to go and that everything was sorted; that won't happen, but I know they will all have rallied round and done all the food that I normally do. Bless their hearts, they so want it to go well and Sue C. has been such a loyal support throughout all this; she is an absolute star.

Spoke to Claire yesterday. I had been sending her texts, but apparently her mobile has broken so that's why she hasn't replied! Still having problems with William at night. Can't help comparing to puppies: if I had a puppy that wouldn't settle, it was either cold, hot, hungry or in pain. Wonder how that compares with a baby? No comparison, I guess. I'm sure he will settle down soon. I hope so for Claire's sake. Apparently Paul is a natural with him and it's Claire that is struggling.

Saturday, 4th, 5.30 a.m. – Actually had quite a good sleep! Went picking up yesterday and managed all except the last drive, which wasn't bad. Jane said I looked frail and I confess I felt it; didn't walk too far, but far enough. Dogs enjoyed it and they were quite good – no dramas. Got the mouth ulcers and cracked lips back today – not very attractive. Danny and Els go home today and Sue and Joe are coming to do the garden, so I should have a relatively quiet afternoon ready for tomorrow. Not leaving until late afternoon, so no rush and then although I am looking forward to it I am also looking forward to coming home. Hospital Wednesday, picking up Thursday, lunch with Lesley on Saturday and that's the week mapped out really. Just taking things easy as I am supposed to! Sam came home with a EuroMillions lottery ticket and I asked him what he would do with the money if he won. He didn't know. I just said, "There are some things money just can't buy." Would a large amount of money make any difference to my life now? No, not a bit, so I would end up giving it all away, which is actually quite a nice thought. I could leave everyone in a very happy, stable financial state and Sam could buy himself a cottage near a river. Alternatively, and far more likely, he won't win anything and life will go on as usual.

I was talking to Rex yesterday afternoon while we were waiting for the beaters to blank Eddies Elbow in. It was an absolutely glorious afternoon and considering it is November the day couldn't have been better. In the space of fifteen minutes we had a red kite soaring round us, three geese flew over on the skyline, two roe deer dashed back and forth trying to find a way out, a hare got up and ran right in front of us and the coveys of partridges started fluttering as they were moved towards the guns. God's country and I wouldn't have wanted to be anywhere else. No matter how ill I feel, this is where I want to be and this is why I want my service outside where the real Creation is and the real place of worship.

4 p.m. – Seriously worried about Windsor as I am having a really bad day. Headache, can't go to the loo, slept most of the afternoon. I have strange pains in my chest and my arm hurts like hell where the line is. To be completely honest I am a bit scared to go to Windsor in case I am ill, but I really don't have a choice, do I? Who could take over for me? Pauline can't go to the trial and now I am worried that she isn't going to be able to take over as field-trial secretary. I really don't know what to do – just wait and see how I am in the morning, I guess, and take it from there. No one is indispensable and if I can't go because I am ill then so be it. Who will take all the paperwork? Chequebook? Pay the hotel bill? Run the trial? Shit.

Sunday, 6.08 a.m. – Slept most of the night. Came to bed at 7.30 p.m. and didn't wake up until 4 a.m., and then just dozed off again. Still feeling grim and now in a bit of a quandary: shall I put the emergency contingency plan into action or just struggle through the rest of the day and see how I feel? I may be OK later; on the other hand, if I'm not all hell will break loose. I think I had better warn a few people to be very aware that there is a strong possibility that I might not make it through the next couple of days. Be positive? I would like to, but at the moment I don't even have the energy to wash my hair. Mouth ulcers at the moment and the corners of my mouth are so sore I can hardly open my mouth. Really do not know what to do. Perhaps the best thing would be to struggle up there today, start the trial tomorrow and then, worst-case scenario, Sarah could bring me home tomorrow evening. Still need someone in the hotel to pay the bill etc. Perhaps John could do that and the club could write him a cheque? Main priority this morning is to get the running order sorted and e-mail it to Paula. What a mess that is. I have never had so many people pull out of an open before. I need to give this up and in a way I am glad I have an excuse, if you can call dying an excuse. Let's see what the day brings.

9.05 p.m. – Made it to the hotel, but have left everyone to it and come to bed. Knackered – just wish it was all over. Paula (bless her) had a disaster with the running orders and for the first time ever they look really scruffy. Not to worry, can't do anything about it now. Set alarm for 6.45 a.m. Roll on Tuesday and let's go home – had enough already.

Monday, 4.45 a.m. – I think I managed a couple of hours! The good news is I have been already! Must have been all those carbohydrates I ate yesterday, so that is a relief! Just made a cup of tea, got a blinding headache already so that probably means I have taken too many sleeping tablets. There has been a bloody generator going all night somewhere beneath my room, which hasn't helped.

John told me last night that he is taking all the guns and judges to lunch at the York Club courtesy of Her Majesty, which means there will be copious amounts of food arriving from various committee members to feed everyone unnecessarily, but what the hell. I managed to ring Sue C. at least to cancel the gallons of soup; anything else left over we will save for Exbury and stick the game pies in the freezer. Just had a sip of my tea and the milk is sour! What else is going to go wrong with the bloody trial?

Worried about the running orders – will have to announce at the beginning that there was a problem with the photocopier. How do I feel? OK? Had a nose bleed – where did that come from? Head aches – take some tablets. Arm uncomfortable – too bad. Nauseous? Don't think so. Bollocks, just get on with it. Breakfast at 7.30 a.m. then off.

I have only brought one pair of knickers! No, not even one! The pair I have are the ones I was wearing last night! I know I have been a tad vague lately, but NO KNICKERS! Perhaps if I phone someone they will bring me a spare pair – oh, God. Now the alarm has gone off because I used my mobile and the clock hasn't been altered to wintertime, so instead of 6.45 a.m. it went off at 5.45 a.m.! Things just have to get better, they can't get any worse. Plus, I have just realised I cannot have a shower as I cannot get my left arm wet and I forgot to bring the plastic cover for my arm. So I shall have to shower with one arm. The other one outside the door. Not looking good for cleanliness. I shall completely smell abhorrent by tomorrow evening, especially if I don't get any knickers!

5.40 p.m. – Back at hotel, had a shower (well, half of me has because I cannot get my left arm wet!), made a cup of tea and just having a lie down before meeting everyone for supper at 7.30 p.m. Not looking forward to that. Could really do without that, but hey, I've made it through the first day. What a glorious day it has been; the weather has been absolutely beautiful. Sue C. actually ran the dogs for me and it was the first time she had done it. She was marvellous and coped admirably (apart from some slight interference from the KC direction, at which point I had to intervene and ask a certain person to treat my stewards with a little respect). Paula and I were left to swan around in style in the vehicle which John had organised – just as well as I would never have been able to walk all day. Eight dogs through until tomorrow, so it looks very hopeful that we may have an early finish and get back home in daylight. Fingers crossed for that. John has been brilliant and took all the judges and guns to lunch at the York Club, which has left us with copious amounts of food. No problem – we can freeze it for the next trial.

Tuesday, 6 45 a.m. – No time to write. Had a good sleep, breakfast 7.30 a.m. then off. Just one thought – what an amazing bunch this A and D committee is. They are not just committee members, they are my friends and I love them all. Great meal last night and I stayed up until 10 p.m. Paid hotel bill etc. and got everything sorted. Onwards and upwards today then home.

Wednesday, 8th, 5.55 a.m. – Got home at 2 p.m. yesterday at the end of a very successful two days. Kept the mask up and put on a good front all through until the presentation. Did the presentation – no problem – thanked everyone, presented the prizes and then, just as I was thanking my amazing committee and friends, I broke down – shit – couldn't believe it. Then Duncan grabbed me by the left arm (the one with the line in and black with bruising) and I nearly shot through the roof! No harm done, just scared me a bit. All in all a huge success so I am delighted that is over and now I have 20th December at Exbury, but not too concerned about that one. Sue C. was marvellous and I hope she can continue when it gets to the four-judge system.

Everyone said I looked well! Amazing what a bit of make-up can do – they should see me now! Sitting up in bed with a cup of tea, no make-up, very pale and look like shit. I think perhaps I am lulling them all into a false sense of security and perhaps I should appear looking as I normally do with no make-up. Unpacked everything last night, so that is all done. I still have to do the paperwork and print off a decent running order and send it to Her Majesty; couldn't send one of the naff ones.

Macmillan centre today followed by BUPA to have this line washed out. Picking up tomorrow? Hope so. Guess with only seven weeks to Christmas I ought to think about Christmas presents, but I really can't get my head around it. Can't see me trolling around the shops somehow. I am going to give mainly money and jewellery from my boxes, but I can't give that to the men, can I?

Thursday, 5 a.m. – Just made a cup of tea. Yesterday Bridget picked me up at 10 a.m. and then we went shopping at Morrisons. Fridge was empty, so needed to stock up. Exhausting. Then on to St Mary's Macmillan centre and spent two hours filling in a form for Disability Living Allowance, which will probably be absolutely nothing but we had to go through the motions. Sat by Canoe Lake – can you believe that? Like I was some frail old lady taken out for a drive and had a sandwich, then on to the dreaded BUPA and I was convinced that we would be there for hours but no, all very quick. Had my line flushed through and my dressing changed very quickly and we were out within an hour! I wish it was always like that. I still get very stressed and tetchy even when it is a non-chemo day. I absolutely hate going as it inevitably seems to take up so much of my life (or what's left of my life). By the time I got home and unpacked all the shopping, put it away and got supper ready I was completely exhausted and just flopped out until 8.30 p.m. then went to bed.

Today – no hospitals, no chores – just going out picking up with my dogs.

Friday, 5 a.m. – This insomnia is dreadful and after the really busy week I have had (Sunday, Monday, Tuesday at Windsor, Wednesday two hospitals, and shopping and picking up all day yesterday) I thought I would go out like a light, but no. Did the whole day yesterday, didn't come home early and didn't miss a drive. All the dogs had a great day and I walked a long way and felt almost normal. It was the Game Fair Dinner last night and I had refused the invitation weeks ago as I knew I wouldn't feel up to it. Plus this next seven days in the cycle is my most susceptible to illness with the dodgy immune system, so there was no way I could go. I sent Alana and Brian in my stead, who probably (no, definitely) felt terribly important, but the nice thing about all of this lengthy screed is that the Game Fair office sent me a beautiful bouquet of flowers yesterday and said they would miss me. I am trying not to think about my next cycle of chemo, which starts on 21st November, because for the next few days up until then I shall be pretty much OK.

I have started thinking about dying again and how it will happen and what will happen. I have absolutely no idea. I have thought, once this chemo is over, that I might join a support group of people who know what it is like and they can perhaps tell me what happens. So if I get two more years, is that two more from now? Do I just die in November 2008? What warning will I get? I seriously don't want it dragging on and on and to become incapable of looking after myself. I couldn't bear to lose my dignity and independence. It looks as though I am going to achieve my first goal of getting through the shooting season – then what? I will have to have some ultimate aim for the summer. I feel really confused and emotional today. Perhaps I am just so tired I don't know what I am talking about. Day at home today, not going anywhere – loads of washing etc. to do and generally catch up with things. Not even going to take the dogs to Butser – they should be tired after yesterday.

9 p.m. – Depressed. Been thinking about it all day – my death. When? How? I am OK most of the time, but today I have worried about what is going to happen. At the moment I can pretty much do normal things. I know I don't have a social life because of germs and I cannot mix with a lot of people, but apart from that during the day on a good week I can walk the dogs, do a few chores etc. and generally manage the house. But what happens when I become really ill and cannot function? When I can't do the simplest things? When I will have to accept help? I will be impossible, hateful. I am so scared of that – not the death bit – the fact that I will lose my independence and probably my dignity. Is it time I stopped worrying about my soul and started thinking about my options? I don't mean right now, I mean when I start to lose my normality and have to rehome my dogs and let other people make my decisions.

Saturday, 5 a.m. – Didn't sleep very much. Still thinking far too much about what is going to happen. Just been down to make a cup of tea and I let the dogs out – when will I not be able to do that? Also concerned that because I have missed one session of chemo and I now have a free week the next session on the 21st might affect me as badly as it did the first time because my body has had a break from it. I didn't ask that question. I am going to have to pull myself together and focus on the time I have left or find myself another project to focus on. I have been so wrapped up in Windsor, I guess this may just be a reaction to it all being over now – onwards and upwards. Exbury on 20th December – let's sort that out. Lesley is coming to take me to lunch today and I know she is just being kind and wants to help, but I really don't feel like going. That's not very nice, is it? I find it very difficult to cope with anything out of my routine and very selfishly want to do things in my own way in my own time, but I guess it will make her feel better if she comes and takes me out. What an absolute cow I am and can anyone begin to imagine what a bitch I shall be when I am unable to function properly?

Need a good shake – will definitely get up and take the dogs to Butser and blow the cobwebs away and get on with things.

Apparently the Game Fair Dinner went very well and they all stood and drank to my health, which, when Alana told me this morning, made me feel momentarily very important. However, I don't suppose they would have done that if I hadn't been dying (bitch mode again). In truth, I was really touched by it and also the flowers.

Sunday, 6 a.m. – Actually, having grizzled and moaned about having to go out to lunch today, I really enjoyed it. It was lovely to see them and they bought me some beautiful flowers and it quite cheered me up. Went to the Thomas Lord in West Meon, which is extremely rustic, but the food is restaurant-quality so we had a good time. MUST STOP MOANING ABOUT EVERYTHING!

The strange thing is that whenever people see me for the first time since diagnosis they are always surprised at how well I look. Forget the fact that it has taken me an hour to wash and dry my hair then another hour for fake tan and make-up. I think people's preconception of lung cancer, combined with television, leads them to expect me to be hooked up to an oxygen cylinder barely able to breathe or walk. Well, I think that will probably come at some stage, but Lesley in particular yesterday said she had known someone with lung cancer and was not at all convinced of my diagnosis because I have no external symptoms. I don't have a cough and the only time I get really out of breath is walking up a hill, and I would imagine fifty per cent of the population are like that. I think that because I was so physically fit to start with it has helped my body cope better, but it still doesn't alter the fact that I have terminal lung cancer which will undoubtedly start showing its ugly symptoms soon enough.

I have made one decision over the past few days. When I get to the end of these six cycles of chemo and possibly go through the radiotherapy afterwards, when Captain Chemo finally gives me some kind of prognosis as to my expected longevity or 'shortevity', if at any stage ET decides to double in size again and reappear, and if chemotherapy is suggested, I won't have any more. Imagine going though this lot then living say six months and being told it has to start all over again. There was a woman at BUPA the other day who had been having chemotherapy on and off for three years! Not for me. Spoke with Brenda yesterday and she has had twelve cycles of chemotherapy and is now going for a complete body scan as she has secondaries everywhere. Doesn't sound too great, does it?

Went on to the Internet yesterday and was looking at a website for holistic cancer cures. Got down to the sixth page of blurb and completely lost interest. I can't absorb facts like that, and get totally bored very quickly.

It's Wendy's sixtieth birthday and Sue is organising a birthday tea and obviously I am invited and would like to go, but I do have slight difficulty making people understand that my life revolves around chemo now. On the 21st I have the big whammy and if I react badly there is absolutely no way I could go out to tea on the 25th, so I have promised that if I feel OK I will be there; if not, I won't. As it is I shall have to get a taxi there or get someone to collect me. I think that because I have just been to Windsor, plus I go out on the shoot, everyone expects me to be fine, but that particular week was a chemo-free week so I could do those things.

Monday, 5 a.m. – I don't suppose I should write much as I am still seriously depressed. Home alone all day yesterday and all I did was work! Washed sheets, towels, normal washing, cleaned out kennels and gave the dogs clean beds, cleaned out chucks and guinea pig, cooked meals for Sam and then felt incredibly lonely. Only one phone call and that was Paula, bless her. Sam came home and I saw him for about five minutes then I went to bed at 8 p.m. Think I will take the dogs picking up and try and cheer myself up a bit by seeing other people. I am obviously spending far too much time on my own worrying about my soul and what is going to happen to me in the future.

Tuesday, 5 a.m. – Dogs woke me up. Thought they would be knackered today after picking up, but they still started messing around. So got up and made a cup of tea. Enjoyed yesterday although it was cold and wet. It doesn't seem to have done me any harm apart from a blinding headache. Still don't feel very happy. The nurse from the surgery is coming to flush my PICC line today and I don't feel very confident about that, but once she has done it for the first time I should feel better. Supposed to be going to Thalia's for supper with Lucy, Bettina and Co. tonight, but I am going to cry off. One, I don't want to drive (and shouldn't be driving) and in the dark; two, I don't feel very sociable; and three, I don't really want to go out in the evenings as I am so tired and usually in bed by 8.30 p.m. So there it is, miserable old cow or what? I am dreading next Tuesday and although I was triumphant about missing the chemo I am seriously worried about how I am going to react having missed one. Seemed such a good idea at the time. Plus I want to miss another one on 19th December, which I haven't told them about yet.

Six weeks until Christmas and for the very first time ever I am not entertaining! I haven't even given a thought to presents and I haven't even considered buying one for Sam. I can't do shopping. I haven't given up; I just don't have the energy! I will give everyone cash and something from my jewellery box and that's that. I don't think I will even get the decorations out. Sam never helps anyway, so it's me that has to lug them all out, put them all up and then a week later take them all down again and I can't be bothered basically. Seriously miserable or what?

Wednesday – Felt better yesterday, or at least I did after the nurse from the surgery had been and flushed my PICC line through. Was slightly concerned she wouldn't know what she was doing and we did have to phone Lou at BUPA to ask a question at one stage, but apart from that it was OK. Before she came I cleaned out the inside of the Frontera as it needed doing and washed the dog blankets. Then I took it up to the car wash and used two tokens to get all the mud off underneath. It will get just as bad on Friday, but if I keep on top of it the rust will not appear – hopefully. After the nurse had been I belted into Petersfield in the Vectra to give it a run – pet shop, paid credit card, Waitrose then back – and Louise was here hoovering. So all in all a busy – normal – day.

Still seriously dreading next Tuesday and the days following. It really isn't such a great idea missing one day of a cycle. I'm worried to death. (To death? That's a laugh.) Jonny rang for a chat and told me that her brother had just started chemo for inoperable bowel/colon cancer and that he has been given three years. The good thing is he had his first dose of chemo last week with absolutely no side effects whatsoever – I wish.

Thursday, 16th November – Had quite a good day yesterday. Took the dogs to Butser, wrote the report for the open field trial, did some cooking, didn't go anywhere and didn't see anyone. Changed all the dogs' beds and washed everything as Fletch and Katy are going to be spruced up at Lynette's. Of course, woke up this morning and it's absolutely pelting it down with rain and the conservatory that was spotless yesterday is now awash with wet dogs, wet feet and wet beds. What is going to happen to these dogs – and Sam? I know Louise comes in once a week and she hoovers and dusts – I still do everything else. Does Sam think the toilet and bath clean themselves? Do his clothes end up in the airing cupboard neatly folded on their own? Does the bed change itself? Who cooks the meals? The cooking fairy? Moaning again – I'm just a bit screwed up and worried about the chemo next Tuesday and my non-existent future.

Christmas – what shall I do about Christmas? It could realistically be my last one. I have said I am not putting the tree or anything else up this year, but it will be very bare. Plus, if I don't do it no one else will. It's me that gets all the boxes out of the loft, unpacks everything, puts it all up and two weeks later takes it all down. No, I am not going to do it; let's make myself even more miserable. Haven't even bought any presents – money in envelopes for everyone. Christmas cards? Shall I send any? Can't be bothered. I am so scared about next Tuesday and it's difficult to explain to anyone, so it just keeps going round and round in my head. It really is like starting all over again.

Meeting Sue C. at Lynette's today and when I have dropped the dogs off we are going to look at some glassware with a view to buying some as prizes/gifts for the A and D. Don't really want to go. Don't really want to go anywhere. I am much better just staying here in my cocoon and just picking up occasionally.

I hate this uncertainty about dying. I would be so much better if I knew the time and date and I could prepare myself for it. Still haven't finished the cupboards or sorted out my jewellery, so it had better not be next week. I seem to have developed a strange cough which I suppose was inevitable, or perhaps it's my body trying to get back to normal having missed a chemo and then that means it really is going to hit me hard next week. Still, look on the bright side – it is only a week. Yeah, right!

I'm thinking about doing one of those tins (there is a correct word for it, but it has gone out of my head at the moment). You put several items in and perhaps a couple of photographs and other things relevant to your life and period you live in then you bury it and someone comes round with a metal detector in 100 years' time and digs it up. Perhaps that's not such a great idea.

Friday, 17th, 5.30 a.m. – Not going to moan about anything today. Met Sue C. at Lynette's, left the dogs there for their shampoo 'n' set and went shopping, but didn't achieve what we set out to do as the engraving for the glasses was too expensive for prizes. Had some lunch and sorted out a few things, collected the dogs, went to Butser Hill on the way home. Fletcher pissed off (but came back), Katy ate sheep shit and waited until we got home and threw it up all over the conservatory. Sam was knackered – been sweeping leaves all day. I wrote the report for the yearbook regarding Ricky-Ross that she has asked me to do for her. Sent off to Annette and sorted out photos and sent them by snail mail. So that should be that – and that was my day. Bearing in mind that this time next week I will be incapable of anything I thought I would write my Christmas cards this weekend – wasn't going to do any, but that would be seriously 'bah humbug', so will just do friends that I never see and a few close friends.

Saturday, 18th November – Slept well(!) with the aid of two pills. Obviously my body is getting used to no chemo, so that on the one hand is good; on the other hand it is not such a great sign with Tuesday looming, so I am even more convinced that Tuesday's chemo is going to hit me hard – PLEASE DON'T LET IT! It is bad enough having it without worrying about all those horrendous after-effects.

Picked up all day yesterday – absolutely foul weather and I didn't really want to be there, but the dogs enjoyed it. Having said that, Fletch isn't too happy this morning and is refusing his food, which is not a great sign. Won't panic just yet and will take his temperature later. Hope there is nothing wrong with him – gives me something else to worry about, I guess. Nothing planned for weekend, just chores, cooking and possibly writing some Christmas cards.

I seem to have developed a cough which I didn't have a few weeks ago. I guess ET is playing up again and I suppose the next X-ray will show that instead of shrinking it's growing and taking over my body!

Sunday, 19th November, 6 a.m. – I wish I could shake off this black mood. I don't want to see anyone, don't want to speak to anyone. I just work until I'm exhausted and then get bored watching the television. I am in bed by 8.30 p.m. every evening, so going out is not an option. I don't feel sorry for myself – just really fed up and miserable and to be honest if I am going to feel like this for whatever time I have left – why bother? Perhaps I need to throw myself into some charitable organisation, but I can't do that as I am avoiding the germ situation. If it weren't for that I would still be doing Buddies and Westbury and I really miss that. Buddies have some really good trips and outings coming up and I daren't go to them in case I catch something. Hopeless situation, but when the chemotherapy is over at the end of January I can begin to do these things again.

Monday, 20th November – Wrote all my Christmas cards yesterday and that was my total achievement. No – forgot – I did take the dogs to Butser and I also went to Waitrose and did a little shopping. Pat has rung me a few times this week and not left a message, so I rang her today. Still didn't get to speak to her, but advised her to ring me during the day as I don't do evening phone calls. However, the phone rang at 7.30 p.m. but I didn't answer it and this time she had left a message. A very emotional one and I can really do without emotion. I think I will text her and tell her I am quite happy to chat as long as it isn't emotional. She was in tears and saying she didn't know what to say to me, but she knew the path I was going to tread(?). OK, we all know I am going to die, but if I can deal with it then so can she. Tomorrow looms ever closer and it is making me feel physically sick to even think about it. I am still really depressed and in all honesty can not keep this up much longer.

The dogs woke me up this morning and it is so not necessary. I am thinking of picking up today – well, that was the plan, but typically it is blowing a gale and bucketing down with rain. So theoretically I shouldn't really go. Why couldn't it have been dry and sunny?

Is it worth all this effort just for a couple of years? Please,

God, the after-effects of this chemo will not be as bad as the first time around. I am really finding it difficult to feel positive about anything any more and not in the least brave. Actually, bravery doesn't come into it; in this position you have no choice and because you just struggle on daily, people think you are being brave – I'm not brave at all, I'm scared to death (no pun intended) and don't know how much more I can endure. The only positive thought I can throw in here is that I am not in pain and I haven't lost my hair. Apart from that I feel like shit most of the time and for some strange reason bruises keep appearing all over my body. Should I mention this to anyone? Also, the PICC line in my arm is very irritating and how that stupid woman at BUPA could possibly say, "You won't even know it is there" I have no idea – she must be completely mad. Of course, I am aware that there is a line coming out of my left arm with a very thick dressing over it so every time I bend my elbow I know it's there – stupid bloody woman.

Tuesday, 21st – This is it, big chemo day, but I am going to be positive. Last time after the big one I was off to Windsor on the Sunday, so I'm just going to take it easy tomorrow and Thursday, take all the medication and pick up next Monday – I won't be too optimistic and aim for Friday; I will just aim for Monday and see how it goes.

Went picking up all day yesterday and was OK. Felt faint when I got up this morning to feed the dogs, but I'm OK now – still depressed with life as I know I don't have much of one left. Going to go up to the garage and wash my car off before I go for chemo – apart from that there is nothing else on my mind as my treatment has taken over my entire life and I have had enough of it. I won't ever do it again. If I am told that I need six more cycles they can forget it – I would rather die.

Wednesday, 22nd November, 5 a.m. – That's that then. Had the poisonous implant – took hours and we finally arrived back home at 6.30 p.m. It all takes forever and as we all know I am not the most patient person in the world and want everything done in double-quick time and then to be out of there. Sadly, it doesn't happen like that. First thing on arrival my PICC line has to be flushed and cleaned, then blood's taken. Then I go for an X-ray to see how ET is getting on (more on that later). Blood pressure, temperature and then wait for Captain Chemo to arrive so that he can prescribe the mix of chemo. This then goes to the lab to be prepared and can take up to two hours. Then the treatment starts with a litre of saline solution flushed through my body (takes an hour, but I can sometimes get them to speed it up). Then the first 500 bag of chemo goes through, that takes half an hour, then another bag of saline, then the large 1-litre bag of Gemzar chemo, which can take anything up to an hour and a half to go through, but I had quite a good machine yesterday and I persuaded the nurse to put it though quickly. Then more saline, then the line has to be cleaned again and finally dressed. Then wait for the pharmacist to bring all the medication up to take home. That's what happens, in a nutshell, and I am normally very impatient, bad-tempered and generally not nice to be around. On a lighter note, rent-a-crowd excelled yesterday and obviously there was Bridget, then Sue, whom I found when I came out of X-ray. She brought a book of jokes with her – she's always good value and had everyone in hysterics. Then Thalia arrived, clutching pineapple (as that is my latest fad). Then Jane arrived with a magazine – not one that I would normally buy (*National Farmers Magazine*), but it looks quite interesting. Captain Chemo arrived and did a complete double take at the number of people, so I asked them to wait outside while he was there.

ET HAS DEFINITELY SHRUNK! It is now almost half the size it was and I have to say it's the first time CC has looked quite so enthusiastic. However, he is now considering going longer than six cycles with the chemo, which I am not at all happy about. I am so looking forward to the end of January, when it stops, and I am seriously digging my heels in about having six weeks' radiotherapy on a daily basis! But I won't dwell on that for the moment as the news is looking good. Not from a lengthy prognosis kind of view, but I am still anticipating another two years.

Let's just hope the next few days do not affect me badly. I am going to follow the rules and completely rest today and take as much medicine as I can to make me go! Then hopefully by the weekend I will begin to feel more normal and can plan picking-up on Monday and perhaps go to Wendy's sixtieth tea party on Saturday – that will be exciting! But I hope to go for an hour. Bridget will pick me up and we will get there at 4 p.m. and leave by 5 p.m., so just for an hour. It will be nice to see Ian and also William, who now weighs 11 lb. I can't wait to see him. So that will be the highlight of my weekend. It's Sam's AGM so he will be going out on Saturday night and all day Sunday. Hopefully I will be capable of looking after myself!

Thursday – Wasn't too bad a day yesterday. Didn't feel too ill apart from nausea, and the dogs were all good apart from the fact that the butcher sent them all a bone! Cracker threw up on Sam's bed, Fletcher threw up all over the conservatory and overnight Cracker shit all over the floor – obviously the bones are not a great idea, but I just thought it would keep them happy as today I obeyed orders and didn't go rushing off to Butser Hill with them. In retrospect they probably enjoyed the bones and then got together and planned the mess so that I didn't try that again. I guess I will have to make the effort and take them today.

Good news is I have been this morning – too much information? Not for me. It's just the best news because I am convinced if I can keep that under control by taking the dreadful gloop then everything else will be OK.

Guess I will spend most of today washing bloody dog beds! Already stripped Sam's bed yesterday, so that is done. Mustn't do too much though – will try and rest today at some stage. It's my bright red rosy cheeks day with the tablets I am taking. It always happens and I look inevitably healthy for a couple of days!

All this fighting with cancer is not the right thing to say really and I think I have said it before; I am not fighting the cancer, just learning to cope with it and the after-effects of chemo. I guess some people say that because they are having the chemo they are fighting it. I don't look at it like that. The only reason I had (am still having) the chemo was pressure from friends and family to 'give it a go', so that's what I am doing. Now, it does appear to be working by shrinking ET, but I am fully aware that this is not a cure and it will grow back again and as far as I am concerned you can't keep fighting it. Breast cancer is different; they have a new drug which has a very high-percentage rate of the cancer never returning. Mine is not like that. It will subside, it will give me a little longer, but apart from that no one knows. Bring on the wonder lung drug! Alternatively, I could have another fag!

Friday, 6 a.m. – Could have had a lie-in, but for some reason Katy, Fletch and Tess decided to start some kind of game and woke me up. It's easier then to get up, let them out, give them breakfast and come back to bed. And I took them to Butser yesterday – bloody dogs are so spoilt and really don't deserve me. Washed all their beds yesterday too, so you'd think they could have a bit of a lie-in.

My depression seems to have lifted and I am now convinced it was just caused by being overanxious about my reaction to the chemo on Tuesday, but so far so good! I've been OK, have rested far more than I normally would, but still managed to do most things. The bowels are fine, plenty of gloop being taken and actually had to get up in the middle of the night to go – enough information on that. My face still looks swollen, but that's the steroids. Eating OK, but still have a most peculiar appetite for strange things. Pineapple is still number one on the eating list.

Being very grown up today and not going picking up as I think that would set me back, so I am planning to go on Monday and I should be fine by then. I will, however, take the dogs to Butser this morning.

Finally had a conversation with P.K. last evening. She had left such an emotional message on the answermachine that I left her one back saying I would be quite happy to talk to her, but as long as it didn't include any emotions or hysterics. She seemed quite happy with that, so much so that I don't recall her asking after me at all. She was intent on telling me about a pig she had swapped for a gearbox, taken to the butcher's in her Land Rover and had now brought home. She started telling me at length what she was doing with it – ham, bacon, sausages, pâté, gammon, some going in the freezer for roasting – like I wanted to know all that. I cannot even bear the smell of pork, and when the hell is she going to eat all that? She lives on her own! Obviously going to grow very fat in her old age. Now I know a lot of people who have always thought she is a bit odd; she was my 'mate' when I lived in Devon, but I have to admit she is weird. I did invite her on a holiday to France once with Wendy and Sue, but that wasn't a huge success as Wendy and Sue didn't really understand her. I guess you can take the girl out of Devon, but you can't take Devon out of the girl. And, what about the time that Wendy and myself went to Cyprus and I had told Pat all about it and she turned up at our hotel room when we arrived having been there for a couple of days already and was an instant expert on everything and insisted on showing us 'her' sights. Fortunately, she didn't stay for very long as she had only booked a few days. I feel a bit mean writing this as I know she just wanted to be there with us and join in and be helpful and, truth be known, she was probably a bit lonely.

Saturday, 25th – Dogs woke me up at 5.30 a.m. Feel like shit. Decided to give the gloop a miss last night so of course this morning I can't go to the loo. The anti-sickness suppositories leave such a vile taste in my mouth that I didn't use one of those either, consequently I feel nauseous. My head is absolutely thumping and I feel as though I have just run a mile as my heart is thumping out of my body, but that just could be coming upstairs! Fourth day after chemo and it has hit me again. Wendy's sixtieth birthday today and Bridget is coming to pick me up to go to the tea party. It will be an effort as I feel so ghastly, but we shall go for an hour. Sam will be out all evening as it is the Nomads' AGM, so let's hope I don't collapse or anything.

Field trials coming up and what shall I do about Christmas? I have never not done anything about Christmas before, but I just cannot trawl round the shops and I just cannot, or perhaps *cannot* is not the word, I just do not have the physical ability or energy to do anything. I am more tired with this cycle of chemo than any of the others and I wonder if it is the combination of the chemo plus all the sleeping tablets I have been taking just to get through the night.

I did take the dogs out yesterday. I was OK then, but rapidly deteriorated through the day and by the time Sam came home around 5 p.m. I was out of it. Watching television is an effort when I feel like this. Washed my hair yesterday; thought it would make me feel better, but it looks a right mess this morning, plus my lips look very swollen and my face is puffy. The PICC line in my arm is really beginning to irritate me and the dressing is far too bulky. When they change it next week I am going to put my foot down and have it done my way. It's so big it catches on everything. Moaning a lot this morning – perhaps I should stop. Gave poor Bridget a hard time again yesterday and she doesn't deserve it – mental note to send her some flowers, I think – feel guilty.

3.30 p.m. – Just waiting for Bridget and then we are going to Sue's for Wendy's birthday tea. Felt like absolute crap all day today and if it weren't for the fact that Ian is coming down from London, Janet and Maurice, and Claire, Paul and William will be there I honestly think I would opt out. However, I have pulled myself together, done my hair and put on some slap so that at least I won't look as though I am dying (hopefully), even if I am. So onwards and upwards, it's only for an hour or so and I want to be home by six as Sam is going out. Also Bridget and Pete are going out this evening, so we have to leave early.

Sunday, 5.45 a.m. – Bloody dogs messing about woke me up, so got up and let them out, fed them and came back to bed with a cup of tea. Enjoyed seeing everyone last night, but I was exhausted after an hour. Unbearable this feeling tired, nauseous, no energy, headache – really cannot cope with socialising especially after my heavy dose of chemo on Tuesday. Constipated today as the thought of drinking that gloop is unbearable, so am putting up with the consequences.

Had great plans for today – dog walk, Waitrose, sort out field trials, but I know I can't do it. Everything is muddy because it has rained constantly all weekend, so all the clean dog beds and conservatory are filthy again. William is adorable and didn't wake up once – just got passed from shoulder to shoulder and barely stirred, but finally settled in a mountaineering position on Great-Aunt Susan's ample bosom and when I left it looked as though he was there for the night.

I think I am worse this time as I was off to Windsor the previous time; although I remember feeling a bit tired I certainly felt better than this. When am I going to sort these trials out? Will I be able to go picking up tomorrow? Chemo again on Tuesday and start all over again, but I am definitely going to get this monstrous dressing reduced on my arm on Tuesday. Either that or the line will have to come out because it is driving me mad. Plus it is all red underneath as either I have an infection in it or I am allergic to the dressing – brilliant.

Must go to the post office next week. Think I will get William a Premium Bond for Christmas; they are £100 each now! I can remember when they were £1. It was funny talking to Claire, Ian and Co. about decimalisation last night, I forgot that their generation had no knowledge of £.s.d. and they didn't know what a shilling was – really strange.

Summing up my feelings this morning – PISSED OFF!

8.27 p.m. – My day didn't improve and when Sam came home about 2 p.m. I finally flipped and cried like I have never cried before. I guess it had to come, but today I was fed up with feeling like shit, fed up with being brave all the time, fed up with myself, fed up with the dogs and everything and I cried. I felt quite calm afterwards, but I am still depressed and just cannot bear anyone telling me to be positive. PISS OFF. I do not feel in the least positive today – today I am crying – for life – for love – for everything and everyone I am going to leave behind, so don't tell me to be positive. I think it shocked Sam and he really was at a loss, but I just cannot permanently soldier on without having some kind of reaction. I carry on cooking, washing, dog walking, shopping etc., etc. and I am tired. I just want someone to wrap me up and look after me instead of me looking after everyone else. I would like to climb out of this black hole, this black place I seem to have landed in, so please let me feel a bit better tomorrow. Actually the bloody weather isn't helping – constantly pissing with rain and blowing a gale. Wet dogs, wet dog beds, muddy conservatory – where is the sunshine? Not going out on the shoot tomorrow – that's how depressed I am. Don't feel up to it plus just can't be assed!

Monday, 6 a.m. – Slept OK, feel a bit better and my decision not to go picking up seems a good one as it is absolutely chucking it down with rain. Might ease off later and I will take the dogs out then. In the meantime, I have come back to bed with a cup of tea.

Tuesday, 28th, 4.15 a.m. – Bad night – chucking down with rain again. Didn't pick up yesterday, but did accomplish a few other things. Cleaned chucks out, changed dog beds, sorted out some things for the Exbury trial – I will be so pleased to hand the field-trial reins over to Pauline. Cancer or no cancer I have held this position for twelve years and it is a long time. Pleased for someone else to take over.

It's chemo day – great – so looking forward to it. Got fed up with watching television last night as all the soaps seem to be running a cancer story and I seriously don't want to know.

I took all the dogs to Butser yesterday – even Nymph and Rhea – and had hopefully planned to do the same today – if it stops bloody raining. Then they will all be OK to leave while I go for treatment. Must give Brenda a call to see what happened with her full body scan and whether all that chemo was worth it. Hopefully she will be clear now. Still haven't had my CT scan appointment through yet; must mention that today. Really don't want to have radiotherapy after this lot and I am seriously hoping to get away with it, but knowing my luck he (Captain Chemo) will think it is a brilliant idea. I don't want any more treatment,

I really don't. After today's session I will have completed four cycles out of the proposed six. On 12th December the fifth one starts and then the last one in January. I can't understand why he thinks it may be necessary to do more. He said initially that six is the norm and only in America do they continue any longer. I just wish he would come up with some figures – like "Yes, it's working and we can say you will live for another two years, but if you have some more you will live for another five years" or "No, it has not worked; you will be dead in six months." Why can't he tell me any of that? I know everyone is different, but he must, absolutely must, have some idea. I think I will dig my heels in and put some pressure on him for some answers.

Wednesday, 29th, 3.30 a.m. – Well, I wish I had seen him (Captain f---ing Chemo) for long enough to talk to him. He flew in as I was getting ready to go home only to tell me that there was a problem with my blood platelets and that if I had a nose bleed or cut myself and it wouldn't stop bleeding I would have to be admitted to hospital immediately. Plus, if I discovered little red spots all over my body then that would also be a dangerous situation and the same thing would apply! So, instead of having a week off next Tuesday, I have to go in to BUPA in the morning to have my blood tested again. I'm really not sure what will happen if the results are still dodgy. Great, just when I thought things couldn't get any worse! I did manage to tell him that I would not be doing Day 8 of the fifth cycle as I had a commitment. He wasn't very pleased and said that when I missed the Windsor one he hadn't intended setting a precedent for me to keep missing them – bollocks. Got home at 5 p.m., which was reasonable.

There was a new chemo patient in the room next to me and I was so tempted to go and have a chat. Poor girl doesn't know what she is in for, but I could have at least told her about the ice lollies. Wonder if I would make a good counsellor? I reckon they need counsellors on the spot. The nurses are really good, but they don't have a great deal of time to spend with you. That's how I knew the person next door was new, because there was a flurry of activity around her all the time and I don't think she had anyone with her. You do need someone there with you – apart from anything else it helps the time go quicker. I obviously had Bridget with me, but Sue called in – clutching fresh pineapple – and she stayed until the end. I shall miss her when she goes to South Africa for three months in January.

Will rest today so the dogs won't get their walk on Butser, but I am sure they will survive for one day. Took all of them again – even Nymph and Rhea – they enjoyed it. I might (might) see if Sam wants to come with me later today and just take them for a quick spin – see how I feel.

Although I am getting used to having the chemo now I still find it unbearable and whereas in the beginning it all seemed surreal, and I managed to focus on things and be very positive, that seems to have stopped. I am seriously finding it difficult to lift my spirits these days and cannot raise any positive thoughts about the future at all. I wake up each morning with a feeling of impending doom and find it very difficult to raise a smile or sometimes even speak.

I know I need to contact EHCC to see if we would now be entitled to a rebate on our council tax and perhaps get assistance with the rent, but I just can't get round to it.

I also seem to have developed a cough I didn't have, which seems strange. If ET is shrinking, why have I started to cough? I suppose it will be the oxygen cylinder next! Don't go down that road.

I was even thinking of not bothering to pick up again on Friday; but you know what, I think I will sort myself out and go. If I don't then it's won, hasn't it? The dogs may as well be rehomed and I can just stay in bed. So today I will rest – tomorrow I will swap the cars around ready for picking-up regardless of the weather on Friday. I will do it. I'm sure it will make me feel better once I get there. This journal is getting quite thick since 12th July – only four months. I shall need a new one soon – wonder how many more I shall fill. Wonder who will read them after I die. Or will they end up in the bin?

Don't know quite what prompted me to get out all the leaflets, information sheets etc. about my lung cancer, but that's what I have just done and lay in bed reading them. Basically – what we all know by now – there is no cure. You do hear of people with lung cancer that do recover; some of these are operable followed by radiation which is very successful. My type of cancer is not operable as the tumour is not suitable and also it has already spread into the lymph nodes in my chest cavity. What my treatment is attempting to do is a) shrink the tumour – which will not disappear completely – and then b) zap the lymph nodes with radiotherapy, which will cause further side effects, to try and stop it spreading into my liver, kidneys, bones etc.

Basically, it's not looking too great and I still don't know what my life expectancy is, but one thing is for sure – this is a terminal condition and there is no getting away from it. Whereas initially I just accepted that I was going to die and that was it, I find now I want to know as much about the condition and treatment as possible. I still don't feel that I could join a backup group of any sort until my chemotherapy is over as it seems to rule my life at the moment, but would like to talk to some like-minded people about it at some stage. Feel quite reflective this morning, but don't intend lying in bed all day. After John the builder has been I am going to try and persuade Sam just to come in the car with me and the dogs to Butser Hill. He doesn't have to walk right round; he could just wait for me. Do I think he will? The percentage chance of him coming with me is five per cent, but he may surprise me and be up for it.

Thursday – Actually I was totally wrong. I asked him if he would like to come with me and he did! I knew he wouldn't be able to walk as far or as fast as me, but it was a beautiful day and even Cracker came too. The views were spectacular and I think Sam enjoyed it. Also, I feel that if anything happened to me when I was there on my own I could phone and he would now know exactly where to find me, so that's a comfort.

I know I was supposed to rest yesterday, but I just couldn't. I seemed to be on a mission all day, but I felt OK so just kept going. Sat down for about an hour in the afternoon and that was it. I'm sure the weather had given me a feel-good, bollocks-to-the-cancer factor. Builders came at 10 a.m. as I want the outside of the house painted. It looks really scruffy where all the ivy came down. Also the window frames and ledges are in a bad way. Also need a new kitchen sink unit and there is some damp coming through one of the walls, so quite a few jobs for them. I did stipulate not starting until the end of January when hopefully I will be able to look forward to a chemo-free time.

What else did I do? Bottled sloe gin ready for Exbury and Bereleigh, washed all dog beds and gave the conservatory a good clean – bloody rain makes everything damp. Did a load of paperwork for trials and input all entrants on computer. Generally started sorting out prizes and gifts and getting my head round things. So not a huge amount of rest as I couldn't settle.

Oh yes – forgot – at 4.30 p.m. yesterday I had a phone call from the radiography department at Queen Alexandra Hospital asking if I could go for a CT scan – like now. Imagine what I said! I have put it off until next week and the ironic bit is that because I am a private patient I have to go after normal hours and when all the NHS patients have been seen, so my appointment will be after 5 p.m. whichever day I go – shit. Not thrilled about that, plus my free week with no treatment is getting shorter by the day. Plus I will have to drink another glass of that disgusting white gloopy stuff before they can do it – joy. One thing, I am not going to tell Bridget about this one as she will only insist on coming with me and I am quite capable of doing this on my own. She does quite enough for me as it is without messing up her evenings. Might even ask Sue just for a bit of company, but I'm not bothered; I can easily go on my own.

1st December – Only five months since the beginning of this nightmare and the treatment and after-effects are really beginning to take their toll. It's mouth-ulcers and cracked-lips time again during the cycle and I'm not sure which medication causes this, but by deduction I think it is the very strong antibiotics I have to take one week out of three. My sense of humour seems to have vanished and I am extremely bad-tempered. This morning it is absolutely bucketing down with rain and blowing a gale, which does not fill me with great excitement to go off picking up for the day. I could easily just stay in bed and keep warm, but I think what I shall do is at least make an effort and go round there and see what pans out. Why couldn't we just have had a dry day? Yesterday and the day before have been lovely and all the dog beds and everything are clean, and now all I can foresee is starting washing and cleaning all over again.

I wore myself out yesterday. I don't do it on purpose, but I just can't rest. If there is something to be done then I have to do it. I think I must have inadvertently upset my sister Wendy (she is so like my mother – I look like my mother, but Wendy is the one most like her in temperament). I can't remember what I said; I have snapped at just about everyone dear to me in the past few weeks and Sam gets it in the neck more often than not. Bridget obviously takes the brunt of it and if I am in a really bad state I avoid talking to anyone. But Wendy, I really cannot remember unless it was the 'who rattled her cage' remark when I was on the phone to Sue last week. I always say things like that in a three-way conversation and always say that it's like having a parrot on your shoulder when Joe keeps chipping in. So I don't know. She hasn't called me all week. I did try to call her yesterday, but she wasn't around. Not much else I can do.

Someone asked me recently what my first thoughts on waking every day were. Difficult to say really. Lung cancer is always in my head, even when I'm talking to strangers who are telling me trivial things about their lives and I have to show an interest. In the back of my mind is the constant urge to scream out I AM DYING WITH LUNG CANCER, but of course I never do. I am always very aware now that I am no longer a normal person – I have a terminal disease and my life expectancy is not great. However, it is not easy to come to terms with. If it was just a fact and you had to get on with your life until the end I think that would be easier. It is the constant reminder that you have a serious illness that plays on your mind. The treatment, the medication, don't forget to take this tablet and that tablet and stick the suppositories where the sun doesn't shine, the large dressing on my left arm, and wrapping and concealing my PICC line, which some idiot told me I wouldn't even notice was there! Then, all this treatment – is it actually going anywhere? Captain Chemo originally said six cycles of chemo and I was already counting down to mid January, but now he is talking more – I can't bear the thought of that. But he never gives out any numbers, never tells me how long this is going to extend my life by and I'm not sure I want to carry on with it. But then the horror of my rapid deterioration starts preying on my mind and I can't bear the thought of relying on other people. So, you see, the state of my mind is absolute shit and I am constantly thinking about it, even when it must look as though I am being brave – I'm not brave at all.

Saturday, 2nd December, 6 a.m. – Yesterday started off very positively and off I went round to the shoot with the dogs – pissing with rain but what the hell. It all went horribly pear-shaped and I don't know what is happening to me. In a nutshell, I walked up a steep hill (which is what I always do although at the moment I do have to stop a couple of times). When I got to the top my head and heart were pounding – again fairly normal. Let the dogs hunt the pen out, which was the object of the exercise, then walked back down the hill about halfway and dropped down into the woods for the next drive. Without going into too much detail, I collapsed and ended up clinging to a tree on my knees for the entire drive. I managed to stagger back to the car. The dogs were working, but I didn't know what they were up to really. Went home and had a sit-down and a cup of tea and then felt OK again, so changed dogs over and went back, had some lunch with the beaters and then went out to the last drive of the day. I couldn't do it; I couldn't even walk 100 yards and I had to come home in a complete state of shock.

What's happening? I thought I would wait and see how I felt this morning, but I am very shaky, head is thumping and I feel wretched. Sam says it is because I am so weak, but this has happened very quickly. I climbed Butser on Thursday with no problem. I can't go out on the shoot any more. I will become a liability and they will just end up feeling sorry for me. I don't know what to do. I will have to phone Nick and talk to him, but what is going on? Why do I feel so ill?

I am supposed to be going out for lunch today with Bridget, Lesley, Glenis and Co., but at the moment I think that is going to be a no. If I still feel like this later on this morning there is no way I could cope with it, so I shall have to phone and cancel. What is going on? I thought all this treatment was supposed to improve my life for a period of time. Do I regret starting it – yes. Would I have been dead by now if I hadn't started it? I couldn't be any worse. I feel debilitated. How do people get through this? Their 'fight against cancer'. I'm not fighting against it as I know there is no point. I have cancer and that's all there is to it. So my question is I have got cancer – has it got me? My answer would be yes, it has. Bollocks to being positive (that's what everyone tells you to do). Know what, I'm going to have a fag out the bedroom window and to hell with everything.

Sunday, 6 a.m. – Well, I didn't go out to lunch. I stayed in bed until 10 a.m. and then struggled with a few chores, but every time I moved my head my heart started pounding in my ears and I found if difficult to keep upright. I can only imagine that this has something to do with the problem with my blood platelets and perhaps some kind of anaemia, but I am extremely weak. There is nothing I can do about it until Tuesday when I go to BUPA to have my bloods done and PICC line flushed. I have no intention of calling the emergency services as I am sure I would just end up in St Mary's or something. I will, however, pack a bag just in case I get rushed into hospital, but I am seriously hoping it doesn't come to that. I did not do anything yesterday apart from rest and I shall endeavour to do the same today. I will not be a hero and go picking up tomorrow and will ring Nick today and tell him he won't be able to rely on me. I can barely walk at the moment without staggering. The poor dogs won't be happy, but what can I do? I just know I am not physically capable.

Sam stayed home all day yesterday, but I really don't think he knows what to do. Still at least he was home and he did go and get some fish and chips, which was what I fancied.

The weather sounds really wild out there today, so I think even a very brief trip to Butser Hill is out of the question. It's Fletcher I feel sorry for. He is the one with all the energy. Katy and Co. will be happy to sleep all day. Perhaps I should give Fletcher some thought. I wonder if Lisa and Richard would be interested in a son of Tello? Sam will go berserk if I even mention it, but he really has to be aware that I am beginning to get to the stage where I can't manage the dogs.

You know what? I am seriously beginning to make the decision that I cannot take any more of this treatment. Each time, each week, another side effect, another symptom and I can't take any more thrown at me. I always said I would carry on and all the time I was capable of continuing to do the things I do then I would continue. But I can't – I can't do normal things any more. Can't just get in the car and go Christmas shopping and now – the worst thing – I cannot take the dogs picking up.

So – you tell me – what now? What the hell do you all want me to do now? Forget positive. Forget brave face. Forget being cheerful – I've had it!

Monday, 4.30 a.m. – I did sleep, but I am awake now and I needed a drink. Yesterday was dreadful. I didn't leave the house all day. The dogs were bored; I was depressed. I'm sure it is going to get to the stage where I am so unbearable people will begin to avoid me. I don't really feel sorry for myself, I'm just so annoyed that I can't carry on doing things I want to do. Felt so ill yesterday that I have actually packed a hospital bag with PJs etc. in case I get rushed in somewhere for a blood transfusion.

Phoned Nick and told him I couldn't pick up today or even in the near future, which was a horrible thing to have to do. What about my poor dogs? That's what they are here for; that is what they live for.

Bridget rang to see how I was and also to arrange to pick me up on Tuesday. I had made other arrangements! I was going to drive myself and then go and meet Carol in the Staunton Arms for lunch, so it looks as though that is a complete no and Bridget has her way and she will be taking me. I HAVE NO CONTROL ANY MORE.

Have made my mind up that I am taking the dogs out today. Even though the shoot is out of the question I am going to Butser and no one can stop me. I know my limitations. If I feel ill I will stop walking. If I collapse I am bound to come round eventually! Watch this space. Jane called last night and actually managed to cheer me up so I was glad I answered the phone.

Have I mentioned the pins and needles before? In my hands and when I have been writing for a few minutes I get cramp and chronic pins and needles, which probably accounts for the appalling writing! This cancer thing and all the treatments – people undergoing it should not be referred to as brave. Brave has absolutely nothing to do with it. Actually it's tolerance levels. When people tolerate enormous doses of chemotherapy for months, people refer to them as brave. 'Joe Bloggs is so brave with his fight with cancer' when actually it should read 'Joe Bloggs is tolerating his treatment for cancer extremely well and people are praying for his recovery.'

In my case – 'Judi Seall accepted the first four cycles of chemotherapy, but not passively, kicking and screaming as they pumped her body full of poison. Now four months down the line her tolerance level is zilch and if she accepts any more treatment it will be a miracle.'

Tuesday, 5 a.m. – What am I doing today? This should be my day off from BUPA – wrong. Bridget picking me up at 10.30 a.m. – BUPA for blood tests and flush PICC line. Captain Chemo has been notified that I have been blacking out, so watch this space. Just hope it is something simple and that by Friday I will be out picking up. Managed to save all my picking-up money to give to the kids for Christmas (obviously some will be getting more than others), but that's good as I haven't had to draw any out of the bank.

Have decided to put the Christmas tree up, otherwise it would just be too miserable for words; and just say I did die next year it wouldn't be very nice for Sam remembering Christmas 2006 with no tree or anything. As it is, things will be very different and for the first time in twenty-three years I will not be entertaining, so on the one hand that is quite a relief but on the other I shall miss all the preparations. So will concentrate this week on doing a bit of present wrapping and put the tree up – that should keep me out of mischief. I do feel like a prisoner in my own body and my own home at the moment. I do hope I am not taking this infection thing too far and missing out on things just because of germs.

Amy came and did my hair last night, which was nice, but it is coming out in handfuls. I have accepted (I think) that I am not going to go bald as that happens very quickly and comes out in great clumps, but having reread the info it does say that it is very likely for the hair to get thin and brittle. Great.

So BUPA today and – almost forgot – deep joy – St Mary's tomorrow for a CT scan. Fantastic. When am I going to stop moaning? No one knows. Didn't go picking up today, but I did drive up to Butser and give all the dogs a run. Just a tad irresponsible as I could quite easily have flaked out – but I didn't. Felt very wobbly and breathless and my heart was pounding by the time we got back to the car, but we made it and they enjoyed it. Apart from that I stayed in (as prisoners do) for the rest of the day. Sent a load of stuff to the charity shop via Carol next door, so that was good. Wrapped the few Christmas presents I have managed to get. Everything is ready for Exbury, so I just need to sort Bereleigh out and I can finish off the trials this season and I am really looking forward to resigning now and getting rid of all this paperwork etc.

Wednesday, 4 a.m. – ALL-TIME LOW. HUGELY DEPRESSED. DON'T WANT ANYONE WITH ME. DON'T WANT TO TALK TO ANYONE.

Spent most of the day at BUPA yesterday, blood tests etc. and waiting to see Captain Chemo. I now have to be admitted on Thursday at 9 a.m. for two large blood transfusions as my body is at crisis stage with my blood. Unless I have these transfusions I will keep collapsing and won't be strong enough to take the next lot of chemo and I should plan on them being given to me over a period of five to six hours each. I have decided to go ahead with it, but I don't want anyone with me. This sounds really ungracious, I know, but I really don't want anyone fussing over me and constantly trying to cheer me up, so I'm going it alone. I also have to go for a CT scan today, but that isn't until 4.30 p.m. and Sue is going to take me to that.

Until my condition improves, no driving – but there is no way I am going to leave these dogs without giving them a run today, so as soon as Sam has gone I am taking them to Butser. If I collapse someone will find me, I'm sure.

So, my week off, my week with no treatment, my week with three days picking-up booked in has gone rather more than pear-shaped. I have had some depressed moments in my lifetime, but this just has to be up there amongst the worst and I can feel myself slipping ever lower and lower and don't know what to do about it. Perhaps after the transfusions (which I am dreading) my mood will improve – let's hope so. In the meantime, I will just stay home alone. I just don't have one positive thought or the energy to even try.

Thursday – I did take the dogs to Butser yesterday, but Sue knew I was going and I had to phone her when I got back just to let her know I was OK. So, that was that. The rest of the day I just pottered and had to keep sitting down, but that was OK.

Today Sue is picking me up at 8.30 a.m. and I am going into hospital for the blood transfusions, which I hope are going to work a little miracle and make me feel 100% better and I can perhaps get back to normal (well, as normal as I can get with this illness). Sue took me down for my CT scan yesterday afternoon, which was OK – no problem – but that short journey and the whole procedure left me with a migraine and my head, heart and ears have been pounding and I can only assume that again this is all caused by my blood problem. I think it is going to be a long day at BUPA, but I am still positive that I don't want any company with me; my head couldn't cope with it. Perhaps with luck I may be able to get some sleep.

My mobility is not great at the moment. Even going upstairs makes my head and heart pound and then of course next Tuesday is a big whammy chemo day – hopefully that will be the last one before Christmas and I may be able to get the nurse to come here to flush the PICC line before the Exbury trial because I am going to miss out Day 8 – fantastic. So I may with a bit of luck feel almost human by Christmas, at least for a couple of days.

Friday – Spent all day at BUPA yesterday having the blood transfusions. Sue dropped me off and I was finished a lot earlier than anticipated although it still took six and a half hours to have the units of blood dripped through. Didn't get much time for sleeping as I was closely monitored all day and saw much more of the nurses than usual. However, I did what I wanted to do and spent the day on my own, which was fine. Didn't have to talk to anyone, didn't have anyone fussing around me and just fended for myself and I was happy with that. Still very relieved when I escaped and found Sue and Joe waiting for me, and I was very glad to get home. I really don't begin to feel any benefit from the blood as yet, but presumably it takes a while for my body to adjust to again having something alien pumped through and of course next Tuesday I have to go for my fifth cycle of chemotherapy and then the sixth after Christmas. I am banking on the sixth one being my last and if any extra are suggested I will need to hear some pretty convincing reasons for why I should even consider having any more. Hopefully next Tuesday Captain Chemo will at least manage to spend ten minutes with me so that I can ask him the results of the CT scan and what his thoughts are. Let's hope he doesn't just fly in and fly out again. Still not supposed to drive, which is so debilitating and completely stops me going to the shops, but I guess it also stops me spending money I don't have so that has to be a bonus.

I won't be going on the shoot today and, being realistic, if I don't improve over the weekend I won't be going on Monday. I seem to have so much to do and get on with, but I just don't have the energy. Really want to get up and running for the next few weeks and at least try and have some kind of Christmas. This is the first time in over twenty years that I haven't had a houseful and have no meals or anything to prepare or think about.

I am hoping to take the dogs for a run this morning. I have told Sue and will ring her when I get back. I also hope my mood improves and that I can shake myself out of this depression. I know I am difficult and absolutely hateful to everyone around me and I don't mean it. That's why I feel I am much better off on my own, that way I don't upset anyone. They are all just trying to help and I do understand that, but what everyone else must understand is that I must do things for myself all the time I can. I know when I can't do something and that's when I shall ask for help.

Sam still gets all his lunch boxes prepared for him, all his meals are done, his washing – everything, and although he has days off when I am really not well he really is happier pottering around doing outside jobs, which is a help, but there is going to come a time when he will absolutely have to start doing some inside chores. I guess we shall cross that bridge when we come to it, I don't want to start nagging him about it now.

This journal is a strange thing. I can't believe how much I have written already and quite soon I shall be on the second book. I wonder who will read it? Will anyone be interested? It makes me feel better and I guess it is some kind of counselling for me. It has been suggested that I join some support groups, but I am really not sure that would be my thing, so I look on this journal as my support group and find it helps to write in it every day.

The thumping headache appears to have gone and I can only assume that is because of the blood transfusions. Wonder whose blood it was? Thanks anyway, whoever you are. It has scared me, this blood thing. Up until that happened I thought I had most of the side effects under control and could pretty much anticipate my body's reactions. Constipation, mouth ulcers etc., etc. and I was coping with all that and dealing with it through various medications, but I don't know about this lack of blood as it is not something I can control. Have resigned myself to eating mountains of broccoli, blueberries, liver – LIVER – YUK. Anything I can eat to counteract this I will, even if I have to liquidise it – LIQUIDISED LIVER? I feel sick at the thought –

perhaps there are pills I can take instead? I'll phone the surgery; pills sound easier to me.

N.B. Just remembered – one of the nurses (I confessed to her about my trips to Butser with the dogs) said a) I shouldn't really do it, and b) if I was going to I should have my name and a contact number on my person in case of collapse. That's OK, I'll do that, but what would happen to the dogs? Hopefully they would stay near me. God knows. It won't happen.

Saturday – Well, this bloody transfusion does not appear to have made any difference whatsoever. I am still so depressed, still have trouble just walking as my legs feel like lead, my head aches and life is just shit. I am finding it extremely difficult just looking after the dogs; they are constantly wanting my attention. I can't just sit down and watch daytime television all day as there's washing to do, and it's a constant struggle to keep the dog beds clean and hoover the conservatory. Then there is the shopping. Some of it I get on line, but there are always other bits and pieces to get, the bank to go to, and I just don't want other people doing everything. I have to have some space. I have to be able to drive into Petersfield and do some shopping on my own. I don't want to be driven everywhere. I don't want people just to come and see me. What are they coming for? I don't want to see anyone or talk to anyone. I don't want to hear where they have been and what they have done, because I can't go anywhere or do anything. I don't want to be taken for a drive somewhere, I don't want anyone doing my washing. I am a prisoner in my body and a prisoner in my home.

The absolute worst thing which has made me slump into this dark cavern is all the time this has been going on I have still been able to go picking up and now I can't and that has made everything just 100% worse. I have always had my picking-up days to aim for and enjoyed seeing everyone and the dogs getting worn out, but I can't do it any more, I just can't and I was honestly aiming to go on Monday as I thought the blood transfusions would sort me out.

Since July I have been active, cheerful, positive and pretty much OK, but these last two weeks have seen such a change and I feel as though I am slipping deeper and deeper into this black hole. I don't expect people to understand and I don't expect anyone to put up with it, so I'm best left alone.

My GP called in today, which was nice of him, and he seemed to think that I have got so depressed because of the blood thing and he also thought it quite likely that I would need more transfusions. I also told him that Captain Chemo was talking about extending the chemotherapy for extra cycles and how upset I would be. My GP agreed with me that Captain Chemo would need some pretty good reasons for doing this and I would need to have some very positive feedback from him before I would consider it. At the moment I am struggling to finish the six cycles and would so readily give it up just to get my body back again. All I wanted when this all started was to get through the shooting season and be able to do what I normally do – it's not happening. I have absolutely nothing to aim for, nothing to get excited about – nothing. I just feel this awful sort of darkness descending as if I am just marking my time here.

Sunday, 4 a.m. – Having had quite a good day yesterday, I felt more energetic than I have all week. The sun was shining, which always helps, and I did escape and take the dogs to Butser. Also managed to wash dog beds and do household chores so felt more human than of late. Having said that, I have had a really bad sleepless night and have not been able to relax and sleep. So much on my mind. I feel guilty with the number of friends who phone and want to come and visit, but I just don't want anyone here. I get so exhausted just talking with people and find it worse when they are exceptionally jolly and try to cheer me up. I don't want to be cheered up – I just want my life back and I know that is never going to happen. Sue and Joe came yesterday and hoovered up some of the leaves, so the garden does look a bit tidier.

I wonder if my blood tests will be OK to have chemo this Tuesday. Part of me hopes that I can't have it and that would mean a complete break over Christmas; the other part of me just wants to get it over and done with. It will be interesting though to see if the tumour has shrunk again and also to hear the results of the CT scan. Perhaps I will need another transfusion, but whatever happens I refuse to let any dates interfere with Exbury and Bereleigh. So once those two trials are over that is the end of my focus and responsibilities as field-trial secretary – what shall I focus on then? Living, I guess.

I will make a big effort today to try and improve my mood with people – especially Bridget as she really does have enough on her plate without worrying about me. Sue has offered to drop me off at BUPA on Tuesday as I have to be there early for X-rays and blood tests; then I will have a couple of hours to spare before Captain Chemo arrives so Bridget could come in the afternoon, which would save her a bit of time. I think Sue has suddenly realised that she is going away on 2nd January for three months and I think she needs to do as much for me as she can before that happens. Also think she is concerned that my condition will worsen while she is away, but to be honest I was hoping that the chemo will have stopped by the end of January and my condition will improve – if only temporarily.

Monday, 11th December, 6.30 a.m. – The plan was to go picking up today, but I'm not sure now as there is a gale-force wind blowing and torrential rain. I am in two minds really as I think it would be good for me mentally to go and see all the guys, but physically I guess not so good. I'll give it another hour or so and see what it looks like in the daylight.

Lucy from Buddies came to see me yesterday and gave me an update on all their activities – it's their Christmas party tonight and I wish I could go. Anyway, it was good to see someone different and have a chat. I am coming to the conclusion that anyone having the amount of chemo I am having should just disappear for six months and then hopefully reappear at the end of it. Most people that have never been involved or close to anyone having chemo believe it is all the same. I did before I unfortunately became educated. Each individual receives different mixes and different types of chemo and there are many, many different types. Most patients have one dose of chemo every three weeks. I on the other hand have 500 GemCarbo chemo and 250 other mixed on one day followed the next week with another dose, so I actually only get one week in three free of treatment and I would never, never agree to it again.

Tomorrow is my big dose and I shall also have another X-ray to see if there is any further shrinkage. I'll also get the results of the CT scan plus blood tests to see if the transfusions have done any good – I may need more. I also need to know the risks of this happening again. Sometimes I just wish it was all over because my quality of life is absolute shit and all I do is moan all the time.

12th December – Chemo day? There is some doubt. Captain Chemo called me at 8.05 a.m. yesterday to ask me to go and see him last night at 7.30 p.m. Because he is always in a rush and never has time to sit and talk for long, he thought this might be more satisfactory! For whom? Certainly not me and I had no intention of improving his timetable just to make him feel better. I asked him about the scan and he said it was 'encouraging' – how encouraging? What does that mean? I asked him if it was likely that I would need another transfusion. Quite likely and if my blood test results are not good today he would book me in for another transfusion and delay the chemo for a week. I reminded him that I had already made arrangements NOT to do Day 8 (as I have the Exbury trial), so that was not an option.

Now I just don't know what will happen today because if I don't have the chemo today I cannot realistically see it being done until after Christmas. So what difference would that make? Will I deteriorate in two weeks? I can't feel any worse than I already do. The upshot of all this is that I am very close to not having any more treatment. I really don't think I can tolerate the invasion to my body and my life any longer. Surely, I can at least get back to normal for a few months even if it brings my death forward by twelve months. I feel sure I will get a few months where I could feel reasonably well and at least get in the car and do my own thing.

The shooting season has been shit. I had been coping with the picking-up quite well until the blackouts started – no one warned me about that, no one warned me that I might get so anaemic that I wouldn't be able to function. February is usually my really flat month having usually had a great shooting season and seeing everyone all the time. In February it is usually dreadful. So, if I feel worse at the moment than I normally do in February, I guess by that time I will be feeling suicidal!

Wednesday, 13th, 6.30 a.m. – OK, I seem to have calmed down a bit today and feel slightly more optimistic. Having worked myself up to fever pitch about blood tests, transfusions, missed chemo sessions, and having gone into BUPA yesterday morning ready for anything and prepared to refuse treatment, I had my X-ray and to my unqualified eye could already see that ET had shrunk again and almost looked as though it was dispersing. I had my blood tests and then all I had to do was wait for Sergeant Chemo (I had demoted him as he had pissed me off). When he arrived (early for once) he didn't fly in and fly out; he actually spent some time with me and was so confident that my bloods were recovering that he wanted to go ahead with the chemo (which he wouldn't do if there was any concern). He was very positive about the CT scan and was excited that the lymph nodes in my chest area had also shrunk. I shall be missing out Day 8 of chemo next week – yes – which he thinks will also be beneficial for the recovery of my bloods and makes the possibility of more transfusions unlikely, but he hasn't completed ruled it out; but if I feel the slightest bit faint I have to ring immediately and not leave it four days as I did (apparently I was too stoic about the whole thing) and then they will rush me in again.

FUTURE PLAN – My next cycle is due on 2nd January followed by a top-up on 9th January, after which he wants another CT scan and a private meeting with me to discuss what happens next. I am very anti going for another two cycles of chemo and in my humble uneducated medical opinion if the lymph nodes have shrunk with the chemo, surely I won't need radiotherapy (I hope). So if all goes well, I will tolerate the chemo I had yesterday and keep all the side effects at bay. I won't be rushed in for blood transfusions and I won't ruin anyone's Christmas by feeling too ill. Exbury will run like clockwork and I can perhaps go picking up on Friday. Can't be more positive than that.

I am interested to see what happens next and when I have my meeting with him in January what he will say about my life expectancy etc. Good news also is that Rusty (one of the chemo nurses) has cut my PICC line off by half the length and taken one of the clips out and then refitted it with a much smaller clip. This is a huge improvement, much more comfortable. It has halved the size of the dressing and I am delighted with that.

Got a bit stressy, but then I always do when I am being pumped through with that stuff, but I wasn't hateful to anyone and Bridget didn't get it in the neck for once. So, actually, I quite behaved myself. Must rest all day today – don't do rest very well, but I will try.

Thursday – Lost a day already! Actually all things considered and bearing in mind I had a huge whammy of chemo on Tuesday I was decidedly chipper most of yesterday! Didn't dog walk, but did go outside with them and do a few outside chores, hoovered the conservatory and made cheese-and-onion sandwiches for Sam's lunch boxes like there was no tomorrow. Did rest for a couple of hours at lunchtime, but then decided to finish all the Christmas wrapping, which I have done, so I'm getting there. Have not taken any gloop as Sue got me maximum-strength senapods and I am very pleased to announce that it is only 5.45 a.m. and they have worked. Great – if that works everything else seems to feel much better.

Also stopped the anti-sickness suppositories as my GP tells me they have to go via the kidneys etc. and can cause other problems, so he has now given me some tablets which just go under my lip and take two to three hours to dissolve (unless they get stuck on my chewing gum). So, I seem to have turned a corner mood-wise. I hope so – I hate feeling like that and I know it is pretty unbearable for those around me. I am on the very rosy-cheek week because I have to take steroids for a week after big chemo, consequently my cheeks blow up and look very red. But I loathe it when people see me and tell me I look well! These tablets also contribute to the insomnia and I ended up taking three sleeping tablets at varying intervals last night, so feel incredibly woolly this morning.

Can't make up my mind if I would be really pushing my luck going to Butser this morning as it is only the second day after chemo, but I probably will. I did have an e-mail from Brenda yesterday, who has cancer in various organs and has been undergoing chemo since July. She recently had a full body scan and was mortified to be told that her main tumour had not shrunk. Surely they could have discovered that a bit earlier and changed her chemo? They are now suggesting they keep her on a tablet-type chemo, which apparently is not such a pain obviously to take or should I say administer, but it looks very involved and on hourly/daily rates. I'm sure I would rather have it all over in one really shitty day. Plus, she doesn't know what the side effects are yet. You see, it's true, there is always someone worse off than you and I feel so terribly sorry for her.

Bettina – another Buddies friend – is calling in for an hour today. It will be nice to see someone different and she will bring all the photographs of the Buddies Christmas party for me to make a collage.

If God is listening up there I would really appreciate it if I could continue feeling pretty much OK for the next couple of weeks and avoid being rushed in for transfusions or anything. Just a couple of weeks, please – I'm not asking for another ten years. Just don't want to ruin the field-trial at Exbury or worry anyone at Christmas – quite prepared to carry on with the treatment in January, but please just let me have this next couple of weeks where I can feel well and be independent.

Friday, 5.30 a.m. – Dogs woke me up and I feel exhausted and slightly nauseous this morning. The plan was to get everything done yesterday and leave today free for picking-up. So – Butser Hill, two visits – Sue and Bettina – as soon as they had gone I hoovered the conservatory then I dashed (yes, on my own driving when I shouldn't be) into Petersfield, paid credit card, shopped at Waitrose, came home, did not sit down for lunch, unpacked shopping, did dogs then finally sat down about 4.30 p.m. and waited for Sid to come and sort the Rayburn out at 6 p.m. Consequently – I HAVE COMPLETELY OVERDONE IT AND DON'T THINK I SHALL BE PICKING UP TODAY!

However, I have made a cup of tea, fed the dogs and come back to bed, so let's see how I feel in an hour or so. Sue C. warned me to 'take it easy', but when I am feeling OK I can't. I'll be fine – tough as old boots really. Seems very strange not rushing around preparing to entertain and thinking about menus this Christmas as it will be the first time in twenty-five years or so that I haven't been entertaining, so there is no massive cooking or shopping to concern myself with – weird! I have wrapped all the presents and all female members of my family have a little extra something from my jewellery box, so I hope I have chosen something they will like and wear. Sue has sorted out Premium Bonds for William, so he is sorted and there is nothing else to worry about.

Hope I am OK for Exbury on Wednesday. I am supposed to be going down the night before and staying in the caravan with Paula – hope I will be OK and that it isn't too cold! Shall I take the wig? Have to go to Petersfield for my optician's appointment tomorrow. I know I need new glasses, but will try not to spend a small fortune on them that I haven't got – I may not need them for long! This last pair I have had for two years – how long the next pair!

Saturday – I didn't go picking up yesterday; could not lift my head off the pillow and felt like shit. You could blame the fact that perhaps I did too much yesterday, but I really don't feel good again today and now I'm seriously worried that I may need another transfusion. I did take the dogs out yesterday, but then spent the rest of the day curled up with a blanket over me watching rubbish on television. Head spinning again, ears pounding – not great. I will do pretty much the same today, I guess, apart from the optician's appointment I have at 11.45 a.m., which I intend keeping. Picking up is also out of the question again on Monday.

I did plan on going, but a call from BUPA has put a stop to that as I have to go for another CT scan – why? I think he (CC) mentioned something about another one last week, but it seems pretty soon after the other one – doubtless I shall find out in time.

Sam is off shooting round with Birkett today and I actually envy him his normal lifestyle at the moment. His life hasn't really changed at all through all this. I know he is shocked and scared at the outcome, but he can still do what he likes. Goes fishing, shooting, sees people, and has normal conversations that don't include tumours, CT scans, blood transfusions.

Bloody phone didn't stop ringing last night. Didn't answer it once – all about field trials probably and when I feel like this I just can't speak to anyone, so they have all probably left numerous important (they think) messages which doubtless I shall have to plough through today. I am so glad this is my last season as field-trial secretary and I must confess that the way I feel at the moment the idea of me taking over as chairman just fills me with absolute horror, but that isn't until March so anything can happen between now and then.

Sunday, 5.30 a.m. – I am beginning to think I need another transfusion and I'm also becoming very aware that this chemo does not have any pattern – it gets worse. You get more and more exhausted and less able to function and whereas in the beginning by the third day I would start to feel better, it doesn't happen any more. I felt OK on Wednesday and Thursday this week (Day 1 and Day 2) after chemo, but since then I have deteriorated and I feel completely exhausted. I am much weaker than I was when I set off for the Windsor trial and now I'm seriously worried about Exbury. Can I in all honesty without putting myself at risk go down to Exbury on Tuesday night, stay in Paula's caravan, run the trial and then come home without any after-effects? I feel so weak even after resting most of yesterday and going to bed at 8.30 p.m. and sleeping for eight hours. Michael rang yesterday and was going to come over this morning with the puppy, but I have put him off. I look and feel like shit and I don't want him to see me like this. I won't be picking up on Monday. I just have

117

to accept that I can't do it any more. I think the most I could probably do would be one drive.

Do I ring BUPA and run the risk of being rushed in for another transfusion or try and ignore it and carry on? One thing is for sure, this stops at six cycles. That's all he wanted to do in the first place and my body just cannot take any more of this. I just want to be able to live a bit of my life – this isn't even an existence. I've started to get that pounding in my ears again and that's what happened when I needed the blood. I'm finding the dogs a chore and that is really a bit unfair because if I do manage to take them for a spin round Butser they do settle for the rest of the day. Sometimes I just wish I only had two dogs and not six. The only reason I have six is to use them for picking up, so that rather defeats that objective as I can't pick up any more. Perhaps I seriously should think about rehoming some of them.

Monday, 18th December – OK, I am going to stop moaning today – well, that's the plan. I must be positive about Wednesday at Exbury. Everyone is rallying round to try and make it as easy as possible for me. All the committee (well nearly all) are really pulling out the stops with the food and Sue C. is going to be dog steward so as long as I can get there, survive the night in Paula's caravan and get through the day, then I can do it. I'd like to be able to say that I can look forward to a relaxing day on Thursday, but I don't think that will happen. Sid is coming to service the boiler and the nurse is coming to flush my PICC line – what I must avoid is a blood transfusion before Christmas at all costs!

CT scan today – don't know what that is about so close after the last one, but I guess CC knows what he is doing. I just hope that he doesn't suggest more chemo after my last whammy due on 9th January because I seriously think I shall refuse it.

Bridget came yesterday and chatted on about where she had been and what she had done. Couldn't respond really as I haven't been anywhere (apart from Butser Hill) or done anything. I tried to explain that actually I didn't want to go anywhere or see anyone until this is all over. I am happier (well, not exactly happy, but more comfortable in my own company) pottering around and doing my own thing. That way I am not relying on anyone, I don't have to be nice to anyone and the only person I can upset is myself. Sam is very quiet lately. I think he is just upset and worried about me. I have completely withdrawn into myself and he does not know how to help or what to say to me.

I haven't just sat around feeling sorry for myself. I got on with chores yesterday even though I didn't feel like it. Washed my Frontera and the dog blankets and generally made it look a bit more respectable. The Vectra needs doing, but I am going to persuade Sam to do that for me on Wednesday. I have swapped them over so that he can take Nymph, Rhea and Cracker to the vet for their boosters.

Not picking up today – it is the only sensible decision to make. I want to go so badly, but I know it would be completely foolhardy – perhaps on Friday or Boxing Day? Let's see how I get on at Exbury and how I am feeling by then – don't want to ruin anyone's Christmas.

Les left me a message yesterday, but I didn't ring him back. He was looking for a flat-coat for Sue as she had just lost her last one and I must admit Fletcher went through my mind and I know it would be the most wonderful home etc., but I just can't do it yet. It would be perfect for him, living in Devon on an amazing shoot with some really wonderful people. Perhaps I am being a bit selfish here; perhaps I will ring Les and just have a chat. Dunno.

Tuesday, 19th December, 6 a.m. – Just when I thought things were beginning to improve the boiler has packed up so no central heating! Fortunately when Sid came to fix the Rayburn last week (because that had packed up) I booked him in to service the boiler and he is coming on Thursday. That is still two days away, but it has put a new concept on sleeping in Paula's caravan this evening – it won't be any colder there than it will be here. Plus, after running out of oil last Christmas I fully intended getting the chimney sweep after the jackdaws nested in it, but I forgot and dare not put a match to the fire as the whole house will go up in flames. Will ring Sid this morning to tell him that the situation is now urgent and a life-and-death situation.

The good news is that yesterday I did start to feel a little better and actually drove myself to BUPA for my – yet another – CT scan. What a sense of freedom and escape! I put the car through the car wash, pottered around the supermarket (with all the germs) for an hour and actually got some shopping. Felt almost normal for once.

Had a really lovely bouquet from Pam in NZ and I was so thrilled with it that I rang her immediately, completely forgetting the time difference. It was 1 a.m. over there and I woke her up, but she was great and, knowing her ability to sleep (and snore), she would have gone straight back to sleep (hopefully)!

Off to Exbury this evening and I doubt that I shall take this with me, so I shall have to catch up and report on my night in the caravan and the field trial when I return. I do hope Paula doesn't smoke in the caravan too much – perhaps she will realise. I hope so.

I wonder why I needed a second scan? Also, they wanted to get my abdomen in the picture. Has ET shrunk in my lung and moved somewhere else? I won't have any more chemo, you know. I really have decided that after the two sessions on 2nd and 9th January that will be it. I refuse to hibernate for another six months on the off chance of another year. Still quite scared about what will happen. Not scared to die, just want to know how I will die, when I will die, will I be able to walk, breathe unaided, and will it be dignified? Poor Sam! Most cancer patients join some kind of support group – I really don't think that is for me. I look on this journal as my support group. I say far more in this than I would say surrounded by 'trying to be cheerful and pretend it's not happening' cancer patients. Sounds a bit mean – they are only trying to survive, but I don't think it is for me. Best wait and see how desperate I get.

Tuesday, 19th, 5.15 p.m. – Let's start at the beginning of the Exbury saga, which materialised into the most extraordinary field trial. Paula picked me up and we set off down to Exbury to spend the night in her caravan, which, even if I was feeling well, would have filled me with horror! When we arrived it was absolutely freezing and Kevin and Caroline were really concerned and wanted us to go to their cottage to sleep (I was tempted). However, once the fan heater had done its job and Kevin had brought in fish and chips, we all started to feel a bit warmer. I actually slept reasonably well with the aid of three sleeping tablets, but we were awake at 5 a.m. and there was no way on earth we would get back to sleep again. So that was it, we just chatted and had some 'quality time' until everyone started arriving for the field trial.

I was quite happy with the way things were proceeding – all the competitors had turned up and we were almost ready to start thinking about moving off. Then I noticed Bob was there and I hadn't been expecting him. Then I saw Barry, Colin, John, Rupert and then SAM! My reaction? What the fuck are you doing here? Who the fuck is looking after my dogs? I had until that moment been happy in the knowledge that Sam was at home looking after my dogs so I could relax and get on with it. I seriously did not know what was going on until it was explained that Kevin (the lovely Exbury keeper), who is such a good friend now, had organised it all as a surprise for me! No – wrong word – their word was 'as a *treat*' for me! I have to say that *surprise* was the better word; *treat* just didn't paint the picture.

It was fantastic of Kevin to go to all that trouble to get all my friends there to shoot for the trial and it really was a great surprise, but the only people that had a treat were the guys! Free shooting at Exbury, lunch provided (by me and the committee), shoot dinner afterwards – you work it out. Not one of them helped load the cars or help pack up at the end!

Anyway – presentation over – then we all headed to the pub where Kevin had laid on a meal. Bless his heart, what a great guy. I did go and have a cup of tea, but there was no way I could make the meal and I had to call it a day as I was completely exhausted and Duncan very kindly brought me home.

It really was a great day, the weather was perfect and Kevin and Caroline and Paula et al had done so much to make it a special day for me and I just cannot believe that so much thought and effort went into it. It was great to have a bath and put my feet up for a while, plus Sid had mended the boiler a day early so the heating was on – huge bonus. I didn't even have a wash in the morning as there was nowhere to have a wash. We had to troop across the yard to the Portaloo to clean our teeth in our wellies! So it was great to think that Exbury was over, I was clean and the house was warm. I was extremely pleased to fall into my own bed, exhausted at 8.30 p.m.

Friday – Spent most of yesterday just pottering about clearing up everything from the trial and doing the paperwork and then started on the Bereleigh trial! I did take the dogs to Butser, but that could have ended in disaster as I started to skid in the car driving up there and only just made it! I had visions of going over the edge with all the dogs in the back! No one knew I was up there, so I could have been in deep trouble! However, I made it and came home the long way round to avoid the steep, icy descent. The nurse from the surgery came and flushed my line out, so that was great – saved a trip to BUPA. Apart from that it was a day at home – there's a surprise. I was in bed by 8 p.m. and slept through until 3 a.m., catching up as I was exhausted.

What I would like to do today is go out on the shoot! Half of me is a bit scared in case I don't feel well and the other half just needs to do it, so I guess that half will win. It is still dark, so I am not sure what the weather is like – whatever happens I won't stay all day, but having missed the last four days I really would like to show my face and take them some cake.

Paula was a bit emotional on the phone yesterday. I think she was just exhausted and thankful that the Exbury trial was over. So much planning had gone into it and I think she just worried herself sick over the whole thing; but she needn't have worried, it all went off perfectly and everyone enjoyed my 'treat'!

Saturday – I went picking up! I only intended staying for a couple of drives, but stayed all day and even managed to come home and change dogs at lunchtime. Everyone was pleased to see me and I really enjoyed chatting to them all. Even Bill said it was nice to see me out. I needed that. Dogs thoroughly enjoyed it although Fletch did get rather overexcited. I can now look forward to another chemo-free week and the possibility of picking up again next week sometime.

I am going to chat to CC (Captain Chemo) because I really have had enough and I want to miss out Day 8 again or even the possibility of having it a week later because that is the one that really finishes me off. Hard to believe that I have been having this poison pumped through my body since August and if he allows me to finish the six cycles – that's twelve chemo sessions – in January, I can see the end of the tunnel and no more chemo. Then what? I really don't know what happens next. Obviously he has radiotherapy in mind, but I am keeping my fingers crossed that he will not think that is a great idea. Do I go on to some kind of medication to keep ET at bay or is it just pot luck and he (ET) is left to his own devices to start growing again? Will I start to develop symptoms? Will I suddenly have a new lease of life and feel bloody brilliant? Wish I knew.

Had more bouquets this week. One from Sam's sister and a really pretty one with a vase from Lesley and Ian. I honestly had no idea how many people cared for me and it really is quite humbling. Now – I have to make a note of this because it is truly unbelievable – I have known Gwen and Mike for over twenty years and in all that time never had a Christmas card. Gwen was always too busy, always too chaotic and it was the norm for her never to get around to Christmas cards. Yesterday, I had a lovely card from them saying they were thinking of me – I must be really ill! Bridget's going shopping for me this morning, so she will be up later. I'm not doing anything much today, but if it isn't frosty I would quite like to go up to the garage and pressure-hose the mud off my car from yesterday.

Sunday – I did go and pressure-hose the Frontera off. Swapped the cars over, so will use the Vectra for a couple of days. I wish Sam would let me sell the Vectra as it is a complete waste for me to have two cars; I never go anywhere. He just doesn't want anything to change, that's the problem, and as long as everything carries on around him normally then he thinks the world, or at least Sam's world, is fine. Didn't take the dogs out – I figured they would be OK for a day as they went out on the shoot yesterday.

Sam has a filthy cold and this is my most vulnerable week where my body is completely wiped out and I need to take antibiotics daily to counteract infection! Not quite sure what would happen if I did catch a cold, but that is the reason I am not allowed to go out to theatres etc. – because of the germ factor. I'm not allowed to go to the surgery or to anywhere crowded and what happens? Sam brings one home. I suppose I could just get pneumonia and die – solve a lot of problems, I reckon.

It's Christmas Eve today, I had almost forgotten. I am usually rushing around like something demented preparing a dinner party, but not this year – have enough trouble boiling an egg at the moment. Feels really strange, everyone else is doing what they always do at Christmas and I hardly know it's happening. I did send out Christmas cards and I have presents for immediate family, but that's about it. The girl members – plus Bridget and Louise – all have something from my jewellery box and William has a Premium Bond. Wonder if I will still be here next Christmas? If I am going to feel like this – forget it. I would rather be dead.

Christmas Day, 6 a.m. – Kids all over the country are already opening presents, turkeys are already going in ovens to be overcooked, people are in hospital too ill to go home for Christmas, children with terminal illnesses are in hospital – some waiting for transplants – some are going to die. There are people sleeping on the streets and it's freezing cold this morning; the fighting goes on in Iran and Basra, Jerusalem is a war zone and it's Christ's birthday. I was talking to a spiritualist recently and asked the question why, if God is so good and Jesus was sent to save us, are there so many horrific crimes committed and so many young people dying? Surely with all that is happening and the 'unfairness' of it all it must put most Christian people's faith in question. How can all these terrible things happen? Why are babies sometimes born with some incurable disease? I have been told that it is a learning curve for us all and in this life what we learn prepares us for the next. I really don't think I believe that.

For myself, I don't feel anger at all. I feel as though I am being punished for something bad I must have done. That's how I have been brought up – my mother always punished me for something whether I had been guilty or not. I don't think I have ever done anything really bad. I may have been somewhat defiant and told a few lies. I only misbehaved at school because I wanted people to like me and be my friend, but actually don't remember having any close friends at school so that didn't work. I guess there is no point in trying to analyse everything – not quite yet, but it won't be too long, I reckon.

We are off round to Sue's for Christmas lunch this afternoon. Apparently Ian has a cold and I am supposed to avoid people with colds! The alternative would be not to go, stay here, have poached eggs on toast and not see my family; and being realistic this could be the last Christmas I am here, so we are going.

Got to Sue's about 2 p.m., had lunch about 3.30 p.m. Very hectic, very noisy, very nice lunch, nice to get out and see everyone. Claire, Paul and William came about 3 p.m. and William had his Santa Babygro on. Left about 7 p.m.; bath and bed by 9 p.m.

Boxing Day – Pretty much the same routine planned for today. Then that is it – nothing else planned for the rest of the week, nothing for New Year's Eve, just chemo on 2nd January looming and he (Captain Chemo) is not going to be pleased because I don't want to do Day 8 again. I'll run that one up the flagpole and see which way the wind takes it! Not long now before he (CC) informs me of what his plans for me are now and what the prognosis is after chemo!

Wanted a quiet chat with Ian yesterday about my funeral as I wanted to ask him to do a reading. I want him to read the poem I did when Dee was buried at sea. I know he was thinking of emigrating to Australia and if that happens before I die then there is no way I want him to make a special journey for my funeral. However, he did give me the impression yesterday that he probably would stay working in London for another couple of years, so that would be good. I will give him a call and talk to him about it as I think it would be apt for him to read out the poem that I read at his father's funeral and I really would like him to do it.

They are shooting here today and tomorrow. I cannot go today, and tomorrow I have to stay home because the nurse from the surgery is coming to flush my PICC line. But it just occurred to me that if she comes quite early I could go out on the shoot after she has gone – yes, that's what I shall do. I'm feeling quite good this week (only because I played truant from Day 8 chemo) so I must take the opportunity while I can. Bereleigh Field Trial is on 12th January and if I manage to do that one then I will have achieved what I wanted to do and that was run all the trials this year – so fingers crossed.

Wednesday – I have been surrounded by people with colds/flu all over Christmas. I already feel as though I am getting a cold, but there is not much I can do about it. I have a headache and a cough, so I'll just wait and see.

Don't know about the shoot today. That was my plan after the nurse has been, but to be honest I'm pretty wiped out after the last two days, plus I did all the driving, so I shall just see how the day pans out. Bridget will be very annoyed when she realises that Sam allowed me to drive for two days and also that I have put myself at risk by being exposed to all those germs.

Thursday – Didn't go to the shoot! The nurse didn't turn up! I eventually called the surgery about 3 p.m. and they said one of the nurses was off sick so they had put me on the doctor's list, which I told them was totally unnecessary, and made another appointment for the nurse to come on Friday. I know how busy they are, but had they called me first thing to explain I wouldn't have been hanging round all day. Rog called in to see me between drives and it was nice to see him. Should have had him and Chris shooting at Exbury and dropped two of the others.

Getting a bit basic – I have a slight concern with my bowels! I always have to take laxatives immediately after chemo as the side effects are horrendous in that department. Usually take the gloop for about ten days in each chemo cycle and then it's back to normal until the next cycle. I find now that it never gets back to normal and I take laxatives continually, which can't be right. Will have to mention that to CC and I must admit I often wonder if the cancer is anywhere else in my body. They never look anywhere else, always chest, but I guess that X-ray must include part of my abdomen or at least the CT scan does. I suppose there is always a chance that it is in my bowels. No one ever checks that out.

Sue C. is calling today, bringing the A and D signs back for the next trial. Poor Sue, she got lumbered with them after Windsor. Also we shall take the dogs to Butser for a run while she is here. I did go yesterday early, which was just as well as we never did get to the shoot. We shall definitely go on Monday before I go to chemo on Tuesday and that will probably be the only one I get to before the field trial.

I have developed a rather nasty cough, which has come from nowhere. I guess it could be the start of a cold. I wonder when the chemo stops, will I go back to feeling normal again? Will I ever be normal again?

Sue C. came down and brought the A and D signs back and then we took nine dogs between us up to Butser Hill. What a pack. Quite daunting for anyone walking one dog, but they were all very good and enjoyed their gallop round Butser. Met Debbi up there with her three minuscule little white dogs, which fascinated Fletch and Flinn, but fortunately the obsession didn't last long and we went our separate ways. Debbi is the girl with the dog-grooming van and she came in the spring and all the dogs had a hydro bath in her van. It was brilliant and I think we may do it again this year. Suddenly wish I had done some illustrations through this journal – Fletch looked great with his head over the top of the hydro bath!

I actually drove into Petersfield after Sue had gone and went to the pet shop followed by a grocery shop at Tesco. Might not mean much to you, but I certainly know that I have missed a chemo session because I feel so much better.

I am longing to know what happens next. I go along, have my X-rays and CT scans etc., and CC appears to be pleased with the shrinkage of ET but never indicates what will happen when the chemo stops or if I decide to stop it. What happens then? What happens when the cancer takes over and I die? Do I just go to sleep? Am I in a lot of pain? Will I have a dignified death? I have a reading with a medium on 8th January – let's see if she tells the truth or indeed is aware of the illness. That will be interesting. Janet, my cousin the spiritualist, recommended her, so I think she must be quite highly thought of. Think I might get Bridget to give me a lift or I guess I could get a taxi. Either way I mean to keep the appointment. I'm not trying to catch her out, but if she doesn't mention my illness or the fact that I am dying I shall be very difficult to convince. I have been to one before with Wendy after Mum died, mainly because Wendy wanted to go, and I confess I didn't believe a word of it. Wendy, on the other hand, was convinced that Mum and Dad had spoken to the medium and she got really upset.

I think, as I know I am dying, I will approach this differently and not be determined that it is all nonsense. I want to go; I want her to tell me things I will believe. I would be very pleased if she could indicate my death timing. I am going with a totally open mind and fully prepared to believe everything she tells me as Janet really does set so much store by her. So on 9th January, the morning after my reading, I look forward to writing it all down.

Saturday – Took all the Christmas decorations down yesterday, which nearly killed me and I ache all over this morning. Such a small task really, but I found it exhausting. Still Christmas is officially over in this house and I am back in my comfort zone. Much as I loved seeing everyone on Christmas Day and Boxing Day, I found actually getting there very stressful. I am so closeted here and have been for some months now – apart from dog walking, hospital and going on the shoot I don't do anything. Finding myself having to get ready to go out two days in a row was surreal and even when we were there I felt almost detached from them all.

Took the dogs out in the morning and the nurse came and flushed my PICC line. Sue and Joe came in the afternoon. They are off to South Africa for three months on Monday and wanted to see me before they left. I may be totally wrong about this, but I think Sue feels guilty about going and I think she was almost frightened that yesterday would be the last time she would see me, but it won't be; I shall still be here when they get back in April. I'm a bit sad because I had planned on being there with them for two or three weeks in March, but of course that is so out of the question now. Nevertheless it doesn't stop me wishing I could be there. She mustn't feel guilty. We can keep in touch by e-mail and I really hope they have a great time.

Had a really nice card from Bob and Ginnie. Sam wasn't very pleased that I wouldn't let him read it, but they spoke very highly of him and I felt it was personal information for me. I hope he stays at Avington for as long as he can keep working. He may not believe it, but it does him good and considering he is seventy in March he looks extremely well. I do get concerned at times worrying in case he became ill – what would happen? I can't look after him. I find it difficult enough now to do what I can and also manage the dogs at the same time. It is time, I know, for some of these dogs to go, but I just can't get my head round it. I do love them, but they are increasingly becoming a chore and there are days when I just cannot manage them. Would it be best to let other people sort them out after I die or would I feel happier knowing that I had found them a perfect home? I really don't know. I guess if the perfect person phoned looking for a particular dog I might, just might, let one of them go.

3 p.m. – I may not get out much, but I don't know anyone else that can sit in their bedroom and watch the beagles hunt out the copse on a Saturday afternoon. They must have had a brilliant day as the sun has been shining most of the day. They are in for a soaking now as the skies have turned black and the heavens have opened. I didn't get out on the shoot this week, but again I watched them from my bedroom as they did Orchard Drive and was envious to see my friends picking up. Not to worry, I am going on Monday – rain, snow or shine!

New Year's Eve, Sunday, 5 a.m. – I have in recent weeks become morose, filled with a strange kind of melancholia, listless and without any energy. I can hardly bear to move and my limbs ache. It is the kind of physical debility that I am unaccustomed to and I feel helpless to do anything about it. In truth, all I really want to do is curl up in bed and sleep. Were it not for the animals and chores I feel I have to keep on top of, I am quite sure that this is what I would do – just curl up in my own despair and deep-rooted loneliness. But of course I don't. I keep going all day automatically doing what I have to do, but the dogs give me no joy at the moment. I so wish they did. It is a constant struggle to walk them and keep their bedding changed and make sure they are OK.

I have developed a cough which I thought was the start of a cold, but as yet no cold, thank goodness. I am, however, coughing up small amounts of blood, but I honestly don't think I am going to tell anyone as I feel sure I would be rushed into hospital and I couldn't bear it.

It's still dark outside, but something has disturbed the roosting pheasants and momentarily they all started 'cocking'. I love that sound, even more in late autumn when they are going up to roost. They have gone quiet again now, but I still hear the owls; they have been hunting all night, no doubt. All quiet now.

I do feel lonely. I spend so much time here alone in my 'cocoon'. Visitors don't make loneliness go away. You can still be lonely in a room full of people. I think this loneliness is something I have created for myself and I have actually got to the stage when I am comfortable with it. When visitors are here, I want them to go. When the phone doesn't ring, I wish it would; then when it does, I don't want to answer it because I don't want to answer any 'How are you?' questions. So my latest answer to that particular question is that I don't want to discuss it.

My daily routine would drive anyone insane, but I do the same things at the same time every day. If this routine is broken by a visitor I find it difficult to cope. I also make a list of things I need to do. Yesterday it included the running order for Bereleigh. If by any chance I do not manage to do all the things on my list by 12 noon then that really puts my schedule out for the rest of the day because I have to finish the list – I cannot sleep if I haven't. How sad am I? It is not until I have written it down that I realise how sad this all is. Actually bored with it all now and would quite like to die.

8.30 p.m. – Bed! Will I die in 2007? Funny thing is when this was first diagnosed I thought in a perverse way, 'How lucky to know that you are going to die. You can get everything organised, clean out all the cupboards, make certain that there are no loose ends and when the time comes you can die happily knowing you have organised everything.' But I have moments when I wish I didn't know I was going to die and wish that I didn't have the responsibility of organising everything before I go. Why not just die and leave everything in a mess for others to sort out? Would anyone think any less of you? Would it matter? If I got run over by a bus it wouldn't matter, but then that's not likely to happen as I have never seen a bus in East Meon or Petersfield. I guess I will just carry on and clear out a few more cupboards.

New Year's Day, 2007 – Bucketing with rain at 5 a.m. Let's hope it eases off before I go picking up, because I am going. Tomorrow and chemo looms ever closer and although it is my sixth cycle, and theoretically the last, I dread it more than any other.

Is there such a thing as an afterlife? For thousands of years religions have preached that there is. If there is an afterlife there must be ghosts, spirits of the dead, who come back to this physical plane for a reason. Why has it never been proven? Why is there no evidence? In this world of ours, this technologically brilliant world, where everything else is proven without doubt, why is there no proof? Mediums and spiritualists believe there is an afterlife, believe that our friends and relatives do come back to get in touch with us, but I am still very cynical. I will wait and see how my reading progresses on 8th January.

Tuesday, 2nd January, 2007 – Chemo day – but don't let's dwell on that!

What a brilliant day we (me and the dogs) had yesterday, out picking up all day! It was a glorious sunny day. The dogs had a great time and worked hard – Katy did one of her famous disappearing acts, which threw me into a state of panic and I dispatched Ra to drive round to see if he could see her anywhere, but by the time he got back she had returned – exhausted, looking vaguely surprised and slightly lame, but to my huge relief. That was fortunately the last drive before lunch, so having gone back to the 'beaters' hut' for lunch I decided to take Katy home and pick up Nymph and Rhea to join in for the afternoon (Flinn was not at home as he had gone with Sam to Avington for the day to be used at stud). So I kept Fletch and Tess with me, collected Nymph and Rhea and went off to Sir William's Hill. They worked hard up and down that hill and it makes me realise how old Nymph and Rhea are. They certainly couldn't do it all day any more, but they so enjoy working and I guess if they dropped dead on the shoot they would die happy. Fletcher on the other hand was still raring to go. The only cloud in the sky produced hailstones like bullets at the end of the day walking back to the vehicle. I thoroughly enjoyed seeing 'the lads' and walking the dogs, having lunch with them all and seeing Bereleigh at its best in the sunshine, and I will try not to get so anxious today and hold the thought of yesterday to get me through it.

Wednesday, 3rd January, 5 a.m. – I really did try and hold that thought and remain calm, and to an extent it worked until about 2 p.m.

Having arrived at the hospital at 10.30 a.m. I had my blood tests and X-ray. Bridget had gone shopping and I didn't expect her until later and I was quite relaxed and prepared for a bit of alone time while I waited to see Captain Chemo. Surprise visit from Sue and Joe on their way to the airport. They only stayed about fifteen minutes, but I was really touched that they fitted me into their schedule. Bridget arrived about lunchtime, her shopping expedition complete and bearing extra gifts she thought I might fancy. Captain Chemo arrived early and things were going to schedule up until then.

We had a long chat regarding two more cycles, radiotherapy, a new drug in tablet form that would have to be approved by the insurance company etc., etc. but at the end of it all I want to live and the radiotherapy probably won't be useful as the tumour and the lymph nodes are in impossible positions and very difficult to zap. We concluded by me agreeing to go to my next cycle appointment (making that seven) and if the X-ray showed significant shrinkage again I would agree to another cycle. If there was no change in the tumour, then I would have no more chemo. I also told him that if we got six months down the line and he wanted to start chemo again, I would not even consider it. I then asked him what would happen next, how quickly would I deteriorate? He said they would be keeping an eye on me with appointments every three to four months and he would tell me if the tumour had become active again. I would start getting pain, weight loss, even more tired etc., but we are not talking several years here. I would say from the conversation we had yesterday that twelve months would be an achievement.

So all I had to wait for then was my chemo to be made up and start the treatment. Louise arrived for a visit. At 3 p.m. they started to push the anti-sickness drugs through and the saline, but my arm started to swell and panic stations set in and all treatment was stopped. I was definitely beginning to stress, I then had to go to X-ray to have a dye put through my line to check it wasn't leaking anywhere because if it was I could not have my chemo put through it as it was too dangerous. Close to tears I returned to my room and suggested to Bridget that she went home for an hour or so because I could foresee a very late departure for me. So she and Louise went and I did calm down a bit when the nurses informed me that the line was safe to use so I could start my chemo. This was at 4.30 p.m. and the actual treatment takes at least three hours. Then the machine broke down and had to be changed. Eventually the first bag of chemo went through in half an hour, twice as fast as it should be pumped, at my own request and risk. The second bag was pushed through in three-quarters of an hour – again at my own risk as it usually takes an hour and a half. I refused half the saline on the promise that I would drink two litres of water during the evening (that would be difficult as it was 6.30 p.m. already and I go to bed at 8 p.m.). Finally had my line flushed and re-dressed by 7 p.m. and Bridget came to collect me.

So I was very tired and emotional after that lot, but much better being left on my own for a couple of hours. I have also agreed to have Day 8. I know I was going to refuse it because of the field trial, but if it is going to be my last one then I really should do it. Plus I have asked them to do it in the morning and they have agreed to a 10.30-a.m. appointment and if my blood tests are OK then I should be able to have the chemo by about 11.30 a.m. and hopefully be home early afternoon. If it drags on and there are any problems I shall walk because I can't cope with it.

So that was my day yesterday and I must confess I thought he was going to be rather more optimistic with my progress than he was. Having gone through all this with the realistic possibility of twelve months, I am absolutely determined – even if I die in six months – not to waste any of it by having chemotherapy again. It would be so different if it were curable, but it isn't. I wish everyone around me were not quite so optimistic as they all think I am going to go on for years. Bridget is the only one that accepts the true situation. Sam most definitely doesn't and that concerns me.

My dogs – I have to do something positive with my dogs, and looking around me there is still so much to sort out. Do I worry myself and start rushing around like a maniac or let everyone else rummage when I have gone? Should I spend my time left sorting out things for others or just leave it? Dunno what to do.

Have I mentioned my taste buds before? Without reading through this journal from start to finish I really don't know how chemotherapy kills your taste buds and leaves you with a revolting taste in your mouth. Six months ago not a day would pass without my eating chocolate, ice cream, sweets, masses of fruit and very little bread. I used to love cereals – now any of these would just turn my stomach. Also coffee and red wine, any alcohol, I haven't touched. Instead I have cravings (must be what it is like when you are pregnant). Feta cheese, breadsticks, bacon, pineapple (at one stage a whole one a day), cheese – and more cheese – crumpets, bread, masses of carbohydrates, crisps, Hula Hoops and chips. Very strange. I kind of hope that when I have been off chemo for a month I might start eating normally (well, normally for me) again. Just thought I would share that with you.

Thursday – Didn't do a great deal yesterday. No dog walk – they were fed up. Cooked a couple of pheasants which Sam had left on the drainer, which made me feel sick. Tidied conservatory and made sure Sam had something ready for lunch. I didn't leave him anything for Tuesday and once again he was totally incapable of doing anything for himself and had a bag of crisps! Makes me mad. What is he going to do when I die? Did have a serious chat with him today and told him that after this lot of chemo I was refusing any more and made absolutely sure that he knew that I would definitely not be around in five years and that I was worried about him, but I still don't know if it sunk in. He never does any washing, cooking etc., so how is he going to survive?

I rested all afternoon, watching television mostly, but rather bored. Couldn't eat yesterday – just didn't want anything, but drank enough liquids hopefully. I didn't have any 'visitors' last night and I had a lot of trouble getting to sleep! I call them visitors, but really I expect it is my imagination. When I close my eyes to go to sleep there is blackness, then after a few minutes forms start to appear and sometimes just faces, some of which I recognise. It's all in black and white and they come towards me individually and then just fade. There have been animals also. I like it. I find it a comfort and I am sure it is just my way of counting sheep, but last night it didn't happen. I was consciously trying, but everything just remained black.

I am almost at the end of this book, but the new one is ready to start and I can't help wondering how many more I shall need.

What started off as a day-by-day journal for my family to read is turning into somewhat of an epic. I have been wondering if it would be beneficial for other cancer sufferers who were diagnosed like me and have absolutely no idea what is going to happen to them realistically. You are given fact sheets galore, but nothing actually prepares you for the side effects of chemo. I wouldn't know where to start if I were thinking of publishing. I would want all proceeds to go to Cancer Research or the Macmillan Nurses and, of course, I can't send my one and only copy away; I might never see it again. I fully intend writing every day until I die, whether it be six months, one year or whatever.

I wish I had something like this to read when I found out though – it would have helped. I guess you could call this my very own 'support group therapy'. I don't think I would be terribly good at that sort of thing, but this writing is my crutch and I just write about whatever comes into my head. Perhaps that is why I have kind of withdrawn into myself and I don't really want to get involved in 'How are you?' conversations – I've already said it all in here.

JOURNAL 2

5TH JANUARY 2007 – 2ND MAY 2007

5th January, 5 a.m. – Had a really bad night, stomach cramps, nausea, sweating, all to do with the chemo and the steroids, antibiotics and everything else I have been throwing down my throat. Tried to cut down on the sleeping tablets last night. I am up to three now so reduced it to two and at 2.30 a.m. regretted that decision. Still can't eat anything apart from dry toast and the odd ginger biscuit and Captain Chemo wants me to agree to an extra two cycles – for what purpose?

I did have a thought – several actually – during my disturbed night and thought it strange that I never think of the past any more. My waking thoughts are always about the cancer and the non-existent future. Perhaps I should think back and count my blessings? I do sometimes, but I find it difficult to remember happy times. I count my blessings for what I have now, not for things that have gone – holidays, parties. I forget it all and just thank God I have the friends and family that I have and for living where I do, the fresh air, the animals.

I am in my 'cocoon' at the moment, those few days during every cycle of chemotherapy when I don't want to talk to anyone, don't want to answer the phone, just want to be left alone. It's difficult for people to understand that, but I hope one day they do. I feel guilty when I don't return the messages that are left for me, but I just cannot bear to have to explain yet again how the treatment is going and how I am feeling today.

I keep thinking perhaps I should try and start painting again.

I am surrounded with all my paints, easel, and masses of blank watercolour paper, but just cannot raise any enthusiasm. A couple of years ago this journal would have had little drawings throughout, but not any more. I wonder if I could if I had a little studio somewhere where I could leave all the art equipment set out and not have to worry about putting it all away when I had finished. Too late now – should have sorted something out years ago. Perhaps in the spring, when I am hopefully NOT HAVING ANY BLOODY TREATMENT, I may pick up the brushes again. Perhaps I will be able to get involved with Buddies again. Perhaps I can take the dogs to Westbury House again and continue my volunteer work. Perhaps I will decorate the bedrooms (I did start and Sam said he would paint the ceiling for me – that was in October, so not looking too hopeful).

Little William was rushed into hospital yesterday with breathing difficulties and was kept in overnight – that's all I know at the moment. Wendy left me a message last night (I wasn't answering the phone). Will call her first thing – that is a very precious little life and Claire and Paul will be beside themselves.

6th January 6 a.m. – I can't do this any more. Yesterday I was ill all day – managed to eat a little soup, but that was it. This morning I feel nauseous and faint and the thought of having to see to the dogs is a worrying prospect. I feel weaker and sicker than ever and I really have made the decision that I do not want any more chemotherapy. As usual it is a weekend and I have no one to talk to this about. If I ring the BUPA hospital there will be no one there to talk to me; they are never available in an emergency. Not that this is an emergency. I think my bloods are down again and I need another transfusion, but where do we go from here? This chemotherapy is NOT SAVING MY LIFE; it is only prolonging it for a while and that could be a short while. I'm not going to do it. I have thrown the antibiotics in the bin as I am sure it is those giving me the stomach cramps – this time last week I was feeling a lot better, even went picking up, I just wish I could have a conversation with Captain Chemo – fat chance. Why am I putting myself through this? At this moment I think dying would be preferable. I CAN'T FUNCTION and there is no light at the end of the tunnel.

I think William is OK. I rang Wendy first thing yesterday and she said she thought he would be fine, but would update me on his progress. Haven't heard anything, so assume he is recovering.

Sam has gone to work and I feel very vulnerable and alone. I can't call Wendy to come and help as she has the flu, William is still in hospital and for the first time since this started I just cannot get up and sort the dogs out – it is unheard of for me to still be in bed at 9.30 a.m., but I haven't the energy. I have to do it. I cannot stay here – the dogs rely on me. I am convinced I need another transfusion and I have the field trial on Friday and Danny and Els are coming over from Belgium and I am too weak to deal with any of this. I have been really good this week and rested as much as possible, but it hasn't worked and I am even contemplating phoning Sam to ask him to come home from work.

Sunday – William is still in hospital, on oxygen and being fed through his stomach. What he has is apparently highly contagious, so no visitors, and he is still quite poorly. I feel so sorry for Claire and Paul and hope with all my heart that the poor little chap recovers.

I, on the other hand, spent all day just resting. Really felt absolutely ghastly all day, but have given the matter a huge amount of thought (because that's all I do – think about everything) and I have decided that I will not be having any more treatment. I am somewhat concerned as to how to go about this as I don't think just not turning up for treatment is an option. As I haven't really spoken to anyone else about this I don't have another opinion, but will doubtless get some advice from Bridget when I tell her.

My feelings on how I go about it are: on Monday I will phone the BUPA hospital and talk to Jane or Rusty (the chemo nurses) and tell them that I have no intention of going to my chemo appointment on Tuesday. Obviously, I cannot just leave it like that, but neither am I prepared for one of Captain Chemo's five-minute chats before he disappears to see another patient. I am going to suggest that I make a private appointment with him to discuss any future treatment he had in mind, a lengthier discussion on prognosis, just so that I know a little of what to expect. He really isn't very approachable – that's just my opinion; he may be one of the best, but I need more information.

I thought I would also phone Ann, who works as a specialist oncology adviser at St Mary's, and I met her on the day I was diagnosed. I am hoping that she will be able to clarify a few things for me.

I will obviously have to go back and have this PICC line taken out unless Jan, the nurse from the surgery, can do it for me. I must also notify my doctors of my intentions so that they will be aware of what I am doing.

I also have to tell Sam and everyone else now, but just writing this down I feel much calmer about everything. I am scared – of course I'm scared. I don't know what is going to happen, but at least I won't have to endure the side effects of chemo any more and however short my life is I will at least – I hope – be able to function.

Because I am not going to chemo on Tuesday I will have to get this line flushed, and if the nurse isn't available I intend talking Bridget through it – she'll be fine.

I hope I manage to organise all this – the joy of no more steroids, no more anti-sickness drugs, no more constipation, recovering my taste buds – I feel better already.

Monday, 5 a.m. – Just when I thought I had this sorted in my head – not having any more chemo – told Bridget and she agrees with me completely. Now I am seriously showing all the symptoms of needing another transfusion, which has thrown me into a state of confusion. Obviously if I need a transfusion I will need to attend my appointment tomorrow for them to give me blood tests. If I do need one this will entail *another* wait and more than likely another day *later* this week for a transfusion. There is no way they could possibly do anything really organised like take me in today for a transfusion – that would be too simple and far too organised for BUPA to cope with.

My quandary is – do I phone and cancel my appointment for the chemo? Do I keep the appointment just for them to check my bloods and take it from there? They may think that my bloods are fine and want to go ahead with the chemo, but that I will not do – one decision made! I may ring Bridget to see what she suggests, but at the moment it looks as though the sensible option would be to have the blood tests. I actually don't mind having a transfusion as it does make me feel better.

Told Sam my decision about the chemo and he was quite upset. Seemed to think I would feel worse without it and I guess he is looking at the chemo as his comfort blanket – all the time I am having it he thinks I am going to live longer. And for him to think I would feel worse without it! I could not feel worse – well, I probably will when I start dying, but at the moment I just want my body back and at least to be able to live a bit of my remaining life as I want to.

Sam is worried about which days he needs to have off this week and I thought it was concern for me. Wrong – he wants to have Sunday off to go fishing, but I have now told him that if I have to have a transfusion he will need to have a day off at very short notice. But hey – let's hope it doesn't interfere with his fishing and perhaps he will finish the truck off so that he can take the dogs with him. I really struggle to see to these dogs sometimes and I'd be glad if he would just take some of them with him. I guess – when I'm feeling better – it will happen.

Going to make a decision about the hospital when I get up. If my heart starts pounding and I start sweating then I shall have no choice but to phone and tell them I perhaps need a transfusion. In a perfect world (but then that's not my world, is it?) I would not need one and I can start preparing for the field trial on Friday.

Tuesday – Made the decision. Phoned the hospital and cancelled the chemo appointment for today. Wrote to Captain Chemo explaining that I wasn't prepared to have any more. I really don't know where I go from here, but I am glad I have decided NO MORE.

Was really careful yesterday as I did not want to be rushed in for a transfusion, so every time my heart started to pound I sat down for an hour and it seemed to work.

How long does it take before my body offloads all the effects of the chemo? How long does it take for my immune system to build up again? If the tumour has shrunk, how long before it starts getting active again? (I do know I wouldn't get an accurate answer to that one.) What happens when I start to deteriorate? Will I be in pain? Where will the pain be? Will it be controlled with drugs? Will I be bedridden? Who is going to answer all these questions? I NEED to know the answers. Captain Chemo should really reply to my letter or at least make an appointment for me to see him, or I guess he would wait until the 23rd, when I have to have an X-ray and blood tests, before sparing me five minutes of his time.

GOOD NEWS – William is home, thank goodness. He is not allowed out for two weeks, but at least he is home. Had a text from Claire – she is very happy to be home.

Wednesday, 10th January – Think I overdid it yesterday. Got overenthusiastic because I wasn't going to chemo. Dog-walked on Butser, hosed out kennels, housework and trial organisation, phone calls, paperwork! Consequently by 7 p.m. my heart was pounding and I had a blinding headache, which I have awoken with this morning.

I look three sleeping tablets last night because I wanted to sleep right through and feel better when I woke up, but it hasn't worked and may possibly be a contributing factor to the ever persistent headache.

Today I will be really careful and just do what I need to do. I didn't rest at all yesterday. Bridget went to BUPA and collected my antibiotics, bless her. Then the nurse came to flush my PICC line (will be very pleased to get rid of that). I had to re-dress that myself, which I shouldn't really touch because it is sterile, but my arm started to react and I had to take it off. Seems OK this morning.

Still pouring with rain and blowing a gale. One of my very favourite things is lying in bed listening to the rain and wind outside. Have made myself a cup of tea and let the dogs out briefly. I intend staying here for an hour or so.

My eyes seem to be giving me problems. Have made an appointment with my optician for a check-up – may just need new glasses. God, I hope I haven't got that degenerative disease that my mother had – that's all I need.

No word from Captain Chemo as yet, but I really didn't expect an instant reply – if at all. Dropped my doctor a note yesterday to let him know my decision. I think it is quite important that he is kept in the loop. Even if I change to the NHS now, I would still have Captain Chemo as my consultant as he works for the NHS as well.

Phoned Claire to see how young William was, and good news – today he is Mr Smiley! Much better.

Thursday, 11th, 6 a.m. – Spent all day yesterday preparing for Friday's field trial and that was exhausting. I have done all the cakes, cut up, all in boxes etc. All the goody bags, booze etc. is already in the car. Normally I would also be doing rolls etc., but dear Sue C. is bringing those and the trophies etc. All I have to do is go and collect the pork pies from Harriotts, do the running orders etc. Sam will put the signs out for me when he gets home, or even on his way home. It is blowing a gale this morning – let's hope it gets it all out of its system today and we have a quieter day tomorrow. I shall have to get up early tomorrow and meet the guns/judges etc. for breakfast at The George. That will be a shock to the system as I usually make a cup of tea now to have while I am writing this. Sam brings me up another one before he goes and then I just stay here until eight or nine depending on the weather and how I feel.

Doing this trial has been worse than usual with people pulling out. I had forty-four entries and last night I phoned number forty-four to offer a run – I have never run out of reserves before.

Had a really beautiful bouquet from Heather yesterday – such a sweet thing to do and they really are gorgeous.

Captain Chemo has replied to my e-mail – very briefly – but then what can you expect from him? Mine to him was about A4 size explaining how I felt etc. and also suggesting that I would welcome a private appointment with him. His reply: 'What about Friday 19th, early evening?' That was it. Actually, I have just had a thought, if I am not going to have any more chemotherapy, what will I have to moan about?

I'm sure I shall still have symptoms, after all it was over a week ago that I had my last cycle and I still haven't recovered from it. Still quite convinced that a blood transfusion would help, but I don't want to mention that as I have no intention of missing the trial tomorrow. Wonder how long it will be before I stop feeling exhausted.

Danny and Els are supposed to be sailing from Belgium to Dover today to come for the field trial, but if the boats are sailing and they do come I think they would be completely mad in this weather. It wouldn't surprise me if all sailings are cancelled. Doubtless they will be in touch sometime today to let me know what is going on.

Field-trial day – Had hoped to stay in bed a bit longer, but the dogs woke me up.

Managed to get everything done yesterday, so the car is packed and ready. Hopefully the weather will be even slightly better than yesterday, which would be good. Text from Els to say the boat had been cancelled and they were driving to the tunnel to catch the train. They must be completely mad – it is just a novice field trial! Romy too ill to come so will have to find another steward. Mark and Jamie (judges) had a safe journey up from Wales – amazingly! So – apart from me deciding what to wear – everything is ready, I think.

Just when I thought I had dismissed the cancer treatment out of hand, I had a call yesterday from another doctor – a radiologist Captain Chemo has contacted and asked to see me with a view to having radiotherapy! I so do not want to do this, but have agreed to meet with him next Wednesday. Apparently, if treatment starts I would have to go every day for a minimum period of four weeks. I don't think so. I need to know if there are any side effects and realistically what it is going to do and just what would I gain from doing it. If he says five years I will do it; if he says one year I won't. I don't know enough about it to surmise or moan any longer, so will leave that until I have seen him. I hope he is more approachable than Captain Chemo.

Got to make an effort today to look OK. Meeting the lads for breakfast – then the trial – so will put some slap on just so that I don't look like a ghost.

Saturday 13th, 5 a.m. – What an absolutely great day we had yesterday. I started off feeling very nervous and twitchy (yes, me!) and snapped at a few people unnecessarily, but as the trial got under way I began to relax and enjoy myself. Poor Sue C. got a tad frustrated as Mark took over the dogs and at times Sue was hard pushed to keep control, but she was fantastic and held her ground all day – what a star! The guns were in very high spirits all day with spirits being the operative word and Chris was in top form and very funny.

I was very touched when David and Matthew came such a long way just to be there and also Danny and Els all the way from Belgium just for the day, especially when I found out that Danny's father had just been diagnosed with terminal cancer. Brian gave me a big hug and said they had missed me picking up, and we had a long chat about Ryan's ongoing illness and vague prognosis. There is so much suffering and sadness about that believing there is a God is sometimes difficult.

Bill and Phillipa both came to present the prizes, which was a first, and I was so glad they had both made the effort. The presentation was packed to the rafters and we couldn't jam another person in. Hugely popular win by Kieran, who gave a very long speech as the winner, and I was extremely touched by the five minutes (at least) he devoted to me.

The guns lunch, prepared by Leanne, is something I would normally avoid, but as it was an occasion – my last trial – I stayed. Paula, Danny and Els, Brian, Dave and Matt also stayed. Huge amounts of alcohol were consumed and it was very rowdy, but I thoroughly enjoyed it until I was just too tired to stay any longer.

The strangest thing happened. I know this shoot like the back of my hand and all I had to do was drive out of the yard, round the top track past the house and down the drive and I just didn't have the courage to do it. I ended up driving all the way round along the main road, but was very shaky and very relieved to get home. How stupid was that? I suppose I really have not driven in the dark for months, and very little driving in daylight, but I never dreamt I would lose so much confidence, especially just driving home from the beaters' hut. On Monday – I am going picking up.

Sunday – I spent most of the morning yesterday unpacking the car, washing out the containers, cleaning my boots etc. Danny and Els were due to call here at 11 a.m., but I called them and they followed me up to Butser Hill and we had quite a good walk. I only had Katy, Fletch and Tess with me, which was much easier than six dogs! I spoke with Danny at length about his father's horrendous diagnosis and prospects and he cried for the first time, which was good. I will think of them constantly and although they want to respect his wishes Danny thinks his father will be pressurised by his grandchildren. The chemotherapy his father has to have is in complete isolation for six weeks with no visitors. Because it is leukaemia they will kill *all* the bone marrow and blood cells and replenish the blood with transfusions. His immunity will be zero, far worse than mine. He is too old for a bone-marrow transplant (sixty-three), but the new blood may give him another two years. No one can tell him what to do; I would imagine he will at least give it a try for the sake of his family, but he is going to be so ill. If he does go ahead with it I pray that it works and he is given more time with his grandchildren. On Tuesday Danny will go with him to speak with the oncologist – he will let me know how they get on.

I, on the other hand, begin to feel slightly stronger each day as the chemo works its way out of my system. It won't last, but at least I can feel normal for a while.

Bridget and Pete came round last night with fish and chips, which was very nice. I had even set the table and lit the candles! While they were here I brought down the file box which contains all the information, policies and insurance plans and I explained it all to them. I also showed them the box in which were all the letters to various people and individual requests, so now that is that and I don't feel the need to discuss it with them any more.

Still not decided about a vicar, but I really am thinking of discussing the whole thing with our village vicar, and realistically the plan of Hascombe Valley just wouldn't work in the middle of winter. I think it may be a decision that will have to be made when I die and see what the weather is like. Well, what other way is there? Can't even plan a funeral in this country without waiting for the weather forecast!

Bear in mind I hadn't cooked anything; Bridget had even made a fruit salad for pudding, but by 9 p.m. I was completely exhausted. Bridget and Pete were leaving anyway as they had no intention of staying any later. I voiced the fact that I didn't think I would ever entertain again; I just can't do it physically. Sam said, "'course you will. You could knock up [knock up!] a lasagne. After all, you only have to put it in the oven!"

Monday – Going picking up today, but I doubt that I shall make it through the whole day.

All my life all I have wanted was someone to care for me and look after me and all my life I have looked after others.

I'm tired. I want a rest. All through this illness I have continued doing the everyday chores I have always done.

Going to phone BUPA to get this line taken out this week. Optician's appointment Thursday, radiologist Wednesday, oncologist Friday – not a very cheerful week.

I'm rambling today – obviously got a very confused mind. Actually, wouldn't mind just dying as I am totally disillusioned with fighting and really don't want any more treatment – it's not going to save me and – actually – what's the point of being saved? If I were saved, what would the future hold for me?

Nothing different to what I do now although staying at Bereleigh wouldn't be an option. I can't look forward to a life of retirement as Bridget and Pete are hoping for at Rose Court. I won't ever retire; I will just die and – at the moment – bring it on.

Tuesday – I took all the dogs picking up yesterday, but had to come home at twelve o'clock. The dogs had a great time, but I just felt so exhausted and could never have done the whole day. I really do not understand – it is two weeks today that I had my last dose of chemo and, to be honest, I really haven't picked up that much at all. I really thought I would begin to feel a bit chipper and start doing a lot more, but my energy levels are absolutely zilch. I don't walk around any more; I have to drag myself around.

My eyes are getting really bad and I welcome the appointment with the optician on Thursday, but I do have a dread of that degenerative eye disease that my mother had. If the optician finds anything wrong and I have to go to more hospital appointments I seriously think I would go completely mad. Hopefully I am being just too pessimistic.

Danny sees the oncologist with his dad today and I feel so sad for them. Brian is still so worried about Ryan, who is still so very ill and his weight has almost doubled with all the steroids he has to take. Life just isn't fair, is it?

Looking out of the window this morning isn't giving me a great deal of pleasure.

God, this bedroom is depressing – why did I paint it this dreadful yellow? Started glossing the window frames months ago, but, of course, I haven't felt well enough to finish so there is a pot of paint on the window ledge and half-painted windows. I have got the paint for the rest of the room and initially Sam said he would paint the ceiling for me. No time? Have a week off then.

Still raining – if it stops when the engineer has been I will take the dogs out, but it looks pretty set for the day. MUST STOP MOANING!

Wednesday – The new doctor at West Meon surgery phoned me yesterday querying the amount of sleeping tablets I had been prescribed. She said it was illegal! ILLEGAL? Who is she? Where did she come from? Is she some kind of sleeping tablet police or what? I told her my doctor had prescribed them and to take it up with him. I am taking 15 mg per night now, which way exceeds what I should be taking, and I confess (not to her) that I am totally addicted to them and have no idea how to stop or even cut down, or do I even want to?

Big day today – going to have this PICC line removed from my arm and I can't wait. To be able to wash that arm properly and put some moisturiser on where the skin is so dry will be an absolute joy. After that appointment I have to go and see the radiotherapy consultant (Dr Radio) who, in my estimation, has already blotted his copybook. I already have no confidence in him, so that's not good. He phoned me last week to talk about radiotherapy and make an appointment. Told me it would be Wednesday (today) and that his secretary would write to confirm and give me a time. NOTHING ARRIVED. I phoned BUPA and they gave me an NHS number to ring; I spoke to his secretary, who then proceeded to tell me she has nothing to do with his private patients and gave me his mobile number. I rang and got hold of him immediately and he told me to meet him at 3 p.m. today. How unprofessional was that? Still – let's see what happens. I will keep the appointment and see what he has to say.

Sam has a day off today, but I shall still have to go down, make him a cup of tea and wake him up to go outside with the dogs. I know it's his day off, but I never have one – forget it. I'm not even going to go down that road!

Thursday, 6 a.m. – I take it all back – I actually liked Dr Radio! He explained everything about radiotherapy and we spoke for three-quarters of an hour, which was good and I think he has (almost) convinced me to go ahead with it. Apparently what he wants to kill off are the cancer cells in the lymph nodes in my chest cavity, which are the most dangerous and could quickly spread to other parts of my body. He amazed me by telling me that the tip of a Biro pen (like this one) could probably hold 500,000 cancer cells and just one of those could migrate and begin to grow elsewhere. How scary is that? He assured me that the side effects are minimal, but because the radiotherapy I would have would be covering a large area of my chest cavity, which includes my windpipe, gullet, aorta etc., I would more than likely get a very sore throat. Also I'll become very tired – which I am anyway. He intimated that he would also like me to have a small dose of chemo once a week alongside the radiotherapy, but I won't have that.

So – it would all start with a 'planning scan', where he begins to plot the area. Then another appointment for him to explain his reading and findings on the scan. Then another scan where they put tattoo marks on the area of my body so the radiotherapy is zapped in the same place each time. Then in approximately four weeks' time, to allow my body to regain some strength after the chemo, the radiotherapy would begin on a daily basis and he actually said I could come each day at a time to suit me, e.g. 5 p.m. each evening or early morning. I'll believe that when it happens. So it would be Portsmouth, St Mary's, on a daily basis for four to six weeks – doesn't bear thinking about, but I will wait and see what he says after the scan.

So after all that excitement I went up to the ward and Rusty took the PICC line out! Still have a minuscule dressing on it, but that can come off today and I can WASH MY ARM!

Had an e-mail from Danny – his father is going to have the chemo for the leukaemia. It is a very brave decision as he has to be in an isolation ward for six weeks and they kill off all his blood cells and bone marrow. He is too old for a bone-marrow transplant and this is the way they treat older patients. This is such a brave thing to do and I could cry even thinking about what he will have to go through, but I so wish him well and I hope it extends his life a little to enjoy his grandchildren.

Friday – Wind still howling – lost two huge trees in the paddock yesterday, but they missed the chickens and didn't touch the kennels. If that big oak tree comes down it will wipe the kennels out completely. Didn't take the dogs to Butser – I wouldn't have stayed upright!

Did go into Petersfield yesterday to keep my optician's appointment. I was informed not only that chemo affects the eyesight, but also that if the tumour is in the chest area it can cause (something beginning with M – can't remember) tumours behind the eyes. Where is that written down on any fact sheet? Why has no one mentioned it before? With a history of degenerative eye disease in the family (my mother) I should have been made aware of this! However, after a very thorough eye test and a new technique for taking photographs behind the eye this has not happened. So – I just needed a new prescription and new glasses. Chose the frames, which I thought were actually quite reasonable at £145, and then they hit me with the cost of the lenses bringing the total to £575! So the credit card took a hammering, but what the hell, you only live once! Just hope I last a while to get my money's worth.

I picked Bridget up – my first night driving for months. Foggy, rainy, windy – couldn't have been worse, but we made it. The appointment with Captain Chemo was at 6.45 p.m. and he was on time and very pleasant and not rushing around like some kind of dervish. I hadn't seen him since I pulled the plug on the chemo, but he was fine and quite understood. He was very much for me having the radiotherapy without any additional chemo. I asked how long I would still feel the effects of the chemo and he said probably six months and hopefully less than that. It will still take months to sort out my blood and the anaemia, but there should be no transfusions – he is going to let my body sort it out unless there is an emergency. The radiotherapy will obviously exhaust me, but it shouldn't affect my blood. I may have difficulty in swallowing, my skin may burn in patches and I will get a sore throat – not sounding great, is it?

The good news is I don't have to see Captain Chemo again until June/July, so he obviously thinks I am going to live that long and then take it from there, but I did emphasise that whatever happens I will not have any more chemo.

Still haven't got used to not taking all that medication – pills for this and that. Not sure if I have to take any while having radiotherapy – hope not. Have had loads of offers to help with lifts to and from St Mary's, which is amazing. Everyone is so brilliant. I still wonder in the back of my mind whether it is worth going through all this as I am convinced it will not give my life extension a great deal. I don't feel positive about five years. I think there may be a possibility that I will be here this time next year, but no one knows the answer. Dr Radio told me that with cancer you need luck, so why am I not walking round with my fingers crossed instead of having all this treatment? Perhaps Cancer Research should develop a luck tablet which would replace chemotherapy in years to come. I will be long gone by then.

PS: Just in case anyone is interested – my bowels are back to normal! But apparently radiotherapy can have the opposite effect. Thought for the day: should I think about incontinence knickers? My friend's ageing father was going on a coach trip and was worried about the toilet and his weak-bladder situation – this is true – so she persuaded him to wear incontinence pads just in case he had an accident. Off he went on his coach trip quite happily wearing his new attire and when my friend met her dad on his return she asked him how he had got on with 'things'. He replied, "It was fine. I went three times and no one noticed." Honestly – a true story.

Monday – The start of an almost normal week according to the diary. No hospital appointments, no medication to take (apart from the sleeping tablets – still can't manage without them). Picking up today, lunch with Carol on Wednesday, picking up on Friday. Bridget is temporarily redundant and I have that surreal feeling again.

Funny old thing this cancer, no wonder they call it the silent killer. I looked and felt really ill all the time I was having the chemo, but as I feel the effects of it gradually leaving me I can feel myself getting back to normal. My energy levels are higher although I still rest every afternoon if possible. I have managed to do 100% more than I have been over the last six months. So I had better make the most of it before the radiotherapy starts and enjoy the well-being for the next couple of weeks as it is bound to change. I still have no prognosis, I still have no estimate of life expectancy, and I still don't know what happens in the lead-up to my death.

Tuesday – Had a brilliant day picking up although it was bitterly, bitterly cold, but I wasn't too cold – had the silk vest and long johns on plus the leather trousers, so not bad at all. Fletcher did the best retrieve on a runner ever and it was worth going just to see him do that. I tried Tess on it first; she failed, but Fletch flew off like a racehorse, followed the line then went on point in the thickest of bramble bushes then threw himself into the middle and came out with the bird. It was one of those joyous, glad-to-be-there moments. Saw more foxes on the estate than I have ever seen in one day – must have been the cold weather bringing them in to kill the pheasants. When they did Orchard, I had four Bambis close enough to touch; they were absolutely stunning. They ran past me to start with then retraced their steps when they realised there was shooting, and they froze momentarily right next to me – brilliant. Wish I had my camera with me.

Stayed for the whole day; didn't wimp off home at all and everyone said I looked so well that they didn't think I was ill at all – I wish. I was knackered when I got home and went to bed even earlier than usual – not as fit as I was and my legs felt as though I had run a marathon. Wouldn't you have thought I would sleep like a baby? Tried without a sleeping tablet, but that didn't work so took one, fell asleep and had the weirdest dream. It involved leaving my car at a train station, running away from Rusty (one of the BUPA nurses), who had a big bag of pink liquid she was trying to pump into me, then getting to Guildford station and not being able to find my car. I ended up in Havant with two very good-looking off-duty detectives that I was trying to persuade to take me to Guildford to find my car. Woke up then. Never did find the car. Took two more sleeping tablets, but still had a lousy night. Overexcited with being out all day, I reckon.

I feel better each day now, but wonder how long it will last.

Obviously I have the radiotherapy to get through, but hopefully that won't be too bad. I absolutely do not regret giving up the chemo and I will definitely never, regardless of the outcome, have it again. It has to be the worst thing I have ever experienced, and I am quite a strong person. I cannot imagine for one moment how really elderly patients cope with it. Young children are so brave, but they are cared for night and day and really don't know much of life, and I think it is this blissful ignorance that pulls them through smiling. My admiration for anyone that has continued chemo is boundless. I wonder sometimes if anyone has ever died while having it. It is quite possible if your blood gets so low and you don't have a transfusion in time. If you catch an infection it can be fatal; plus, if your PICC line ever gets infected you could lose an arm!

Wednesday – It's snowing. Supposed to be meeting Carol for lunch, but will have to wait until it is light to see how thick it is. May just be a sprinkling, but the car looks pretty white!

Watched a programme on television last night about lung cancer, which was pretty horrendous. You actually saw the tumour once it had been removed. I wouldn't be surprised if some of my friends/relatives etc. watched it and wondered why mine couldn't be removed. This woman's tumour was the size of a tennis ball, and once they had removed it, and the bottom section of her lung, they told her she was completely free of it and they had removed all of the cancer. Unfortunately, mine is different and at the top of my right lung and almost looks as though it is attached. It is inoperable and removal is not an option. Added to this I already have cancer in my lymph nodes in my chest cavity which will never be cured. They may be able to shrink it with radiotherapy, which will actually kill the cancer cells, but I will never be cured.

Have I ever mentioned smoking in this journal? Not sure that I have, but here goes. Although I always say to everyone that only fifty per cent of patients diagnosed with this cancer are non-smokers, I know that I am one of the fifty per cent who are. Do I regret smoking? I am not sure that I do. It was that era when it was cool to smoke. I started when I was about sixteen or seventeen. All my friends smoked, but they have all given up long ago. My sisters both smoked, and my parents both smoked – Mother cigarettes, Dad cigars, the bigger the better. I know very few people that do smoke now, but it is the young ones I wish wouldn't. In my generation we were encouraged to smoke by all the adverts – movie stars, pop stars, absolutely everyone. In this day and age the teenagers – and younger – know the pitfalls of smoking, they know how dangerous it is, they are discouraged by adverts, they see famous people die from smoking-related diseases, so why do they still do it? I so wish they wouldn't.

Have I given up? I will always be a smoker, and why bolt the stable door when the issue of whether I smoke or not is irrelevant now. I guess most people think I have stopped. I never smoke when anyone else is around. It makes them feel better, plus I couldn't cope with the patronising nagging I would have to put up with. I wonder if anyone thinks, 'She's smoked all her life – she can't expect anything else.' I really can't imagine any of my friends/family saying that; I'm sure they would stick up for me.

Do I feel guilty when I smoke? I suppose I do, but only because I know how absolutely horrified some people would be.

Thursday – Feeling stronger every day and more up to speed. Getting on top of household chores and paperwork to hand over to Pauline. Drove to Petersfield and did some shopping then met Carol for lunch at the Bat and Ball, so that was pretty normal, then drove home, unpacked all the shopping etc., and I am pleased to say that I was tired but definitely not exhausted and have made arrangements to meet her again on 7th February.

I am fully aware that this feeling of well-being will be short-lived, but I'm just going to go with it. Carol amazed me. I knew that she had become a Christian after her scare in hospital a couple of years ago, but had no idea how serious she was about it. She apparently now has accepted the Holy Spirit into her body and she can now speak 'in tongues' through the Holy Spirit. Unlike my cousin the spiritualist, Carol does not believe in spiritualism, but believes that only our bodies die and not our minds and we move on to another place when we die. What about the mind of a murderer, rapist or someone with dementia – would they take their minds to another place? I am always so sceptical and I so wish I wasn't. I was brought up as a Christian and always loved going to Church and singing the hymns, but have never achieved that complete belief and devotion. I have always envied the look of rapturous joy on the faces of people who truly believe and so wish I could feel like that, but it has never happened to me. If we do move on to another place, where do we go? Will we meet others there that we knew on earth? Why has it never been proven? This one has beaten the scientists – why doesn't anyone that has died try to contact someone on earth to prove it? Tell you what – when I get there I will see what I can do; I must be able to organise something. Perhaps because I am 'on the edge' with my feelings about the afterlife, I won't be allowed in. I'll be kept in some kind of holding area till I have made my mind up. Perhaps instead of reading a novel before I go to sleep I should read and understand my Bible – yes, I do have one, my Bible from Sunday school. The trouble with that is that you need an interpreter, so perhaps what I need is a Bible class – so back to the local vicar. I have been thinking of having a chat with him for ages, so perhaps this is the time.

Friday – It suddenly occurred to me, and I have no idea why, but what happened to Sundays? Sundays aren't really Sundays any more. High Streets are open for business, garden centres and DIY stores are full of bickering couples, cinemas and estate agents are all there open and waiting for business. When I was a child Sunday was the Sabbath. We went to church, we were not allowed out to play and we always had Sunday lunch and Sunday tea. My dad was never included in the churchgoing as he was a complete atheist, not that I completely understood what that meant as a child. The only times he ever entered the church were for weddings (including his own), christenings (we were all christened) and funerals. My mother was ashamed of him being an atheist and would never discuss it. Come to think of it, she really didn't ever discuss anything with me; she told me what to do and when to do it. I don't remember my mother with any affection at all and I know that is a dreadful thing to say but it is the truth. She was a demanding, strong woman who was not averse to beating the hell out of me. I know Wendy and Sue find this so hard to believe, but it is the truth and although she had miscarriages before finally conceiving me, I know I was wanted. I think the truth is that my mother really didn't like me and she was never my 'friend'.

I went to piano lessons, ballet classes, Brownies and Girl Guides, but never really excelled at anything. I wanted animals. I wanted a pony, but I think my complete love for animals stems from just wanting something to love and something that would unreservedly love me back. I had white mice and a guinea pig, and always had a dog. I have had animals all my life – dogs, ponies, horses. I always had something relying on me to be there and look after them. For this I was rewarded with their love, their complete trust and their loyalty. Now? The horses are all gone – Blueprint, my bay, had a tragic death ten years ago and I have never had another. I still have dogs, though, the chickens and, of course, Gary the guinea pig.

Actually, this is supposed to be a daily journal not a reminiscence of my life, so before this turns into some kind of autobiography of a very unfamous person I think I will stop.

I usually relish the thought of cleaning the car out. I scrub every little bit until it is absolutely spotless, but I can't get excited about it this year. It really doesn't matter if I don't get it done for a month. It is a big chore and I need to get it done, but perhaps not today. Anyone with any sense would really take it easy today, but I am back in the 'I am not ill' world because I have been feeling OK.

Anyway, I would like to say that I have had a great season and been on every one of the thirty-four days, but I doubt that I have done twenty. I have kept the shoot cards, which are in the filthy Frontera, so will count them up later to see how many I actually made it to. I have, however, managed to run all the field trials and feel pleased I have at least managed to accomplish that. The field trials and the training day were all hugely successful, so I can hand over my duties as secretary to Pauline in the sure knowledge that the A and D is up there with the best and I have every confidence it will stay there.

I hardly dare think of next season – will I still be here? If I am, will I be capable of picking up? Helping at the trials? It is just over six months since I was diagnosed and look at the state of me now. A lot can happen in the next few months, but personally I wouldn't make any plans for more than a week ahead at the moment. Not that I think I am going to suddenly drop dead, but I know I am not the person I was and that anything can happen inside my body to cause me to deteriorate. Plus I start radiotherapy soon – joy.

Sunday, 5.30 a.m. – All other normal people would still be in bed – but actually I am in bed. I have, however, been up, let the dogs out, cleared up as one of them had thrown up overnight, made a cup of tea and, having fed the dogs, come back to bed. But I won't stay here for long. As I begin to feel better the list of jobs in my head just gets longer and, although I didn't make a start on cleaning the car out yesterday, I did wash my shooting coats, saddle-soaped my leather trousers and boots, made three shepherd's pies and then made a start on the paintwork in the bedroom.

At the moment, and for how long I cannot guess, I have no ailments, no ghastly side effects from anything, no depression, nothing – so let's all take advantage of it for as long as possible and, until I have anything further to report on medical statistics or my next treatment, this journal will have to contain general rubbish of my day-to-day living and a possible reminiscence of the past here and there. Can't discuss the future for obvious reasons.

Monday – Builders coming today. Hope they are going to start outside as I don't think I can handle them in here all day. The whole of the outside needs painting, so let's hope they start with that.

My hair has suddenly started coming out again. It is so thin it looks a real mess. Having had a bit of a hair-and-nail afternoon yesterday to try and perk myself up, I have woken up this morning and it looks a real mess. Don't want to put any heat on it as I could lose even more. Why now? It's very depressing.

I'm going to Buddies Club to help out this evening. Really looking forward to seeing all the kids as it has been months since I have been there. I have missed all the Christmas and Halloween parties, but perhaps I can get there on a Monday evening for a few weeks now. Tonight we are doing arts and cooking toad-in-the-hole, so that will be an experience.

I wonder why I am so obsessed with decorating and cleaning out cupboards. I will be making a start on the Frontera this week, getting it clean and back in pristine condition for next year. Why do I care? Why don't I just leave it and not concern myself with making sure everything is as I want it? Anyone else in my position would be contemplating a trip round the world or some kind of last fling before they die. I wonder if it is because I don't think that is the reason. I personally think that if I was given three months from today I would still want to finish painting the bedroom, and do the car and probably plant up the hanging baskets. I have no great desire to go anywhere exotic. My only dream would be to see the primates, but that will never happen.

A couple of days at a health spa might be quite nice. I might see if Thalia and Linda fancy it, perhaps before I start the radiotherapy – don't know. Haven't spoken to Bridget all weekend. I wonder if she is relieved not to have to take me to chemo any more. Poor Bridget had a lot to put up with, but she was with me all the way, bless. I don't think I will need someone with me all the time for radiotherapy and I fully intend driving myself. First appointment tomorrow for my planning CT scan and then onwards and upwards.

Tuesday, 5.30 a.m. – Had a slight run in with a boxer dog, his owner and a Frisbee on Butser Hill this morning. Aforementioned owner and boxer dog were happily playing fetch with the Frisbee when Fletcher arrived and legged it 200 yards to beat the boxer to the Frisbee by a head. Owner not at all amused – and boxer trotted up to me and waited for me to grab the Frisbee off Fletch and give it back to the rightful dog owner. Quite happy, I think he would have liked to make a day of it with Fletch and Co., but his owner just made a grumpy noise and walked off in the opposite direction.

I went to Buddies Club last night – first time in months and I half expected them all to have forgotten me, but everyone got terribly excited. Jackie and Amanda wouldn't let me go, and Michael and Chris were completely uncontrollable. We did art and it was great fun. I hadn't realised just how much I had missed them and was very touched with the way they greeted me and remarkably all remembered my name.

For those who don't know who the Buddies are, they are a group of children or young adults with either Downs syndrome, autism or severe learning difficulties who attend Highbury College to learn social skills etc. Buddies Club is held on Monday evenings and we do cookery and art, go to the movies and eat in restaurants. They generally improve their social skills and they love it. I am a volunteer who helps with them as there are some who need one-to-one attention all the time. We also do trips out to the supermarket etc., and they all have an input on the curriculum for the following month. I love it and I love the kids and always come away with the rest of my life's worries put firmly in perspective. I have really missed not going all these months, but perhaps I will be OK for a few months. Bettina (another volunteer and friend) and I did them a picnic in the country in the summer last year; they haven't forgotten seeing all the dogs and they want another one this year, so that will be great.

Still haven't finished decorating the bedroom – there is still one yellow wall and one yellow door, but it will have to stay like that now until I have the time and energy to start again.

Wednesday – Collected my new – cost a fortune – glasses. Still not sure that I like them, but that's just vanity and I cannot believe that I am still concerned so much about how I look! Felt good yesterday though and did manage to go out looking relatively smart. I made a bit of an effort, but it does take longer to even remotely feel that I look OK. Why do I bother? sixty-one years old, dying of cancer and I still want to look good.

Have been experiencing some pains in my chest which are quite alien, right down the centre of my chest, almost through my windpipe. I guess that's the cancerous lymph glands working to spread round my body. However, having gone for my planning CT scan yesterday and been given my dates for radiotherapy, perhaps they will be zapped into oblivion soon. Yeah, right.

Now, I have always fancied a little tattoo somewhere, but as the years have passed it just hasn't seemed realistic. Always wanted a little ladybird or butterfly in a not-too-obvious spot, but I guess as the skin gets older and wrinklier the poor little tattoo would look like a dead ladybird or butterfly.

Having digressed somewhat, my point (no pun intended) is that before my scan yesterday I was covered in coloured markers by the two radiologists. Felt really vulnerable lying on my back with my chest bare and two radiologists having an art attack on my body. This is why it is called a mapping scan, although it doesn't include any motorways or Little Chefs. Getting to the point now – having been back and forth through the machine several times, and scared myself silly as I had been concentrating on the little orange beam above my head when I suddenly noticed a very small sign saying, 'DO NOT STARE INTO THE BEAM – RADIOACTIVE', I thought, 'SHIT, just spent a fortune on the glasses and now I'm going to go blind.' Anyway, once all the back-and-forth was over, one of the radiologists came back and said she was just going to tattoo me! They do this so that the beam is aimed in exactly the same positions for each appointment, so I now have (undoubtedly boring and certainly not ladybirds) permanent needle-inflicted tattoos under my arms, which I cannot see (and now think they have made a mistake and have to go through it all again), and one in the centre of my chest (where my cleavage should be, but I have never had a great cleavage). I have decided that if it shows in the summer I may have it enlarged to look like a ladybird or a butterfly.

The next surprise was the efficiency with which they gave

161

me a printed list of all my appointments. They start on 20th February and the final one is 26th March. EVERY DAY, apart from Saturday and Sunday, for just over four weeks. What a chore having to drive to St Mary's every day. My consolation is that after 26th March my destiny will be in the lap of the gods as I will have no further treatment after that.

Compared to the BUPA hospital and the nightmare waiting-around etc., yesterday at the NHS hospital the efficiency was amazing. My appointment was at twelve; I was seen at twelve, scanned immediately and was out by 12.45 complete with my list of appointments. At BUPA I was lucky to get my next appointment handwritten on a piece of torn-off paper – that is no exaggeration.

Went to Homebase on the way home to get some more paint and a new lampshade for the newly painted bedroom and finally called in to Bridget's for a cup of tea before I went home.

Thursday, 1st February – Wednesday was a bit of a non-day really. I didn't go anywhere to see anyone or even talk to anyone on the phone – to be honest, I didn't feel great and I don't feel great this morning either. I am wondering just how much extra time I am going to get. Bear in mind I have already 'lost' six months doing chemo and am about to embark on radiotherapy for another month. So that totals seven months and I probably won't live for another year, so what's the point? I suppose I could have died having a heart attack, so being given time to think about it is a luxury. But – what am I going to do? I have no desire to go rushing off round the world. Sam is convinced I will just carry on as normal. I'm just not going down that road; I think I have been there before – I don't want kid-glove treatment, but I would like a little care. I appear to be rambling this morning with nothing definite to say, so I think I will call it a day. I still have these strange pains in my chest and a cough and a general unwell feeling which I don't think I should have at the moment. Shouldn't I be feeling great not having chemo any more? Or – haven't I given my body long enough to recover from chemo before rushing around like a lunatic? I suppose painting the bedroom could have waited, but it's looking so much better and if I have to lie in bed (fat chance) it doesn't look so depressing. Only two more walls to do and then it's finished.

I am going to pack up all this unwanted medication, syringes, needles, dressings etc., and take it all down to the surgery – it fills a drawer at the moment! I will make an appointment for next week to see my doctor and 'put him in the radiotherapy loop'. I'll also give him a copy of my living will, which I have to get witnessed (three copies) so I will get Ron and Carol next door to do that over the weekend. Then I can have a chat about the sleeping tablets because I have tried to cut down, but it just doesn't work so I am totally addicted to them now.

Going to take the dogs to Hayling Island today, meeting Sue C. and the dogs and then off to the beach. That will cheer me up.

Friday – Had a great time at the seaside yesterday. The waves were high and the dogs absolutely loved it – Fletcher especially – he is the best surfer. Had a pub lunch on the way home, so all in all a success.

When I left the house yesterday morning I also left Ron P. investigating a leak coming from underground somewhere just outside the kitchen window. So very glad I left him to it because when I got back the hole he had dug was big enough to bury me in and the really good news is that it has to stay like that until a new ballcock can be obtained. Apparently the leak is coming through a 'post-war' fitting which is not made any more. So – yep – in true builder style a new one – which won't be in until Monday at the earliest – can be fitted.

It's the shoot dinner at the Bat and Ball tonight and I was planning on going – in fact I have been paid for and will be expected. My bravado and intentions have left me, as the more realistically I think about it the more I know I cannot make it. It doesn't start until 7.30 and we probably won't eat until 8–8.30 (which is normally my bedtime) and, much as I hate to give in and admit it, I am really not fit enough for a big night out; even if I got a taxi to collect me at 10–10.30 it would still be too much for me. I managed Buddies on Monday, but I was home by

8.45 p.m. and went to bed later than usual. I was exhausted the next day, so I am being really sensible and not going to go. I am actually not sure that I could cope with the crowd either – how pathetic.

I am finding it more and more difficult to write and have to keep stopping with the chronic pins and needles in my right hand. It's probably a repetitive strain something, but I have no intention of talking to the doctors – I may need some treatment and I am not prepared to have any.

Three weeks of freedom till I start the treatment then four weeks of treatment and that's it – no more! I shall have to have the odd X-ray or scan for them (well, probably CC) to keep a check on ET and see when it becomes active again. I actually don't know what happens when the cancer starts growing again. I don't know how quickly it takes over and you die, but I suppose each individual is different. I can't realistically expect the consultant to answer that question, but I would expect him to give me an estimation after finishing the radiotherapy.

Have you noticed how I chat on about all the everyday things, but always come back to the cancer without actually realising what I am doing? It's because it is always there on the edge of my mind trying to get through my normal thoughts and take over my mind as well as my body!

Saturday – Still on the same subject, I think that people around me – family and friends and especially Sam, who see me quite a lot – see at the moment someone who is looking quite well. Without the chemo my spirit has lifted and although I still have an extraordinarily vile taste in my mouth and I am still quite weak due to the anaemia and I still get extremely tired, to all intents and purposes I look better, even to myself, although I see several more wrinkles and I look as though I have aged ten years. I still find myself tackling jobs and working most of the day as I used to. Yesterday I cleaned windows, started cleaning the Frontera, cleaned out the chickens, cooked, did loads of washing etc., and still didn't collapse in a heap. My day went horribly pear-shaped when Sam came in.

SAM: Did you know that your washing machine was leaking; there is water all over the floor
ME: Did you turn it off
SAM: Don't know how to.

He then stomped off to have a bath and watch a television programme on otters. The otters at that particular time would have been very at home in the utility room. So instead of relaxing and taking it easy watching television I was surrounded by wet towels and a dripping washing machine. Having discovered that it was the rubber seal round the filter, I took it and showed Sam, who obviously felt guilty at this time (and the programme about the otters had finished). He went to see what he could do, but it leaked again and I told Sam on my way to bed. I have had a look at it this morning, but as yet have not turned it on – a bit early in the morning for paddling. I shall try it later and then do my usual thing. If it isn't working I can see myself going online and ordering a new one. Can't manage without a washing machine.

Didn't go to the shoot dinner. I had already decided I wouldn't cope with several factors, the late night, the noise and the large number of people. I am usually 'up for it', but I just couldn't face it – don't suppose I was missed. Strange thing is I thought Sarah (my friend and next-door neighbour) would have called me and offered me a lift – or perhaps she was waiting for me to call her and assumed that when I didn't I wasn't well enough to come.

Sue and Joe phoned from South Africa yesterday to see how I was. I had sent them a round-robin e-mail, but they just wanted to check up on me.

Busy week socialising next week. Buddies on Monday evening, which I am looking forward to, lunch with Carol and Angie on Wednesday, so quite a lot on. Taking the opportunity of this three-week window before I start radiotherapy to do as much as I can.

Theo phoned me from Belgium; bless him for being so concerned. He was so pleased that Wader – a Labrador dog bred by me – was now the top field-trial dog in Belgium. We spent a long time discussing Danny's dad, who has now started his marathon chemo treatment in isolation. I so feel for him. Danny e-mailed me earlier this week to say that the treatment had started, but his dad was so very ill already. With no immune system left at all, as they have killed all his cells, he has caught an infection in his lungs and is really unwell. Danny and Els are allowed to visit, but only if they wear masks, gowns etc.

When my treatment is over I would quite like to go away for a couple of days – not bothered about flying off to exotic places (don't think that is an option), but a health spa would be quite tempting. Will see how I feel.

Actually managed to alter the A and D website yesterday. First time I have actually felt like concentrating on it, so that is an achievement.

Still getting those chest pains, but haven't told anyone. My left hip is worryingly painful, possibly because I am more active again. The prospect of having to have another hip replacement on top of everything else just doesn't bear thinking about, so I won't.

Sunday – Still no washing machine, but have discovered (yes, me, not Sam) that it is just the rubber seal on the filter which has perished somewhat and it needs a new one. I did ask Sam to phone around, but in the end he phoned me with a phone number to call and there should now be a new seal winging its way to me early next week, so the washing will have to pile up until then, I'm afraid.

Something I had on my mind was my living will, which I bought, and there are four copies that have to be signed and witnessed. Then I have to take them to my GP and he has to sign them all to prove he has discussed it with me, and he retains a copy. Once it is all done I keep a card in my wallet with contact numbers on it in case of an emergency. I sat and filled them all in yesterday and put Sam down as my health-care proxy, which means any treatment I am offered has to be discussed with him first. When he came in I was sat at the table and I would have liked him to sit down and discuss it with me. As it happens, I gave him a brief résumé and he remained standing. I asked him to sign them, but he said he would do it later and wanted to read one first. Fair enough, I thought, but they are still in the same place this morning – he hasn't read one – he hasn't signed them. Now this is important for me. I want it done and dusted – not just because I have cancer, but I could have a heart attack next week or an accident and now I have got this far with it I want it finished. I want to see my GP next week, leave a copy with him and that's it.

Monday – Feeling very low in spirits all day yesterday although once again I spent it working. Beautiful sunny day when most families would be out together or having lunch together. I spent most of it attempting to clean out the Frontera, having used it for picking up, and the inside and out are both filthy. I spend most of my life on my own; Sam is never here. Sometimes I am quite happy in my comfort zone on my own, but other times I wish I had someone to talk to. I am quite lonely, but most of that is my fault. I have spent the past six months not answering the phone and discouraging visitors and now I very rarely see or hear from anyone unless I make a point of it. My fault – I have some fantastic friends, caring friends and dozens of them have offered me lifts to radiotherapy and I appreciate that. Sometimes I wish that Sam and I had a more 'together' relationship. We hardly ever see each other long enough for a conversation and we never go anywhere together. This is our relationship; this is what we have made it, but it doesn't stop me wishing for more. I would love him to just take a day off and, instead of just doing chores around the place, I would love him to just be spontaneous and just take me out for lunch somewhere. Or even a bunch of flowers – all this time I have been ill he has never bought me any flowers. I must stop moaning about Sam – he will never change and that is my main concern.

Back to yesterday – I actually managed to start the cleaning of the car and at least inside I removed all dog beds, towels, jackets etc. that stay in there during the shooting season. Opened the garage to get the little Hoover that we use, or actually I use, for car cleaning and it went OK for a short time and then it blew up! Black smoke everywhere, so that helped (not). Had to use a hand brush because I couldn't be bothered to get the household Hoover. Anyway, having scrubbed, brushed and polished the inside it doesn't look too bad; it's in such great condition for its age and I still love it. My impulse buy because I loved the colour and nicknamed by Sam the Fucking Ornament as when I first had it I didn't take it out much in case it got dirty.

There was a hunt here yesterday with bloodhounds, great amusing animals and hilarious to watch. I had a great view from my bedroom window as they all galloped across the field. The hounds didn't quite keep together and were nowhere near as neat and businesslike as the foxhounds. They were constantly yelled at by the whipper-in, but an absolute joy to watch on such a beautiful day. Stopped me feeling sorry for myself and found myself thanking God I live in such a beautiful setting and if I get really fed up I just have to look out of the window or go for a walk with the dogs.

Which reminds me, we saw some oystercatchers at the seaside last week and I have never seen them before, so I keep meaning to ask Sam if they normally get down this far from the Highlands. Also saw a flock of similar birds which were smaller, and I need to ask him what they are – he's very good at that sort of thing (ornithology).

Still haven't spoken to the vicar – must do that – want to do that – want to sort it. I feel a bit embarrassed to phone him really; perhaps I will just go and sit in the church and hope he pops in.

Tuesday – Not functioning very well this morning. My hands and legs are so painful and I think it is all because over the last few days because I have felt so much better I have done so much more and I am paying the price, so probably won't write much this morning.

I have completely cleaned the inside of the Frontera by hand since the Hoover blew up and yesterday I cleaned all the windows inside and out. They came and mended the leak in the water pipe yesterday, so the hole in the drive has now been filled up.

My day culminated in going to Buddies, where cooking was

the plan and we made cookies and spaghetti bolognese. The pans of spaghetti and bolognese were quite heavy as we were cooking for sixteen people – ten buddies, two teachers, two teaching assistants and two volunteers (me and Bettina). We had a lovely evening and the kids thoroughly enjoyed it. What they don't understand is that Lucy (inventor and person in charge of Buddies and my friend) has been relieved of Buddy duty and asked to do a different teaching rota. The kids will be absolutely devastated – Lucy is Buddies.

I am pretty depressed about my hair at the moment as it is still falling out in handfuls and is so thin that you can see my scalp on the top of my head. All the front has broken off so there is virtually no fringe left. Why now? It is almost five weeks since I had chemo and I don't understand why my hair is getting worse instead of better. Can't write any more – hand too painful and also now have pins and needles. Will try again later.

Wednesday – Avoided cleaning too much yesterday, and didn't paint as my hands and legs were too painful. Also I think my hair is falling out now because of my anaemia (caused by the chemo). Don't know how long my blood will take to be OK and I might mention it to my doctor next week – perhaps I need another transfusion. In the meantime, I am trying to eat properly – nuts are good (they have iron) and spinach, but I don't think that will help. I might be willing to take a tablet now as I am not on any other medication and I don't feel quite so anti pills.

Claire and Wendy came to see me yesterday with William and we did a bit of off-roading with William in his pushchair. It was a glorious day and not muddy at all, so the pushchair held up quite well and William loved it. Dogs came with us, but they were very good with him so all in all a success.

The really hot news is – the washing machine is working! The new seal arrived yesterday and after trying to sort it out Sam came to the rescue and told me I was getting in the way and he fixed it – score ten Brownie points. Amazing how much washing can pile up in less than a week. Wasn't too worried about the sheets, I don't panic if I can't change them every week, but I was getting concerned about my 'everyday' knickers and thought I might have to start on my 'best' ones – now why was I worried about that? Does it matter if I wear my 'best' holiday ones? When am I ever going to need them again?

More hot news from yesterday – the chickens are laying again! May not mean much to anyone else, but I love it when they are. The best thing is going to see how many there are when I collect them. I may let one of them sit on some this year so that we have some babies – sad, isn't it? I need to get a life. Yeah, right – I think I have actually had my life.

I usually come back to bed when I have made a cup of tea, write this journal then go back to sleep. Sam usually leaves me another cup of tea before he goes. I can't do that this morning as my mind has gone into overdrive and I keep thinking about the vicar and I must get to see him – will phone him today. The doctor – must get to see him and give him my living will to sign and keep a copy. Dying – I keep thinking of dying – actually don't mind dying, but want to die neatly with no fuss, no dribbling, just go to sleep; but my thoughts and imagination, I'm afraid, don't agree with that. I really don't want to end up pathetic and helpless – why can't they just give me an overdose? It should be legal! Can't cope with this – I'm getting up. Let's do something positive like put the washing machine on!

Thursday – Thank goodness I have no plans to go anywhere today – thick snow outside – the forecasters got it right. It's still dark outside at the moment, but I can't wait for it to get light so that I can see what it looks like over the fields. Normally with snow I dread it; living here it always looks so beautiful but makes life so difficult with the animals and getting out of this side road. This time I shall look at it in a different light. Being in the position of knowing you are dying will make me look at everything as if I am seeing it for the last time and this most certainly could be the last time I see snow or have the opportunity to take the dogs out for a run in it. I would love to go to Butser Hill with them, but would never be able to get up there in the car; but we can walk round the estate.

Went and met Carol and Angie for lunch yesterday. Angie was late – she's always late. She lives the nearest to the chosen pub, but had to go to yoga first then obviously had to go home and completely change, do her hair and make-up and then come to meet us looking – as always – ready to go to the Hunt Ball!

Nearly forgot – very important – not only have I made an appointment to see my doctor next week to put him in the picture regarding the radiotherapy and get him to sign my living will, I have also spoken to the vicar of East Meon's All Saints Church. He was really nice and I am going to see him next Tuesday at 10 a.m. I am having doubts about the funeral service being held in Hascombe Valley on several points really. I still think it's a brilliant idea, I would still like it to happen, but it just doesn't seem to be a sensible thing to do and should I perhaps think about the church instead? This is what I want to talk to the vicar about. I know people have services at sea – we did with Dee, and although it was only family present it was very moving. I know I cannot possibly assume that there will be a lot of people wanting to come to my funeral and although I said initially it would be perfect if it rained when they were all standing in Hascombe Valley in their wellies, I don't mean it and would hate for it to happen. I can't plan the weather and although Hascombe would be perfect and beautiful on a dry day, and that is where I really want it to happen, I have to be realistic. That is why I am going to talk to the vicar and see what he thinks about it. I planned all this and rewrote my will etc. in somewhat of a rush not long after diagnosis, but I have had a long time to think about it now and I want to talk to someone close to God and see what his views are.

Sam's alarm has just gone off – hope he decides not to even attempt getting to Avington today and stays home. The last thing we need is him stuck in a snow drift somewhere.

I do still keep thinking about dying and what will happen to me. I wonder if perhaps I should talk to someone about how I will die and what path this illness takes. I really would like to know so that I know what to expect and I won't feel so scared. I know I have mentioned this before, but never done anything about it. No good asking Captain Chemo. I am going to phone

Ann at St Mary's oncology unit and I may even get to make an appointment to see her when I go for my appointment on 20th February. Yes, I will do that today.

P.M. – Spoke to Ann today, lung specialist nurse from Queen Alexandra's Hospital. I have met her once, on the day I was diagnosed, but as I then went privately I haven't seen her since. However, she did give me her card and told me I could ring her at any time and I did because I thought she maybe could give me some answers. We had a long chat and she was really straightforward and really nice and I feel I could really relate to her. There is absolutely no doubt that I am going to die, but when is anyone's guess. I could go on for quite a long time and I know that everyone wants me to be positive, but between you and me I really don't think I am going to last two years. However, as each case is different it is difficult for anyone to say how I am going to feel and how it is going to happen. We did get down to the nitty-gritty of whether I wanted to die at home or in hospital – that was a difficult one to take on board, but I think my decision would be hospital. I have too much to worry and think about here, so I think hospital would be the best place for me.

Another decision I have made. As soon as the radiotherapy treatment is finished I am going to cancel my BUPA membership and go back to the NHS. Two or three reasons really. One is that my membership is up for renewal in April, so that would save about £100 a month; two is that I don't want to die in isolation in a BUPA hospital; three is I think the Portsmouth Cancer Care Team is brilliant and I just know that I would be looked after. That's it for today – profound or what!

Friday, 5 a.m. – Can't get dying out of my head. It's the first thing I think about every morning when I wake up, during the night and if I sit still too long during the day. I just wish I knew what was going to happen so that I can picture it in my head and deal with it. I have dealt with the dying, but not the how and where. I definitely don't want to die here at Orchard Cottage, I would be too agitated every time I heard a dog bark and there would be too much here for me to worry about. Has the washing been done? Has Sam got his dinner? Have the dogs been fed? etc. I would be far better off in a hospital or a hospice – which hospice? Would I be allowed to go and look around the Rowans, for instance? Just so that I could picture it in my mind. I am scared now and worried. I honestly think it is going to be much sooner than people are expecting because at the moment I look so well. But – I know my own body and I know I am not well and I am concerned now that this radiotherapy is going to take away another few weeks of my remaining life. I can't help wondering what would have happened if I hadn't had the chemo – that certainly wiped out six months and I am at least owed that much.

Started worrying about my dogs again. When should I start to think about rehoming them and could I really even contemplate rehoming Katy? She is devoted to me and I absolutely adore her.

I was talking to Michael yesterday and his father is in hospital, been there for four weeks already, and it sounds as though he is in the last stages of bowel cancer. And what is he worried about? His little dog. On top of this Michael's mother had a stroke ten days ago and now he has both parents in the same hospital. How sad is that? Plus to add to Michael's upset and worries, his two sisters are already arguing and wanting to sell their parents' house! You see, Michael's parents had no warning, had no time to plan and organise what they want to happen. I am lucky (lucky?) because I have the opportunity to sort everything out, although I must confess I am getting tired of worrying about everything, but I know I won't be able to rest and enjoy whatever time I have left until everything is straight in my mind. I have to have another talk with Sam; he has put everything to the back of his mind because I look so well, but he really shouldn't do that. I told him my decision to go back to the NHS last night and his immediate reaction was horror – he really doesn't understand, so I may get Bridget (yes, St Bridget) to come over the next time Sam is here for the day and we can go through everything. Not just skim the surface, but prepare him for what is going to happen. God I am so sick of worrying about everything and everyone else.

Do you know that when I was first diagnosed and the consultant told me I had six months if I was lucky, I thought I would kill myself? Not then, not that moment, but when the time came and I found out what I had to look forward to I made up my mind that I'd rather die before I reached that stage – it seemed like a sensible decision. I had always had a feeling that I would get something dreadful and kept a stash of sleeping tablets for that purpose and I actually have quite a large stash at the moment so I am sure I have enough. It's a strange thing though; I think a lot of people think like this and I wonder how many of them do actually commit suicide. I wanted to do it, but now I can't. I don't think it's a matter of being brave or cowardly; I just can't contemplate doing it now. Is it the self-preservation thing that kicks in and you just think, 'One more day, one more day'? I think I would worry about my soul. Isn't it a sin to commit suicide? Would my soul never rest, just like my mortal body?

I think since I have stopped having the chemo I have obviously felt physically better, but in the interim before starting the radiotherapy I have started to constantly think and worry about my death and when it will be. I have come to the conclusion that all the time I was having the hated chemo it must have also been like a subconscious crutch and all the time I was going through the horrendous treatment I must have been convinced that because the tumour was shrinking so significantly I was going to be told at some stage that I was in remission and could probably live for at least another five years. That hasn't happened and although I start the radiotherapy in two weeks I know, don't ask how, but I just know that I am not going to live for another two years. I just have this feeling and it's nothing to do with being pessimistic. I am pretty sure this feeling is why I am so agitated at the moment. I'm not ready – I haven't finished everything. There are more cupboards to clear out. Shall I sort my clothes out or leave that to someone else?

11.10 a.m. – I have been in tears for the past hour – cannot stop crying. Sam is home today and I know when he got up (I took him a cup of tea at 8 a.m.) he was in a bad mood, but I didn't take much notice really – best left alone. He went up to the garage to get a paper and I went outside to see to the chickens and guinea pig and when Sam came back from the garage I took the dogs – all of them – for a much longer walk than usual. Consequently I was knackered when I got back. I have had a very unhappy day. I wanted so much to talk to Sam about all sorts of things, but it isn't going to happen and I feel really upset and lonely.

Sunday, 5 a.m. – I don't really feel like writing anything today as I am still really upset. That triggered off all my emotions yesterday that I had probably been holding back for weeks. I thought I was emotionally exhausted when I went to bed but still ended up taking three sleeping tablets, which is not a great idea, and here I am awake. Made a cup of tea, fed the dogs and it's still only 5 a.m.

Sam is going fishing today with his friend Lazlo and I am glad he is going out. He probably doesn't quite deserve this amount of venom, but that's how I feel.

Pauline is coming this morning to collect all the field-trial paperwork etc. I must just let go and she must find her own feet, but if she has a problem I will help. I am really not sure about taking over as chairman. I know I have agreed to do it, but I seriously don't think it will be that long before they have to find a replacement for me. Still, I suppose once again that will not be my problem as I won't be here.

Tonight I feel extremely lonely and confused and it's almost like I am just waiting to die. I start radiotherapy next week and I really don't want to. The brief euphoria I felt when I gave up the chemo and started to feel better has vanished. I really don't feel well, I keep breaking out in hot sweats and the next minute I am shivering, but I haven't got a cold or anything. Basically tonight I really think I would prefer to be dead because my life is shit – just me, the dogs, this house, the chores. Shouldn't I be enjoying the time I have left?

Monday, 5 a.m. – I am reduced to this morose, unhappy person and all I have left to do is clear out a few cupboards and live this nightmare until I die. I think about it all the time now. I'm really confused about it and confused about my beliefs and wondering what I am going to say to the vicar. Will he think I am just turning to him because I am scared of dying? Am I? In my head I am going to talk to him about my funeral, but do I need more from him? I was brought up with the Church – we had no choice, my mother insisted on it. I know every hymn off by heart and I love the feeling of reverence being inside a church gives you, but do I believe in God? Do I believe in life after death? I thank God every time I look at the countryside around me, but I don't pray. I don't pray to ask for help, to thank God, count my blessings, pray for others, and yet I am comforted in the knowledge that others are praying for me.

Tuesday – Slightly nervous today as I am going to see the vicar this morning. Not sure why I am nervous, but I think I am expecting to go there and he is going to solve all my problems and I am going to leave there with a weight lifted off my shoulders; but of course that just isn't going to happen. Hopefully I will have something more realistic to say when I have been.

Do you know, I am really getting to the stage when I want this nightmare to be over. I just know I am not going to last another two years, so why is God dragging it out? Why can't I just fall asleep one night and not wake up in the morning? Why is there so much suffering in the world? Why is dying such a long drawn-out process? I need to be at peace with myself and I'm not; my mind is in constant turmoil. I just want inner peace so that whatever time I have left I can face it peacefully and happily and not worry about anything else.

P.M. – I went to see the vicar today and I cannot believe how nervous I was before I went. The anxiety is obviously contributing to my inability to sleep without the aid of two or three sleeping tablets. He was so nice and I immediately felt relaxed with him and told him of my initial plans to have my funeral in Hascombe Valley and the doubts I was beginning to have. He completely understood and suggested that people attending might be more comfortable in a church and I could at the end of the day have my ashes buried at Hascombe. So consequently I listened and he suggested a private family cremation in the morning and once the ashes had been collected he would then conduct a funeral/ thanksgiving service in the church with the ashes in a casket. I am really happy with this idea and he assures me it can all be done on the same day, so that's fine. (Obviously, this new decision resulted in rushing home and changing my will to include the new instructions immediately. Could it wait until later? Of course not – it had to be done now!) We talked a lot about how I was feeling and how I long for a feeling of peace but felt that to turn to the Church after all these years just because I am going to die made me hypocritical. He was great and put no pressure on me at all and I really think I will start going to church on Sunday mornings just to see if I can start feeling a bit calmer and a bit more at peace with myself and the world. He asked me if I had ever been angry about my diagnosis and I said I hadn't. I can't remember ever feeling angry about that. I know I got really bitter about the treatment at BUPA, but that wasn't because of the cancer; that was about the total inefficiency of it all. But don't get me started on that – I am supposed to be working on my inner peace!

He has promised to call in and drop me off some ideas on things to read which may help. I told him I had a Bible in my bedside table and he asked if it was a modern one as apparently (approximately thirty years ago) a translation was published in modern-day English (cool!), which made it much easier to understand, so I will give that a go. I told him about my concerns for my soul rampaging around in the heavens and not being able to settle anywhere and wondering whether I really believe there is life after death. He assured me that a lot of people feel like that; even devout Christians have doubts about their beliefs. Anyway, to summarise, because I obviously cannot scribe the entire conversation, I am going to start going to church and meeting others there who hopefully will help me to understand and feel more at peace and I'm going to try and read the modern version of the Bible.

Wednesday – Doctor's this morning. I have a load of unwanted medication, syringes and needles etc., that I cannot just throw away so I shall take that back. I also have my living will, which needs to be signed by him and he has to retain a copy, so that will be another job ticked. Need more sleeping tablets!

I haven't mentioned Butser Hill lately and doubtless you are wondering why. I haven't been neglecting the dogs, still taking them out every day but because the shooting season has finished I can walk anywhere on the estate and as there are 3,500 acres I am spoilt for choice. I still can't manage a really long walk like I used to and I am wondering if this is as good as it gets. I still get really tired and that's before the radiotherapy, which I am now dreading. I have come to the conclusion also that I just don't like having any treatment.

I haven't told Sam any of this or about visiting the vicar yesterday. Since last Saturday's upset I just don't feel I want to tell him any of this. He is quite happy as long as I don't moan about anything, and when he comes home and asks if I am OK I just say yes and he's happy with that. One day he is going to realise I am not OK, but I really cannot worry about that any more.

I am still concerned that I have not met up with Pauline to hand over the field-trial information. When she didn't come on Sunday I was gutted. I got it all ready for her and now it is cluttering up the house. If she doesn't get in touch by the weekend – guess what? I am going to have to start getting judges etc. myself. I really don't want to do this, but I just don't want the club going down the pan. Why isn't anything ever simple? Why can't I just get all this offloaded and not have to worry about it any more?

Thursday – Panic over – Pauline is coming on Friday morning and I will finally be able to hand over the reins of field-trial secretary – great. I get myself in such a state over such things, but it seems that everything is such a big deal these days and I just can't take everything in my stride any more.

I saw my doctor yesterday and he signed off the living wills and retained one for the surgery records, so at least they know my wishes now. As ever, he was really great and he seems to know that I am not going to live for long. I told him how I felt – so sure that I was not going to go on for two years – and he didn't contradict me, just asked me how I felt about that. I said I was OK with it, but obviously a bit scared about when it would happen and how, and he said he didn't know the answer to that, but 99.9% of the time people in my condition would be fully capable of making decisions at the end so I would still be bossing people about!

I am not giving up all my dogs, but I think I have decided that it is time to find a home for Fletcher. It is going to be such a difficult one and it will have to be a perfect home, but I think I should do it. He needs more than I can give him and it won't improve. I am never going to be the person I was again and he needs a lot of love and attention – and the seaside! I think I will take them to the seaside again next week if the weather is OK.

Can you believe the doctor has recommended I start taking the HRT tablets again? I thought he would be pleased that I stopped taking them during chemo. I was throwing enough junk down my throat without adding to it. He thinks that taking them may help my sleeping problem and also may help my thinning hair as I obviously need the oestrogen. Fingers crossed it works – would like my hair back! He listened to my concerns about the amount of sleeping tablets I was taking and the fact that the amount being prescribed to me was way over the surgery's licence. He wasn't concerned, didn't attempt to try and cut them down and gave me an increased dose in my prescription. That's when it hits home that you really, really know you are dying.

He's a great doctor and I am really comfortable with him. Told him of my decision to revert back to the NHS and he thought it would be a wise move at this stage. Seeing a consultant privately is fine for quick treatment, but they have no team behind them for backup and aftercare and the NHS does. I am going to write to Captain Chemo today and ask him what to do and how to go about transferring. The BUPA insurance comes up for renewal on 1st April, so I will just cancel it then – I won't need it again.

Friday – Met Sue C.'s family for lunch yesterday at Selborne. I really didn't want to go and it seemed such a huge effort to get ready, but I did and once I met up with them I enjoyed chatting with them. But everything is such a big deal for me and I was completely exhausted when I got home. Beginning to have doubts about driving myself to radiotherapy every day, but still plan on doing it initially. Seems strange that Sue and Joe will be away all the time I am having it. They will be counting down the days to the end of their three-month holiday and I will be counting down those same days to the end of radiotherapy.

E-mailed Captain Chemo yesterday to get an answer to reverting back to the NHS, but have had no response as yet. Dr Radio left a phone message at 7.30 p.m. last night to ask if I could meet him at St Mary's this morning between 9 and 9.30 to chat about my scan – forget it. My other option was to meet him at St Mary's on Tuesday. These private consultants and their consultations! He is obviously completely unaware that I already have an appointment at 9 a.m. on Tuesday at St Mary's. I will have to ring him this morning and sort it out and I must admit I am secretly hoping he is going to tell me that he has looked at my scan and he doesn't think I am suitable for radiotherapy – I wish. The downside to that would obviously mean the cancer has progressed too far and there is nothing else to be done – whatever.

Sam came home last night and told me he had been invited to the wedding party of one of the guys at the fishery and if he went he would stay the night. He also told me that Bob (his boss) had booked him in to go to a conference and that would mean another overnight stay. I was not happy about this. Under normal circumstances it would have been fine, but these two occasions were slap bang in the middle of my radiotherapy. So instead of making it even easier I would have had to cope with extra. Sam always puts the dogs to bed for me and always lets the kennel dogs out for me before he goes to work, so normally I don't have to worry about the early morning or the evening with the dogs outside. Plus, I would have all seven dogs to see to as Sam usually takes three with him every day. He's been doing this for the past few weeks to make life easier for me. Last but not least, and it seems pretty pathetic, I don't want to be here on my own at night, so I have asked him not to go.

I just wish I hadn't had to explain all this to Sam and that he had thought it out for himself. He said he didn't know what was going on and when I was having the treatment. I feel a kind of lonely despair at times and I can feel depression kind of settling on me like a suffocating shroud (no pun intended). I need a bit of warmth in my life – I expect Sam does too. No one should have to live without it – just a hug would do.

Pauline is coming to collect the field-trial stuff this morning. I shall be very relieved to see her take it all away and I just know she is going to do a great job.

Saturday – Yesterday was a bit stressful initially because Pauline cancelled again about half an hour before she was due to get here. I actually lost it slightly and insisted that all this information had to be handed over, and she said if I left it on the porch she would come and collect it at some stage during the day. I put it all on the porch and it started raining, so I rang Pauline again and arranged to meet her in Waitrose car park in Petersfield at 2 p.m., which did eventually happen – more of a chuck-over than a handover. I have my doubts as to this being a long-term thing and I think the committee will have to think again before too long. I did the job for eleven years; I doubt that Pauline will do it for two. It has to be a long-term commitment really and I don't think she is prepared to do that. However, I am sure she will do a great job.

I spoke to Dr Radio yesterday morning and didn't really get much information over the phone. He is going to meet me at St Mary's next Tuesday to discuss my scan, but the radiotherapy is going ahead so he must think it is worth doing.

Had a very nice e-mail from Captain Chemo – I bet you thought you had heard the last of him. I e-mailed him a couple of days ago telling him of my intention to revert back to the NHS and he just replied saying he would be pleased to have me as an NHS patient and he will put everything in place for that. Another box ticked.

Also had my new will through for checking, so once I have approved that and my new one is sent to me and witnessed, and sent back etc., that box will be ticked again. I hope I don't start changing my mind again as it costs £25 every time I change it and money is tight. Going to start putting a few things on eBay again – just to get a bit of cash!

I put the double bed in the spare room on eBay and it looks as though it will sell – it has to be twenty-five years old, but it's OK. Anyway, to cut a long story short, it has 'storage under', so I thought I should empty that before someone came to collect it. What a Pandora's box that was. I was completely exhausted when I had finished. There were fifteen fleeces (mostly my shooting ones that I put in there when the season is over), one single duvet, two electric blankets, two double blankets, two throws, four cushions, two new pairs of trousers, a beach mat, a boxed over-mattress fleecy thing and four 1980s Hamells dresses, all wrapped. It was all very well getting it all out, but where to put it all? The dresses are going on eBay. I thinned the fleeces down to approximately half and everything else went into black bags for the charity shop, but fortuitously Jacqui came round to deliver some hay, straw etc., and she took the lot for her daughters to have a look through and anything not wanted would then go to the charity shop. I forgot to mention there was also a plastic box under there which contained three pairs of shooting breeks, one pair of jodhpurs, one hunting stick and two sweatshirts – unbelievable.

So all that pretty much took up the rest of my day and I ended up knackered and fed up. I have decided to take the dogs to Butser this morning for a treat as I plan another day cleaning out cupboards etc. Looking forward to seeing Fletch do a round trip of the hill.

Sunday, 5 a.m. – He certainly did do a round trip and made a new friend – a collie called Bobby, who, much to his owner's horror, took off in hot pursuit of Fletcher. They came back still running like whippets and the owner of the collie was fine about it and said Bobby enjoyed playing with other dogs. I don't think playing came into it – Fletch was on a mission.

I seem to be on a bit of a mission myself and find it difficult to sit down and relax for even an hour. Yesterday I cleaned out all the kennels, changed all the bedding, hosed them all out and generally tidied up outside. Indoors I managed to do some cooking and cleaned out a couple of kitchen cupboards, getting rid of anything that was over the sell-by date.

My hair is still upsetting me as it is still falling out in handfuls and, even when I wash it, it looks lank and straggly. Can't even begin to feel better until my hair improves – if ever it does at this rate. Feel like shit. Look like shit.

Still got things on eBay and will sell the bed ('storage under') and the Ercol chair today so I plan on putting those 1980s dresses on that I found and will try and put a few more things on each week if I can. Sam won't like it if I start getting rid of too much, but it will help him in the end.

I cannot believe that this time last year I was well into organising the Game Fair. There is no way I could have coped with it this year; I have trouble organising a trip to Petersfield at the moment.

Getting a bit screwed up about the impending radiotherapy treatment, which is imminent. I have never been to the oncology department at St Mary's and actually dreamt about it last night – how sad is that! The treatment at BUPA was so insular and isolated it will be a shock for me to see other people in the same situation. I know the treatment will be nowhere near as horrendous as chemo and people keep telling me that. It's just having to go for treatment on a daily basis, and the fact that it is yet more treatment for what? This is the problem – never knowing the end result. It's only five weeks I am encouragingly told by my nearest and dearest – but it's still five weeks of my life. I have already lost six months of my life having chemo and it's all for what? Three months? Six months? Twelve months?

I always think other people have nice Sundays – perhaps going out together or just having a family day. I usually spend Sundays as I spend every other day of the week – on my own (with the dogs), not relaxing with my feet up – usually doing chores.

Monday, 5 a.m. – Spent a boring Sunday, but did manage to clear out the puppy kennel and move some of the dog food etc. over there – my dog storage shed, where I keep all the dog food etc. has been leaking like a sieve and ruining the contents, so something had to be done. There will never be puppies again, so I may as well put the kennel to good use. Could do with a man to shift all the stuff, but hey, they say that hard work will never kill you. That's a laugh – maybe not, but cancer will.

Watched a television hospital programme yesterday which featured a twelve-year-old girl who had had a liver transplant and was on the point of being allowed home. Before she went home she had to learn how to take and administer her twenty-five doses of medication, which had to be administered six times a day just to keep her alive. Some were tablets, some were liquids to be taken by mouth, and some had to be pushed through the line into her stomach. She was so positive, so pretty and so happy that she was going home and you saw her waving as she drove off in the taxi. At the end of the programme it was announced that she had died not long after the film was made and the film was being dedicated to her bravery. That puts everything into perspective.

I have sold the double bed and chair in the spare bedroom. I put them on eBay and the bidding finished yesterday. Once they have been collected my plan is to put my easel and paints etc. in there and hopefully start to do a bit of painting again. I will have room to spread it out and I won't have to put it all away every time I use it. That's the plan – do some more painting if I am up to it.

Before I even think about that I have a few more cupboards to clear out and I would like to get rid of that large deep freeze quite soon. I need to get that moved and clean underneath it before I die. There must be a thick mat of dog hairs underneath it, probably dead mice as well, and I would hate anyone else to have to clean it out. I know it's completely mad, but I can't help it; I am not going to be able to do everything, but I will do as much as I can. My mind often drifts back to those days helping Davina to clear out Amelia's cottage. Actually it was hilarious some of the things we found. Bless her; she kept everything – a bit like Sam really. I have the opportunity to lighten that burden for my nearest and dearest, but I am quite sure they will have a good laugh at some of the things they find – hope they do. I hope they manage to find something useful.

Tuesday, 6 a.m. – Have to leave home at 8 a.m. this morning to get to St Mary's oncology department by 9 a.m. Going to see Dr Radio followed by a simulator radiotherapy just to make sure that all the marks (tattoos) are in the right place before starting the treatment properly next week. I will leave it at that until I get back as I don't really know what is going to happen until I get there.

Arrived at St Mary's for 9 a.m. and was slightly early, so went for a look round and ponder in the chapel on my way to the oncology department. I have often walked past it but never gone in, and amidst all the hustle and bustle of a busy Portsmouth hospital it is amazingly tranquil. I could have stayed longer, but – onwards to Dr Radio. I took a seat at reception and felt quite alone although there were already a lot of people waiting, but they were all couples, husbands supporting wives, wives supporting husbands, mothers and daughters, mothers and sons, and I think I was the only one on my own – my choice. Bridget had offered to come with me, but she hasn't been well so I made her stay at home. Sam? Sam was at home looking after the dogs; I'm not absolutely sure he knew where I was going.

However, I met with Dr Radio, who immediately put me in a bad mood by telling me that instead of four weeks' radiotherapy I had to have **six weeks** and the last day of treatment would now be on 17th April. Having firmly fixed 26th March as my last day in my head, I was a bit upset. He also suggested (again) that I had a 'small' dose of chemo each week alongside the radiotherapy as it would help 'kill' the remaining cancer, but I refused. I won't have even a teaspoonful ever again. Then I was taken into the 'simulator' room. Once again flat on my back naked from the waist up, arms crossed and over my head holding on to two grips and four radiologists hovering over me with marker pens and

185

rulers and laser beams projecting from the ceiling. Then they all leave the room and I am left in this position while the bed moves up and down. Various parts of the machine move above and alongside constantly taking pictures so the radiographer can line up exactly where the radiation is aimed. Three-quarters of an hour in that position and my arms had gone completely dead. Finally, after much toing and froing, the radiographers were satisfied they had the complete map and pictures and measurements for Dr Radio to approve. I actually couldn't move and it took a few minutes to get my arms moving and sit up on the table. It was quite a scary experience. If they worked on it a bit more and included a few flashing lights and perhaps spun the whole thing around it would make quite a good theme-park ride. (I know all about theme-park rides – Matt and I have done them all. We used to go to a different one on his birthday every year while he was growing up.)

Called in on Bridget and Pete on my way home and took Bridget some flowers. She asked what they were for and I said nothing – what I meant to say was "because you are the best friend anyone could have". Told them all about the appointment etc. Pete gave me some 'go faster' pens – I am writing with one of them now – brilliant. I won't run out of pens ever now. Got home and took shopping in (went shopping on my way home). Dogs were fine.

Wednesday – Was going out to lunch with Carol and Angie today, but have to go back to the hospital so lunch is cancelled.

Thursday – All sorted at the hospital. I start the radiotherapy proper next Tuesday, 27th February, through to 11th April.

Apart from that I am feeling fine; my energy levels are almost back to normal, so falling asleep in the afternoons does not happen any more. John and George came to measure up for my new kitchen yesterday. You wouldn't think that kitchen was big enough to get excited about, but I can assure you it is. It will be great to have drawers and cupboards that open properly and are easier to keep clean – I can't wait. However, there is a downside

– I think I shall have to make arrangements to leave home for a couple of days while they do it – I don't think I could stand the noise and the mess. It's such a tiny kitchen. Perhaps they could do it like a *60 Minute Makeover* – that would be good. In my dreams! Plus the outside of the house is being painted in the spring. Amazing – just when I am going to die the house is getting a facelift.

Actually, the way I am feeling at the moment all this dying talk is complete rubbish. I feel sure that I shall still be here in ten years. That's how I feel today because at the moment I am functioning – I am doing everything I usually do.

Friday – Walked the dogs on Butser yesterday in the torrential rain and got absolutely soaked, but they enjoyed it and I'm feeling pretty good. The weather was so appalling all day that I decided, in eager anticipation of the new kitchen, to paint the pantry. Have run out of paint now, so only managed to get half of it done.

I was feeling fairly optimistic about the radiotherapy appointment until I had an e-mail from Sheila yesterday wishing me luck but at the same time hoping the machine did not break down too often, leaving patients hanging about for two hours while the radiologists played catch-up with the appointments. This has put the fear of God in me and we all know my stress level accelerates beyond belief when equipment breaks down. So should I rethink my plan of going to treatment at 5.30 – out by 6 and straight to the A and D committee meeting at 7? Or should I try and calm down as this mild hysteria could be a bit premature and everything could go swimmingly.

I watched a programme on television called *A Child in a Million* and it was about a four-year-old girl with a very rare cancer for a child of that age. I can't even write about it really, but that little girl (and her parents) were so incredibly brave. She survived endless chemo and had operations to remove tumours from her lungs and one that was attached to her heart. She recovered from that and actually started school, but died two months later. It shouldn't happen to such babies. I don't really mind dying – I have had my life, passed my sell-by date – but that child – why? What happened to "**Suffer the little children to come to me**"? What exactly does that mean?

Saturday, 5 a.m. – It is six weeks since I had any chemo and I feel stronger every day; my energy levels are almost back to what they used to be. I don't think I could take on the Game Fair at the moment, but I am getting back to normal with dog walks etc. and don't get so weary now. In fact, my next-door neighbour said I stride out over the field and you would never know there was anything wrong with me.

This is where the silent killer comes back into play, I think! Remembering this time last year, when it is obvious now the tumour was active and growing inside me, there were no external signs, no symptoms. So perhaps this will happen again. I will have the radiotherapy – obviously – then I assume I will be called in for check-ups and they will be able to tell when the cancer goes on the rampage again, but this will be the time when I refuse any further treatment and from then on – who knows?

Sunday – It's Sunday – again – already and it's only 5.30 and I have been up, fed the dogs and am now back in bed with a cup of tea. I was quite enthusiastic to wash my hair yesterday as I had especially been shopping to see what products I could buy to improve the state of my rapidly balding hair. It hasn't worked – I didn't expect miracles, but it doesn't even feel any better. I just do not understand why, after finishing with chemotherapy six weeks ago, my hair is just getting worse and worse. The fringe has all broken off, I have a bald spot on the top and the rest of it is so thin you can see through it. Very depressing – I can't even make it look even halfway decent any more and my bad hair days are now every day. I look dreadful and I really care about looking dreadful, and I can't adopt a couldn't-care-less attitude because I do care and I don't want anyone to see me like this.

It was so quiet here yesterday. I had one phone call from Carol in the morning; the guy came to take the bed (with storage under) at about 11 a.m. and apart from that I didn't speak to a soul (only the dogs) all day. Did a bit more pantry painting, but it's not the right paint – can't be doing with two coats and need to get to the shops to get some 'one coat' Dulux to finish the whole thing. Chucked a load of oils and spices out and it all looks a bit fresher. What else did I do? Cooking, cleaning, dog walks – unsuccessful hair wash and that was about it, and now it's Sunday. I hate Sundays.

This time next week I should have been flying out to join Sue and Joe in South Africa – they have already been there for two months and don't come back until the end of March and I was supposed to be going out for a couple of weeks, but of course that is impossible now. I am not allowed to travel until six months after treatment has finished and even then travel insurance is quite doubtful. I suppose – if I am still alive – I could go next year, but probably won't have any money by then. I spent this year's flight money on my new glasses!

Going to church this morning after I have walked the dogs – perhaps that will stop me feeling sorry for myself.

Monday – As Sundays go, yesterday wasn't too bad. I didn't see anyone and spent the whole day alone, but I did go to church in the morning. It was the first Sunday in Lent, so the hymns were not as jolly as usual, but nevertheless it was a nice service and the sermon was very good. On my way out the vicar handed me an envelope and said he had hoped I would be there. When I got home, inside the envelope was a letter from him listing some ideas on what I could possibly read to perhaps calm me down and hopefully restore my beliefs. Strangely enough amongst this list is Psalm 121 (I will lift up mine eyes unto the hills etc.) and I had already chosen this Psalm to be included in my funeral service. There was also an old newspaper article, about twenty years old, written by John Robinson, the Dean of Trinity College Cambridge (formerly the Bishop of Woolwich). He wrote the article after being diagnosed with terminal cancer and the headline was 'God Is to Be Found in the Cancer As in Everything Else.' It was a very long article, far too long for me to attempt to summarise, but I am reading it again for the sixth time. I agreed with quite a lot of what he said. He said in one paragraph, "making one's will and other dispositions, which is no more of a morbid occupation than taking out life insurance". The whole article is obviously centred on his beliefs and Christianity, for the Christian impending death is preparing for eternal life, which means real living, more abundant life, which begins when you die, continues, doesn't end. I find that so hard to believe, and why is there no proof? And this means it is about quality of life rather than quantity. How long it goes on here is secondary, so preparing for eternity means learning to live, contributing and enjoying what matters most. Giving the most and getting the most while it is on offer. Seek first the kingdom of heaven and who knows what shall be added.

My friend Lesley has given up alcohol for Lent – I am not giving up anything; I am going to do more, I'm going to start visiting Westbury Hospital again (I had to stop because of my low immune system and the germ factor) on a weekly basis. I usually take one of the dogs with me, and that cheers the patients up. I am going to do more with Buddies and organise the picnic here at my home they have been asking for.

One question I cannot answer – if Christians are not preparing for death but for eternal life, why do Christians get so upset when someone dies? They might be expected to react differently if they are convinced that person is going to a much better life.

On a much lighter note – we are off to the seaside today – Hayling Island – and meeting Sue and Romy – Fletch has already packed his surfboard!

Tuesday, 27th February – The start of the radiotherapy, six weeks, and I shall be ticking away the days until 11th April – the last one. I'm not scared of the radiotherapy; it's the intrusion of the treatment on a daily basis, it's the forty-mile round trip to the hospital and being slapped on that table like some offering to the gods, the two or three hours taken out of my day and to what end? No one knows. As for the side effects, only time will tell. I do have the option of refusing radiotherapy, but I won't do that; if it was purely my decision I wouldn't have it, but everyone else wants me to so I shall give it my best shot. Knowing me, I wouldn't be surprised if I didn't make the whole six weeks, but I will try.

Had a really super seaside trip yesterday with Sue and Romy and all the dogs. The weather was perfect; unbelievably it was sunny and warm, which considering it has been raining for the past two weeks was a miracle (and it's raining again this morning). Had lunch at Langstone afterwards – really enjoyable – the dogs were exhausted from all the surfing and walking for so long on the pebbles and my legs have aches in muscles I didn't know existed this morning.

Started an initial clear-out in some of the outside sheds. Have donated most of my dog training dummies to the A and D and also the tea urn. I fully intended giving them my dummy bags, but there was a mouse nest in one of them! I have turned it inside out and left it hanging in the rain to clean it off.

While I was fighting to get the tea urn out I noticed several dog-related items that I may put on eBay – two travel carriers, one collapsible dog cage and a plastic dog bed. I think I will put them all on as one lot and the next non-raining day I will photograph them together. Also a brand-new rabbit hutch which I had for Fiver (my little black rabbit) when I first had her.

Thought for the day: I really hope that this radiotherapy is going to be an absolute breeze, giving me no cause to grumble and hopefully not making me feel unwell and, again hopefully, being able to drive myself there and back for the whole six weeks without having to depend on others. In other words – I'm just going to get on with it!

Wednesday – That's the first trip over. Left the house at 4 p.m. (appointment was 5.30), I was seen at 6.10 and home at 7 p.m. I don't regret my decision about becoming an NHS patient; I am still a private patient until 1st April, but the treatment I am receiving now is exactly the same as the NHS patients'. Nothing is any different for me, no jumping the queue or anything. The only difference is that the consultant (whom you don't see) is getting paid for it.

I did get there early as I was concerned with the traffic, but it was no problem at all. I went and sat in the little chapel for a while before my appointment; in the midst of this bustling hospital it really is very peaceful.

Met another lady slightly older than me who was also there to have her radiotherapy for the first time (with her husband). She also has lung cancer, pretty much like mine. Hers isn't in her lymph nodes, but there may be a problem with her kidneys so she may need more chemotherapy aimed at her kidneys. The sheer horror of more chemo! She is a non-smoker and had the same as me. Statistically fifty per cent of the people that get lung cancer do not smoke, but they don't publicise that fact, do they? Just ostracise the smokers. Anyway, we (my new friend, don't know her name yet) put the world to rights and discussed our 'common topic', and I guess I shall get to know her over the next few weeks – probably find out her name tonight.

The radiotherapy was fine, obviously doesn't hurt and lasts just a few minutes once the monster machine is set up with the right measurements. Again, covered with marker pen, which is apparently a daily ritual so I don't think I will wash mine off – perhaps at weekends.

My hair is bothering me – I am seriously thinking of getting Amy to cut it all off and then start again. It is still coming out in handfuls and getting thinner on a daily basis. My new friend lost all hers and they told her she wouldn't! It looks really nice now as it has just started to grow back. If Amy cut mine off I wouldn't be worried about it, would I? No point – wouldn't have any.

Apparently – and Bridget is not going to like this – the radiotherapy should not affect my driving and I should be able to drive myself for the whole six weeks. Unless I am really, really exhausted.

Thursday – Second radiotherapy over and done with. The downside is extra appointments throughout called review appointments. I suppose I may get to see Dr Radio at those –

plus I have to go for regular blood tests – why? Something to do with my anaemia, I suppose. There was a young woman there last night – early thirties, I would guess – with four children, the youngest about eighteen months, eldest nine-ish at a guess. Her husband was with her and they were such a lovely family. She obviously had finished her chemotherapy. I felt so sorry for her – she just has to survive.

Dragged myself to the A and D committee meeting – Pauline, the new field-trial secretary, couldn't make it as she had a migraine! I am getting seriously concerned about the field-trial situation and wish I could just walk away and forget it, but as they have bamboozled me into becoming chairman I can't just walk away and forget it all. I wish I could think of someone else to take over as chairman, but I can't.

Got home exhausted at 9.30 p.m., so was very late to bed (late for me) and those wretched dogs woke me up at 4 a.m. I really don't like driving in the dark any more – pretty pathetic really, and the way I am feeling at the moment the daily drive to Portsmouth is going to wear me down. However, up until now the traffic has not been too bad. One lady there who comes from Stubbington said it took her three hours to get home – three hours! I would so be on another planet.

Bernard rang me yesterday – said he had tried several times, but no one answered the phone! Apparently there is a reunion of everyone that went to Portsmouth University and we had the flats in Netley Terrace, so I think he said Anna was organising it, but Cliff, Geeves and Co. were all helping with the organisation. So they are coming from far and wide and making a weekend of it and Bernard suggested I try and make it on one of the days. That would be great – some of my happiest days were living in Netley Terrace and being friends with all those guys.

Friday, 4 a.m. – Really bad night. As soon as I start treatment I seem to get a bit agitated and have even more trouble sleeping. I think I also, after just four days, have a side effect – diarrhoea! Lovely.

Upset the apple cart with the A and D with only three weeks to go until the AGM. I have decided to take a real back seat. I cannot continue to stress myself out like this, so I am not accepting the chairman's position. I just do not want any responsibility at all. Duncan was less than thrilled as he only has three weeks to sort it out, but it really isn't my problem. That club has had fifty per cent of my life for the last twelve years and I have done enough. I don't know what this will do to the structure of the club. Paula is already 'in bits' with losing Annette from her working test team. I really hope the A and D stays right up there where it belongs, but if it doesn't and if standards fall I cannot interfere. I am glad I made the decision, but why do I still feel guilty and worried?

Saturday – How pathetic – I am so pleased it is Saturday and I have two days off driving into Portsmouth for radiotherapy! I am already feeling the effects. I have developed a really chesty cough already. This is because the treatment not only kills the cancer cells, but it also kills some of the healthy cells surrounding the cancer so actually kills some of the lung. My windpipe feels clogged and sore and I can already feel very tight around that area, plus I am experiencing some difficulty swallowing and all this in the first week. I hate feeling like this and just cannot be stoic about it all – again. The treatment is making me ill! I felt OK before it started and now I am going to lose another six weeks plus however long it takes for my body to recover (or not) from radiation treatment. There are people there each evening in their seventies and eighties putting themselves through this – why? Why are they clinging on to their frail lives and subjecting their frail bodies to all this treatment? I wouldn't. I know life is precious and all that, and I appreciate that, but if you feel too ill to enjoy that precious life then why bother?

I am moaning again and I so wanted to sail through this without complaining and without feeling too ill, but it isn't going to happen, is it? I do feel lonely when I am there. OK, I have refused everyone's kind offers of lifts etc. But it's not that kind of lonely as there are plenty of others waiting for their treatment and we do talk to each other and compare notes – like you do.

The one nice thing about going to the hospital is that on my way to the oncology department I always spend five minutes in the chapel. I just go in and sit there quietly for a while and it has become a daily ritual. Do you know, I even question that – would I go every day if I had to put myself out and walk a bit further? Would I go if it was on another level? I don't know the answer to these questions – perhaps I should just be happy that it isn't on another level and I do have to go past it every day. It is a lovely chapel and I noticed yesterday that some of the windowpanes are in remembrance of people. The more you look, the more you see. Someone had been in and scattered rose petals all over the pew in front of me, so they had obviously lost someone in the hospital. There is a book you can write in (I haven't yet) and I always look at it. Children write, 'Dear God, please make my mummy better.' Do you think God reads those daily messages? How does He have time to read all the message books in the land and listen to all the prayers being said in the land?

Sunday – Got really depressed yesterday – started coughing up blood, and there were pains in my chest. Tried not to let it get me down and tried not to think about it, but actually in truth I plummeted to the depths of despair and didn't want to speak to anyone. It's not that I don't want to speak to anyone really, I just don't want them to know how miserable I am and have to listen to my moaning.

Think about it, the chemotherapy knocked out six months of whatever time I have left. I had five weeks with no treatment at all and started to get on with things again – seeing people – doing things and generally feeling better. I now have it all on hold again with the prospect of another five weeks' radiotherapy (and apparently it takes six months for your body to recover) when I don't feel like doing anything or seeing anyone again. Why? I am so seriously thinking of chucking it all in. I am going to ring Ann tomorrow and ask for some truthful answers as to the benefits – short- or long-term – of this radiotherapy and why, when in all the literature it states you have radiotherapy for two, three or four weeks, is mine now extended to six weeks?

Sam went to his party at Avington last night – managed to

get Pete to come and give him a lift. They were sitting down for their meal at 8 p.m. What was I doing at 8 p.m.? Going to bed! The only good thing about yesterday was not having to drive to Portsmouth for the treatment!

Had a really lovely long phone call from Ian, bless him, and he has agreed to do one of the readings at my funeral. There was no hesitation, he just said, "Of course I will do it for you." He is such a great guy.

The garden is such a mess after all this vile weather and under normal circumstances I would at least attempt to keep it a bit tidy, but after I have finished all the day-to-day chores I kind of run out of steam. Thank goodness Sue and Joe come back at the end of the month. I don't suppose they are looking forward to it one little bit, but I am. I have missed Sue really. When all else fails she can usually make me laugh and I'm looking forward to seeing her again and looking forward to seeing Joe with the lawnmower going! Hope I feel well enough to make him a BP!

Shall take Fletch and Co. to Butser this morning and then go to the family service at church – perhaps that will lift my spirits. Also I will ring all the people who rang me yesterday and I didn't answer the phone – sometimes I just can't put on a cheerful tone and I don't want them to know I am miserable!

Monday – The weather yesterday was enough to depress anyone although getting up as early as I usually do does sometimes have its advantages. I was up on Butser with the dogs and back by 8.30 a.m. – completely dry and rain-free walk. Within ten minutes the heavens opened and it absolutely torrented down all day without a let-up. There is a temporary water feature (pond) in the field and when I took the dogs out p.m. (this time in the rain) Fletcher (who else?) dived straight in and obviously thought I had arranged a special delivery for him.

I did go to church and I did enjoy it. Family day so all the children were there and the vicar allowed them all percussion instruments to bang or shake during the hymns. It was hilarious. Saw Gill and Wilson there and had a chat – the churchwarden came up and introduced herself. I was momentarily nonplussed (it happens quite a lot these days), so she obviously thought I was a complete gibbering idiot seeking refuge or something. There was soup and rolls for everyone in the church hall afterwards, but I didn't go. Now I wish I had, but there were a couple of reasons why I didn't – the main one being I don't know where the church hall is! I think it's probably attached to the church, but never having been round the back I don't know. How stupid was that? Why didn't I just follow everyone else? I will next time. The other reason was that I didn't really feel like socialising, telling new acquaintances who I am, where I live etc., but also – knowing me – I probably would have volunteered for doing something, like church cleaning on Wednesday evenings! I still feel vaguely hypocritical as I am still not absolutely certain on my beliefs – I look on it at the moment as 'having the banns called'. At least when the vicar delivers the funeral service he will know whom he is talking about! It's not just that really – I must want to go to church, I must want to visit the chapel every day at St Mary's. I don't do it just to reconcile myself with God; I go because it makes me feel better, more peaceful, not so agitated.

Just when you thought I wasn't going to moan about anything – this time last week (go back a few pages) I felt fine, my energy levels were returning and I was feeling stronger! This week I have a hacking, wheezy cough, headache and backache and my energy levels have dropped by fifty per cent. That's after one week – supposed to do six weeks. Chances of that happening? You work it out.

Tuesday – Spoke with Ann (lung-specialist nurse, part of the NHS backup team) and she told me that the radiotherapy was just as traumatic as the chemotherapy and that it could be quite debilitating if the patient reacted badly. I asked what would happen if I didn't do the six weeks and she said it was my decision, but that my level of care wouldn't drop and it was my body and if and when I felt I had had enough then I should just say the word. That made me feel a lot better – knowing that my exit route was quite safe.

The radiologist was not bothered about the hacking cough.

(Well, she wouldn't be, would she? It's not her that's coughing!) She said in some cases patients react very quickly to the treatment – or should I say patients' bodies react differently? – and whereas side effects don't kick in under normal circumstances – or should I say normal patients – for two to three weeks, in my case they have kicked in early and will probably settle down quite quickly. Let's wait and see!

Not so depressed this morning, and considering it is only 5.30 a.m. I am feeling quite optimistic and I am in quite a good mood. I didn't go to Buddies last night; I just felt that I would be pushing my luck going straight from treatment to the college, but I have quite made my mind up that I shall go next week. I should have settled into a routine by then and not find everything so tiring. I think I got really down last week because I pushed myself going straight from the hospital to the committee meeting and then not having a very satisfactory meeting all contributed to my exhaustion and black depression.

This week I am determined to sail through the appointments and carry on with everything else as normally as possible. Wendy called in to the oncology department at St Mary's yesterday while I was waiting for my appointment. She had been to an appointment for physio over the road – repetitive strain injury in her shoulder from constantly answering the phone at her job. She has offered to take me to a health spa for the night – her treat – but I don't think so. I'm quite happy to go, but not until I have finished treatment and she's not paying for me. She needs all the money she can get.

I have actually managed to cut the sleeping tablets down – at the moment just by one tablet, but over the next couple of weeks I am hoping to get it right down and just take one tablet per night. It occurred to me also that taking three sleeping tablets per night obviously makes a detrimental contribution to my moods during the day. So, with a bit of luck, I'll cut right down to one tablet then I shall be cheerful, positive, optimistic etc. on a daily basis. (That will be a first then! Pre-illness I was never like that!)

Popped into the chapel again yesterday. It has now become a bit of a ritual and I think I would feel really guilty if I walked past it now without going in. I felt a bit self-conscious the first time I went in, but now I don't. I am really comfortable going in there and just being quiet for five or ten minutes.

Wednesday – Halfway through the second week. They were running an hour late last night, but I didn't get agitated, remained very calm and took it all in my stride. The woman sitting next to me kept giving long drawn-out sighs – you know – a bit like a horse snorting. I can do those quite well, but not with my new calm image. She did have a bit to snort about actually as she had been locked in the changing room! One of the nurses blocked her in by wheeling a patient on a trolley and backing him up against the door until I noticed the woman frantically scratching on the door and drew the nurse's attention to it. She (the woman not the nurse) was extremely grateful and came and sat next to me, wanting to be my best friend, but she wasn't really my type so I didn't encourage her. As for the man on the trolley, I think he was dead. I was riveted and watched his chest for signs of breathing, but in the hour I was sitting there he didn't move a muscle. I can't help wondering how long the woman would have gone unnoticed. I was right on the end and could hear her, but I guess once they had moved the man (or the body) on the trolley she would have been OK.

Was given another blood-test appointment last night and told that I have to have one every week because of the chemo effects still in my body. That's a bummer. I thought having had the blood test last week that was it – should have known better.

Saw Dr Radio and told him about the hacking cough. He said to take linctus (which I have been doing) and was going to prescribe me some steroids, which I refused. He was concerned as they are treating a large part of my lung, but I don't want steroids. Anyway, have agreed to see him on 20th March to discuss my progress.

The weather was stunning yesterday and prompted me to give the chickens a good clean-out – not easy when one of them insists on helping! Gary the guinea pig had a good spring clean and the dogs had two walks – amazing what a bit of sunshine can do to lift your spirits. I can hear the birds outside already singing (5.30 a.m.) and in a few weeks' time the dawn chorus will reach fever pitch here. If it is going to be another brilliant day I may just run the dogs over to Hayling Island so Fletch can have a surf!

Thursday – Another stunning day, warm (well, about 12 degrees) and sunny and you could see for miles from Butser Hill, where the dogs had a great time. It's Crufts this week, which always prompts me into remembering the years Amelia and I spent up there manning the Working Gundog Forum and the masses of collages we prepared to decorate the information stand. The last time we did it was 1999 and I couldn't drive as I had my hip operation in February, so we decided to hire a transit van to take us and all the artwork up there. It was hilarious. Amelia, being four foot nothing plus a possible half-inch, couldn't see over the steering wheel – very scary – plus she ploughed down a centre line of bollards at the NEC because we couldn't get round the back of the building, where we normally park.

Seems a lifetime away now. Amelia died very suddenly in 2001 and I still miss her friendship. Now and then when I look at Fletcher it reminds me of her. One of Amelia's dogs, Othello, is Fletcher's father. I mated him with Katy after Amelia had died – it just seemed like fate and the right thing to do.

Which brings me on to Fletcher himself. I had a lovely letter from Nigel and Mo yesterday regarding Fletcher etc. because when they wrote previously to tell me of Sedge's death I did write to them and ask them to have Fletcher. Their immediate reaction was "couldn't possibly" etc. so I decided to ring them and have a chat. I explained that I wanted this to happen – they would give Fletcher an absolutely perfect home and it would put my mind at rest. Whether I die in six months or six years is irrelevant and it really isn't me that counts in this decision; to know that Fletcher was in a marvellous home and that he was going to be thoroughly spoiled for the rest of his life would make me so, so happy. It is going to happen – not immediately – but when we are all ready. I haven't told Sam yet – now why does that bother me? Because he won't just accept this decision; he will fight me all the way and it will make it unpleasant. What I need him to do is support me and back this decision because it is important to me, but I anticipate trouble and it's something I can do without.

The journey to the hospital and back each day is a nuisance, but I have tried just to grit my teeth and get on with it. I have been caught up in the traffic once or twice, but nothing to cause too much grief. Having listened to some of the other patients telling me about their 'horror' trips, I have vowed never to complain even if I feel like it. People are travelling miles to get there each day from Bognor Regis, Worthing and the New Forest. From Stubbington it takes one couple three hours to get home! I now consider myself lucky to be able to get there normally in forty minutes. There are apparently very few of these radiotherapy machines in the country, which is why people travel such vast distances. There are two in St Mary's Hospital, Portsmouth; the others available to me, living where I do, would be Basingstoke or London. This illness doesn't give me much to be grateful for, but suddenly I am grateful that I only have to go to Portsmouth.

Romy, bless her, called in yesterday just as I was pulling out of the drive to go to the hospital. She had bought me some flowers to brighten my day, she said. I couldn't even stop and make her some tea – had to go for a blood test before radiotherapy. She is so kind – I really do have some fantastic friends in her and Sue C. – not a day passes without a message or phone call from Sue.

Just listen to those birds this morning – sorry – forgot you can't, can you? They are singing their little hearts out this morning. Not another sound – complete silence apart from them singing, just for me.

Friday – Just this afternoon's appointment and that is two weeks completed, plus Saturday and Sunday to look forward to with no appointments. Most people look forward to the weekends for different reasons – no work, Friday night out on the piss or the pull – me, I am just grateful that I don't have to drive to Portsmouth hospital.

My new image – the patient patient – was tested to the limits last night as I was sitting next to a couple from Bognor Regis in the waiting room. He (Alan) was a nervous wreck and kept checking his watch to make sure the radiographers were running on time (they were); she (don't know her name) regaled me with stories of the traffic on their daily journey, their bungalow, the estate where they live and how it was beyond her that people on the estate should even consider selling their back gardens as building plots, and his (Alan's) bone cancer, which isn't funny but she was giving me too much detail. I didn't get up and move, I didn't tell her to shut up and I did my very best to smile and say, "Really?" or "Oh dear!" or "Hmmmm" in the right places. I was so pleased that my appointment was called absolutely on time, but couldn't fail to notice that she had collared someone else when I came out! They were early for their appointment – sometimes it takes them two hours; sometimes they just sail through. Bridget would have been proud of me – amazed actually! Bridget on the other hand would have made friends with them! Strange thing was they were completely self-obsessed, didn't even ask me where I lived.

The weather was glorious again yesterday and you could see for miles on Butser. I had planned to watch a bit of daytime television with a cappuccino and some peanut cookies, but we had another (the third in as many days) bloody power cut, so that put paid to that. Having phoned the electricity company to find out what was going on, whined miserably at the guy (child) on the other end and discovered it was a major fault and would probably take two to three hours, I then had to keep myself occupied instead of slobbing out in front of the television.

I had already walked the dogs, so I actually started to have a bit of a garden 'tidy'. Went up to the garage, filled up with petrol, checked the air in the tyres (yes, I really did) – they are all pumped up to '30' now. This is probably totally wrong, but I couldn't be bothered to look in the book, which was probably buried under a mountain of dog blankets and towels. Washed the car in the jet wash – I actually like doing that, it's therapeutic somehow – and having got all the mud off I discovered several more rust spots, a dent in the door and red (red?) paint on the wing mirror! Sometimes it's best to leave the dirt on.

When I finish my radiotherapy on 12th April it will be nine months to the day since I was diagnosed. Nine months of treatment and, as far as I am concerned, nine months of having no life at all, so I think at the very least I should have nine months treatment-free and spend my time as healthily as possible.

What shall I do? I don't have enough money to go rampaging off around the world – I wouldn't want to do that anyway. Start painting again? Do more with the Buddies? Go back to visiting Westbury House patients? Offer to help at the church? It will seem very strange. Obviously I will have to have check-ups on a fairly regular basis, I would think, but there is one thing that is absolutely certain – NO MORE TREATMENT.

Saturday – Two weeks down, four weeks to go, and on my way home from the hospital last night I felt exhausted. It really wouldn't be so bad if I could rest more during the day, but because I know I have to have a bath and get ready to leave the house by 3 p.m., and before doing that I have to take the dogs out for their second run, I find it difficult to relax during the day. I'm on edge all the time. But today I don't have to go and I am not rushing around anywhere. Did some shopping yesterday plus took a load of things to the charity shop etc. – non-stop really.

My legs and back are particularly painful at the moment – all my joints are killing me and I don't know if this is a reaction to the radiotherapy or just arthritis. I can only sleep in one position at night because everywhere else is too painful and I have a horrible suspicion that my good hip needs replacing, but I don't think we shall go down that road. It takes a year to recover from that and I am pretty sure that is a year I haven't got. Swallowing is difficult at the moment. It feels as though there is a lump in the middle of my chest when I swallow, but that is definitely the radiotherapy.

They were there again yesterday – the Bognor Regis people – but I spotted them coming and averted my gaze plus I put my handbag on the chair next to me – not very Christian of me, but she (Mrs Bognor Regis) soon collared someone else and was chatting away happily, so I don't think I upset her. I did say goodbye to them on my way out. I felt quite charitable on the way out – the operators were running early (a rare occurrence), so I was out before I was supposed to go in plus it was Friday and the weekend off – so there you go.

Wendy left a message about a pill that has been in the news recently. It has been developed for lung-cancer patients, but is incredibly expensive so not as yet distributed through the NHS. I actually know all about it as Captain Chemo had already mentioned it to me. In fact BUPA insurance had already agreed to pay for it after I had finished radiotherapy. *I don't want it.* The side effects will be chemo-like as, after all, this tablet is a form of chemotherapy and I just don't want it. It suits me that everyone thinks it is not available – well, actually it isn't available to me any longer. I had quite forgotten that. I have cancelled my health insurance, so I really am just an NHS statistic now and couldn't get the pill even if I wanted it. So no campaigning for the pill – I don't want it.

I'm going to take the dogs out this morning and then I'm going to have a nice quiet day – plus no cooking – Sam is going to get fish and chips tonight.

Sunday – For some strange reason I have been unwell all night. There was a stage when I did consider calling an ambulance, but when I thought about it I don't think I would have called one under normal circumstances (by normal I mean if I didn't have lung cancer). I could not sleep and had chronic stomach cramps, sweating then diarrhoea then sickness, so this morning I was praying that the dogs would not want to get up early – but they did, so here I am at 5 a.m. feeling like shit and it looks as though the day is going to go pear-shaped before it's even started. The plan was – dog walk, church – then round to S and R's for Sam's seventieth birthday party. The way I feel I won't get any of that done. So I have decided to get a couple more hours' sleep and see how I feel after that – although I really do want to go to church this morning. So, in the interests of self preservation, I am not going to write much this morning and will try and get some more sleep before the kennel dogs wake up – Sam usually does those,

204

but you can bet your life he will lie in this morning.

I think it was the fish and chips – I ate rather more than I should have, later than I should have, and I don't think my injured gullet could cope with it – BLOODY RADIOTHERAPY!

Monday – Sam's seventieth birthday yesterday – very busy day. Took all the dogs on Butser first thing then went to church. Then managed to sit down for an hour before going round to S and R's for a little party for his birthday. I couldn't possibly have managed to organise anything this year. S was great – made a fantastic spread – and Bridget and Pete were invited so it was really nice. M rang while we were there, bless him. I'm looking forward to seeing him at Easter. G showed us her prom dress and it is absolutely stunning. She looks gorgeous in it and I have a perfect pair of earrings to go with it! She won her race again yesterday. She just gets better and better and I am just sad that I won't be around when she makes it, because she will. She's only sixteen and already fourteenth in the UK, so it is going to happen and I am going to miss it. R is taking Sam to the movies tonight as part of his birthday present. He had loads of cards and bottles of brandy, so he did rather well – no card from Wendy and I did remind her last week.

Still finding it difficult to swallow and after Saturday evening I don't think I will ever be persuaded to eat fish and chips again – it doesn't take much to put me off food and that was enough. However, I haven't got to the stage where I can't eat – heaven forbid – just when I had started to get fat!

Back to the hospital again today – the start of another week's treatment. I have been warned that as time goes on with the radiotherapy my skin in the areas that are being zapped may burn – like sunburn, I suppose. There is definitely a smell of burning flesh while the machine is operating, but as yet no burn marks – I guess that is something to look forward to.

Sam has another day off today – two consecutive days! I am so used to being here on my own that it seems strange to have him around – not that he has offered to run the Hoover round or anything, but he did give the kennels a good clean yesterday (I'm thinking of taking a photograph and putting the metal kennels on eBay). Sold the nest of tables from the hall and Sam hasn't even noticed they have gone!

Tuesday – Feeling exhausted and nearly had an accident on the Eastern Road on the way home last night – narrow escape at a red light. Must concentrate more. Finding it more and more difficult to swallow and having had an appointment with the clinical nurse last night for a review she told me that the situation would get worse as it gets more and more narrow as the weeks go on – plus it takes some months for everything to return to normal when the radiotherapy has finished. I see Dr Radio next week and will try and persuade him to cut down my weeks from six to four again, but I don't think he will. Apparently had I agreed to a small dose of chemo each week alongside the radiotherapy then four weeks would have been OK, but as I refused the chemo he upped the radiotherapy to six weeks.

Mr and Mrs Bognor Regis weren't there last night, in fact none of the people I had got to know were – I suppose they have all finished! So I just closed my eyes and listened. There were two people there who could have been talking about me! "She used to always be out and about somewhere", "loved going to the theatre", "holidays", "never goes anywhere now".

Why do people always say, 'sadly …….. lost his/her battle with cancer'? Why do they call it a battle? I don't feel as though I am having a battle with cancer; I feel as though I am having an endurance test with the treatment. To be honest, I don't want a battle; I just want the treatment to be over, and if I thought I wouldn't cause a complete uproar with everyone around me, I would willingly give up the treatment now. People say, "You should do what you want to do, it's your decision, your body," but you can't because everyone else wants you to at least give it a go, so I am actually doing this for others, not myself.

It's so peaceful here at 6 a.m. in the morning and all I can hear are the birds singing their hearts out. I would like to record this and play it when I am really ill and dying, but I'm not sure if my portable CD player can record. I'll have to check that out. I know

I could probably buy a recording of birds, but it wouldn't quite be the same as the birds from my bedroom with the odd pheasant in the background.

Wednesday – Don't really feel like writing this much. I'm getting increasingly tired and have to eat very slowly as it feels as though there is a brick wall stuck in my gullet! Apparently this takes quite a long time to recover from after treatment – it hasn't stopped me eating, but I have to eat really slowly. Also I'm getting really bad headaches, but I think that may be due to the driving and it has been really sunny this past week so I have been driving into the sun. Seeing brilliant Dr Radio next week, so will ask him. *But* I don't want any steroids – I have already put weight on and do not want to get any fatter. My skin doesn't appear burnt yet, but I guess that will come. There is most definitely a smell of burning flesh when the machine is in action!

Feeling really fed up and grumpy about finances. There is never any money to spare and I am paying £167 per month for my funeral plan – how crazy is that? It finishes in October. We are just about surviving here and there is no extra money coming in for anything. At least when I was well I had the money from dogs on holiday, but now I can barely look after my own let alone anyone else's. I shouldn't actually be worrying about money in my condition, but I have to. Sam doesn't do any of it, so that's something else he will have to sort out for himself when I am not here. It doesn't bear thinking about. Wendy met me at the hospital yesterday (Tuesday) and brought a box of chocolates for Sam's birthday.

I'm also beginning to wonder whether Sam and I should look for something smaller. It's the last thing I need at the moment, but at least Sam would be sorted before I die. He can't stay here on his own.

The radiotherapy is beginning to take its toll. I am very weary, but still managing to drive myself. Still walking the dogs every day and I am convinced that is what keeps my lungs (lung) open, and I think the more exercise I can take the better. Once I have tomorrow's session under my belt that will just leave three more weeks to go – counting the days! Apart from anything else, it's costing me £30 a week for petrol!

Friday – I'll just do this afternoon's session and that's three weeks done! No debilitating after-effects (at the moment), just the horrible pain when I try to swallow anything. They suggest you liquidise all your food. I don't think so – roast potatoes and lamb just aren't the same in liquid form, so I shall just carry on eating normally (but very slowly and well chewed).

I have decided that on 12th April – when I finish this treatment (have I mentioned that before?) – I am going to stop writing this (unless something extraordinary occurs) and not write all the time I am feeling well and until such time as the treatment wears off and the cancer takes over again. Then I shall start to write again until the end, I guess. I am hoping for some kind of prognosis when this has finished, or at least an educated guess at perhaps minimum and maximum life expectancy. Blimey, that's a bit scary – what if after all this treatment they only give me six months – wouldn't even get to the first day of the shooting season at that rate. I have nothing I want to make long-term plans for, but I would like to go to South Africa in January or February and would also like to go to the Blenheim Game Fair in July 2008 – not in an official capacity, but as a guest (for once) and perhaps I could (for once) just enjoy the Game Fair. So that's it – a 'little tiny' plan until July next year and that would also include M's twenty-first so there you go – not much to ask for, is it?

"Oh-my-God-I-forgot-to-mention-something-really-important-and-about-to-happen!" – that's all one word said very enthusiastically! I AM HAVING A NEW KITCHEN! OK, I know it's not big enough to swing a cat in, but it is still an event! It has all been purchased – still in flat-packs at the moment. I've just got to organise when and I'm thinking it might just be better to wait until after Easter. It's maple and it will be so good to have a new sink and surround – a shiny one!

Saturday, 5.30 a.m. – Still getting up early, but the clocks go forward next week so perhaps that will be the opportunity for the dogs' body clocks to alter (and mine) – let's hope so. Three weeks completed and it's rather sad, but I am actually crossing off the days on the calendar – doesn't quite compare with opening the doors on an Advent calendar, but crossing the days off the calendar at work when you have a holiday looming works for me and now I only have fifteen left to go.

I am still being a model patient, but the process has been very quick for the past week – no long delays and back in the car on my way home before you can blink. I meet quite a lot of people there – mainly women with breast cancer (who kind of give you the impression that they belong to some kind of exclusive club!). They have all lost their hair. Some have stunning wigs (I'm quite tempted to get one), some have appalling wigs (obviously not tempted) and some don't bother with wigs at all. What they do all have in common is they like to talk about it and compare notes. I also found out that they didn't have chemo like me. They weren't lying in bed for hours with the chemo being dripped in over a period of time; they were given theirs by the nurse straight into their lines and it was all over in an hour or so. One woman there was being treated at the BUPA hospital in Havant, but she never had a room for the day; she was treated along with three others at the same time in room 210 (the room with the big leather chairs), so her experience of chemo at BUPA was so different to mine. It has made me very aware of just how aggressive my chemo was and what massive doses I was given. However, I was somewhat gratified to hear that the constipation was just as bad! Rather late for me to pass on my notes on 'how to deal with the constipation' though. Perhaps I should do a 'short notes on surviving chemo' a bit like H. Reginald Cooke's *Short Notes on Choosing and Breaking a Retriever*, or the title could read *Cancer, Constipation and Captain-Fucking-Chemo*. It sounds good to me.

I am constantly shocked at some of the patients waiting to be zapped on these machines. Some are really elderly – would you bother? I know I wouldn't. Some are barely alive and arrive pushed in wheelchairs by porters. Some arrive in their hospital bed attached to drips etc. (probably chemo) – would you bother? I wouldn't. But perhaps they don't have a choice; perhaps they are just wheeled there and just accept everything they are given. I am so glad to have written my living will – I don't want to be pushed around from treatment to treatment, just accepting everything in a complete comatose state.

There was one man there yesterday whom I had never seen before and he looked filthy. He had a moustache and his nose was running. He stank of booze and fags. Do these poor girls really have to deal with this kind of person? He was obviously having radiotherapy, which is a hugely expensive process, and it was probably totally wrong of me to think that he shouldn't be just as entitled to the treatment as anyone else in the room – not very Christian. Hold that thought.

Sunday, 5.30 a.m. – I am beginning to hate weekends. I just seem to work all the time, take the dogs out and do various other things, whereas weekdays are much the same. I always feel so lonely at weekends. I long for Saturdays to get here so that I don't have to go for treatment; then when it arrives, in a strange kind of way I miss the disruption of having to go for the treatment – how sad is that?

Nick died on Saturday – Mickey rang to tell Sam. Now, I don't know (didn't know) Nick terribly well, but Linda and Joss, Sam etc. were all good friends and the last time Sam and I saw Nick was at Joss's sixtieth birthday party in July last year. Nick died of cancer and had been struggling with all the treatments etc. for six years. He thought he had been completely cured by a faith healer in Belgium – obviously not. When we saw him at Joss's party eight months ago he looked terrific and a picture of health, and now he is dead. It has actually brought it all home to me and made me sit up and think about death again. I have been feeling fine for the past week, weather has been glorious. I have felt quite strong, and were it not for my dreadful hair I would probably appear to most people the picture of health. When I am feeling good like that I don't believe that I am going to die; that funny surreal feeling creeps back and I convince myself that it isn't going to happen to me, but it is!

I don't think I should spend all day on my own today – whom can I go and visit? Whom can I phone to visit me? Remembering it is Mothering Sunday I expect most families will have plans. Sister Sue is still in South Africa; Wendy is probably going to a girls' lunch – see, that is the problem with Sundays, let alone Mother's Day. I might go to church after I have walked the dogs, then I may give Lucy a ring to see if she fancies a coffee or something – or I may just get so fed up I won't do anything and just slide into a deep state of depression – mustn't do that! Wonder what Michael is doing? Probably going day shooting with Bob!

I could get on and start emptying cupboards etc. ready for the kitchen, and it all needs painting but I really don't have the energy or the inclination today.

Wonder when I am going to die. Wonder how many years or months I am going to go on. I seriously believe that realistically it can only be twelve months – perhaps two years. I won't have any more treatment so— It is absolutely dreadful not knowing, not having a clue. I don't mind knowing I am going to die; I just want an educated guess at when.

Monday – So yesterday – Sunday (that makes it Monday today) – I looked on the Internet, typed in 'lung cancer' and up came page after page of websites, backup groups, absolutely everything, including every tiny bit of information that your average person with lung cancer needs to know. I was somewhat overwhelmed by the choice and I had no intention of visiting all the sites, but I did look at 'Cancer Backup' and 'NICE', which are both recommended by the NHS. I wasn't interested in diagnosis, treatment or follow-up treatment; I was searching for prognosis. I did find it – in most cases once lung cancer has been diagnosed, and with no treatment, generally patients do not survive more than two or three months! (Got past that stage, then.) When chemotherapy has had a reasonably good effect (yes – we can definitely say that ET has shrunk) and radiotherapy has shown an improvement (not sure about that yet), there is a fifteen per cent chance that some patients may go into remission for five years. More generally it will extend patients' lives for one or two years, but it could be as little as six months. How do I feel after reading all that? No different – it's pretty much what I already knew, but obviously I still want to know.

Did I spend the day on my own yesterday? Yes! Did I go to church? No! Did anyone phone? No! Well, that's not strictly true – Paula phoned in the evening. Did I phone anyone? No! Did I take it easy? No! I did what I said I had absolutely no intention of doing and started emptying drawers in the kitchen and also started painting it. Wore myself out and didn't feel as though I had achieved anything apart from the fact that at least when I die the kitchen will be clean and tidy. Must get rid of that huge chest freezer. If anyone tries to move that it will be disgusting underneath – probably enough dog hair to stuff a mattress!

What's happening today? Amy is coming to do 'something' with my hair (what's left of it) and I think cutting is the only option, so this time tomorrow I could be hairless! Plus, of course, the usual radiotherapy appointment p.m. – quite looking forward to it. It's the only bit of a social life I have at the moment.

Tuesday – Amy cut my hair yesterday – quite short, but not as short as I asked her to. I asked her to cut it all over, but she didn't think that was a good idea! Anyway, I'm loving what she has done and she assures me that there is a lot of new hair growing. It looks tidier and much better than it was. Amy tells me that fifty per cent of people go through life with really thin hair – how? I guess it is because I have been used to having thick hair all my life that I can't cope with it. Spent so much time on my hair I was almost late for my radiotherapy appointment – I get so stressed out these days if I have to rush anywhere and I have to put my foot down on the motorway, which these days – frankly – scares me.

Since when have the NHS been employing schoolboys? You don't get to see who your radiographer for the day is until they call your name and you walk round the corridor and go into the 'room'. There were two twelve-year-old boys in there! "Come in, Judith. How are you today?" I thought it was a wind-up, but no – how embarrassed was I? Loath to take my clothes off, that's for sure, but it had to happen and I ended up in the usual position, naked from the waist up, flat on my back with these two kids marking me up with their pens. Before the illness I probably would have taken it in my stride, but I was mortified. Stupid really as if the group in the waiting room were anything to go by there was a lot worse to come! Let's hope they are not on duty today.

Wednesday – Bit manic yesterday (Tuesday). Saw Dr Radio first – asked him what happens when the radiotherapy finishes. Apparently I go for a scan to assess the situation then a three-month appointment with him for another assessment, then as I am now going to be an NHS patient I go back to the respiratory centre at Queen Alexandra Hospital and under the consultant I originally saw. Ann is based there, so presumably she will come into the loop at some stage. I asked him about a prognosis.

He said, "Should be good."

I thought, 'Good?'

Then he said if I was lucky, and you need luck especially with lung cancer, it would be as long as one to two years – and that's lucky? Of course, I had to appreciate it may have slipped off and spread somewhere else – fantastic! Then he sent me off for a chest X-ray and told me to call in and see him next week to see it. Then I had my radiotherapy and came home!

Feeling exhausted this morning, but have to pull myself together as it's the A and D AGM this evening and I just have to be there. So my appointment for radiotherapy is 10.40 this morning instead of this afternoon as I have to leave here at 6 p.m. for the meeting. I just wish some fairy godmother would come in the meantime and make Sam's lunch and supper, take the dogs out, run the Hoover round and generally do everything I have to do. Is this what it is going to be like right up until the end? Am I going to be flogging myself until the last minute? I am nowhere near ready for them to come and do the kitchen. I started a few drawers, but exhausted myself – wonder if Sam would paint the ceiling for me today? I will leave the paint and brush in a very prominent position!

I need to look presentable tonight (for my sake really). I spend all my time looking like shit, but I am going to make an effort tonight. At least my hair looks a bit better now it has been cut. I was going to do my nails last night, but just didn't have the energy. What shall I wear? Have put on a bit of weight, so it won't be the leather trousers!

So, do I do a group newsletter with an update confirming that I have one to two years? There is only a fifteen per cent chance of five years – do they all want to hear that after all this treatment? I just know they are all expecting me to recover and I don't know what to tell them – I guess it's best they know the truth. Better phone Bridget and book my bed at the Rowans!

Went to the hospital earlier than usually today as I have to go to the A and D AGM tonight. Puts a different perspective on things going in the mornings and, although the traffic was almost non-existent and I got there in record time, I still prefer my usual late-afternoon stint. Also you definitely get different patients at that time of the day and the hospital, instead of winding down for the day, was just building into a crescendo. The place was packed and the walls lined with patients on trolleys waiting for X-rays etc. Have I made a mistake cancelling my health insurance? My highlight? Mr and Mrs Isle of Wight! Daily ferry crossing – nightmare. Their main topic of conversation? Their bird bath was frozen solid this morning! I do try to be pleasant to people, but sometimes . . . Plus the man sitting next to me couldn't wait to tell me he only had one or two years to live! Really! Well, whoopee doo!

Thursday – Late night last night – I mean really late. Didn't get in until gone 10 p.m. and didn't get to bed until 10.30 – two hours later than usual! Didn't fall asleep at the meeting, but almost nodded off through Ricky's talk!

That's it, then – the end of an era – no more field-trial secretary and I must take a step back. I would really like to resign from the committee, but will leave the dust to settle. I can't imagine being here for the AGM in March next year, but you never know. Made a huge effort with hair, make-up etc. so people won't remember a frail, sick-looking person hopefully. I do hope I am fit enough to help out at all the field trials this year, taking a back seat – unheard of, and I will undoubtedly interfere if something isn't as it should be.

Friday – I should be quite pleased as once I get today over with it means there are only two weeks left. *Only!* I just can't bear it – another ten days back and forth and my energy levels are getting lower and lower. I just about manage to walk the dogs and just can't face much else. The sheets need changing, I need to finish cleaning out the kitchen, and the ironing hasn't been touched. They asked me at the hospital yesterday if I was getting plenty of rest – how does that work? I can feel myself sinking into a deep depression. I think also I built myself up so much for the A and D meeting that now it is all over and I have resigned it feels a bit strange. I know I haven't really left the committee, but a bunch of flowers would have been nice. I expect when I die I will get some then, but I would rather have had them at the meeting – I guess I just felt a bit flat.

Incidentally, not only are they employing schoolboys as radiographers, they are also importing them now. I had a really nice black lad yesterday with the most gorgeous soft black curly hair and he was fourteen at the most! I am seriously past embarrassment or self-consciousness – just strip off and let's get it over and done with.

Sue's birthday today – they only have one more week in South Africa. She won't want to come home, but I will be pleased to see her.

I CANNOT WAIT TO FEEL NORMAL. I wonder how long it takes for the effects of the radiotherapy to wear off? Apparently I don't have to see the consultant for six weeks after my last treatment – WONDERFUL!

Saturday, 4 a.m. – Can't sleep. Keep thinking about how long I have got to live and, more importantly, what will the quality of life be? Have I gone through all this just to exist for the next twelve months or so or will I gradually deteriorate or become an invalid? It scares me, the not knowing, and sometimes I think I am talking about someone else and not me. I just wish I knew what was going to happen. I know I have said that before, but it is the not knowing. Sam doesn't know what to do or what to say – I'm not sure that he really understands the full implications. I have been really low this week and completely drained of any energy and that is the radiotherapy taking its toll. I wish Sam would just give me a hug now and then. I do feel very unloved. I know I am so difficult to live with at the moment – well, I have always been difficult, I am just worse now. I feel as though I am on a knife edge and could go either way.

The birds are already singing. Clocks go forward tonight, so the dawn chorus will soon be at full pitch once all the summer visitors arrive. The cuckoo will be here mid April. I always look forward to hearing the first cuckoo and then after a few weeks it drives me mad!

I have a new friend, Sandi. Met her at radiotherapy a couple of weeks ago and we just clicked. She's been through the mill – operation to remove a breast lump, chemotherapy now radiotherapy and then she has to have a mastectomy and reconstruction at the same time as they have found another lump. She's great. We get on really well and her stories of constipation are on a par with mine. She's great to talk to – great sense of humour and because she has been where I have been we understand each other. Wonder if we will see each other after radiotherapy has finished? We haven't exchanged phone numbers or anything, but I would quite like to – don't know if she would. Hopefully see her next week if our appointments are close.

John (the builder) wanted to come and fit the kitchen on Monday, which threw me into a complete state of panic as I haven't finished emptying or painting and Sam couldn't have Monday to help me as he is going to Nick's funeral. If Sue was home she would have helped me, but I couldn't ask Wendy (bad shoulder) or Bridget (bad neck) or Carol (on holiday) and I couldn't think of anyone else that might give me a hand over the weekend. Lucy – she might have done it! Anyway, to cut a long story short, I put the builder off and now it isn't likely to be done until after Easter! My fault – got stressed, too major for me to cope with.

Have chronic pins and needles in my hand, so have to stop writing. Going to phone Nigel and Mo over the weekend to see if they have discussed having Fletcher. If they have and they are prepared to give him a brilliant home then it is what I want for him and I will let him go. Sam doesn't understand, but I want Fletcher to have a wonderful, happy home life and Sam can't give him that. I have also asked Lynette to take Katy when I die, and I know she will either keep her or find her a really good home. Tess will go to Sue C. I will be so happy with that. Nymph, Rhea and Flinn will be quite happy with the lifestyle Sam gives them. They will be his responsibility and he can take them to work every day with Cracker.

Sunday – It's 6.30 but really its 5.30, so I'm up at just the same time as usual but lost an hour. Most normal people will stay in bed longer on the day the clocks go forward, but try telling my dogs that.

Sam took Fletcher and Flinn with him yesterday and regaled me with stories of Fletcher disappearing down the river and taking Cracker and Flinn with him, which makes me even more determined to get Nigel and Mo to have Fletcher. It will break my heart, but at the same time I will be really happy if they have him. Sam isn't looking at the bigger picture – he can't cope with them all and talks of me not worrying. He says he will just put all of them in the truck and take them with him if I can't manage. Then not only would Fletcher and Flinn take off with Cracker, but Katy would definitely be there with them and Nymph is quite capable of doing a disappearing act – nightmare.

Planned on doing nothing much yesterday, but ended up doing loads and although I was tired it was so good not to have to drive to Portsmouth. Fletcher has a stud this evening; the bitch won't be ready, I'm pretty sure of that, but we shall see. Sadly, the money I earn will go on the council tax and pay for the oil!

Think I will go to Butser this morning and then to church – didn't go last week. Need to go and see the vicar again soon and show him my order of service.

Monday – Nick's funeral today. Sam is home and he will be going, but I'm not. I did go to church yesterday and I enjoyed it, but I'm still not sure what I believe in. I believe in evolution and that the Bible is made up of fables told by storytellers, but do I believe in life after death, everlasting life, the spirit world? I don't know and wish I did.

Roger came round yesterday unexpectedly just to see how I was. It was great to see him, but I was so aware of my appearance. If I had known he was coming I would have definitely put some slap on and looked good (well, as good as possible), but I looked really rough – no make-up, hair a mess, eye bags – absolutely knackered. And what did he say? "You're looking good." I could have killed him – I looked dreadful. We talked about the picking-up next year and I said I couldn't see it happening as far as I was concerned. I think the best I could possibly hope for is being able to go out for a couple of mornings. Another thing gone from my life – no more puppies, no more field trials, no more picking up – and now what will happen is the dogs will gradually go, I suppose.

The good news is that Nigel and Mo are definitely going to have Fletcher – it will break my heart, but at the same time make me very happy to know that he is going to have such a good home.

Back to radiotherapy today. It is beginning to take its toll. I am so very weary and can just get through a normal day, but couldn't even contemplate going out for lunch or going to Buddies in the evening. I just want to get back to normal, but I know that isn't going to happen ever. I think all I can hope for is just some kind of quality of life that I can enjoy perhaps a little.

Sue and Joe will be home on Thursday and they won't be looking forward to coming back down to earth with a bang. Haven't heard from Wendy all weekend. Claire goes back to work today after maternity leave and she is dreading leaving William.

I couldn't do it. I know if I had ever had children I couldn't have worked. I was bad enough with puppies. I guess in this day and age needs must and money is tight – mortgage to pay etc.

Tuesday – Sam had the day off yesterday to go to Nick's funeral. Left here at 10 a.m. and got home just after 5 p.m. While they were in the church someone broke into Mickey's car and stole his mobile phone – marvellous! Hard to believe that someone was lurking about outside that quiet little church in Catherington just to steal Mickey's phone!

I wish Sam would have a few days off and just generally help me. I am seriously exhausted and I told him yesterday that the doctors think I should rest more. When I told Sam he just agreed, but I still have to cook, wash, and do the dogs, and the kitchen is still only half prepared and half painted and it is really getting me down. The garden is a mess; they still haven't been and cleared the fallen tree. Perhaps I should give writing in here a miss for a few days as I am not in the best humour and I really haven't got the energy for this.

I should really send out a newsletter, but I am just not in the mood. Apparently, even when the treatment is finished, it takes weeks for your body to recover (again) – perhaps by the summer I will feel better and then – I wonder – how long before I deteriorate again! Once I get to that stage, the stage where there is absolutely no hope and nothing else to be done and I am admitted into hospital, I don't want any visitors – well, apart from family and family includes Bridget but absolutely no one else – well, perhaps the vicar!

Smoking – am I still a furtive smoker? Well, I have really done my best to continue smoking as at this stage it can't make any difference, but this bloody radiotherapy which kills healthy cells as well as the cancer cells has stopped all that! Amazing – smoked a fair bit during chemo when I felt like it, but this is different. I am only operating on one lung at the moment and my chest feels very tight. That's why I keep walking up Butser, because I think it expands my chest. Anyway, I digress. Smoking – it nearly chokes me to have a cigarette and would recommend radiotherapy to the lungs as opposed to hypnotherapy or nicotine patches to stop anyone smoking. However, once I feel better – oh yes, I will, and there is absolutely no use anyone tut-tutting or shaking their heads – if I want to smoke till I die I will. Why give anything else up? I kind of think l might like to go on the Orient Express – never done that. Not that that has anything to do with smoking – it just came into my head.

Wednesday, 5 a.m. – Just made a cup of tea. Saw Dr Radio yesterday as he texted me to ask me to see him regarding my X-ray last week. He was very disappointed with the results. He was! How does he think I feel? Bottom line is that the radiotherapy has not made any impression on ET (the tumour) and it is the same size as it was when we started. I am on my fifth week now and still have another six treatments after this week is over, with the Easter weekend in between. That's four days next week and two days after Easter and he wants me to have another X-ray on Monday for him to assess again. Basically this is very bad news as the one-to-two-years prognosis goes down the pan and at this rate I shall be lucky to get six months.

Dr Radio said I was very unlucky as if ET had not been in the position it is (on the side of my lung and not in a good position) they could have cut it out, but I thought they didn't cut it out because it had spread to the lymph glands in my chest cavity? So why didn't they take the whole lung out and zap the lymph glands with the radiotherapy? Dunno. There are so many different types and I know they have done what's right, but nevertheless having gone through all this it is rather depressing (to say the least). I haven't told anyone other than Sam yet, but will probably do one of my e-mail round robins today if I feel like it. I told Sam when he came home, but he never said anything. He doesn't know what to say. He never asked the question 'How long?' He doesn't want to know.

One day I shall be taken into St Mary's when I become really ill, and I guess from there to the hospice. I just cannot believe that I shall be joining those grey wheelchair people clutching oxygen cylinders. There must be a better way. If I had a month's warning it would be good.

Thursday – E-mailed everyone with the 'good news' and phoned Bridget to tell her as she hasn't quite caught up with e-mails and computers yet (don't think she ever will). The only other person I should tell is Thalia, so will ring her today.

Was amazingly energised yesterday, but I don't think it was so much energy as agitation that motivated me. Did some gardening and some kitchen painting, but I shall suffer for that today as every bone in my body aches. So I reckon it will be dog walk and not much more until the dreaded drive to St Mary's this afternoon.

My heart is absolutely pounding in my ears like it's having to work really hard to pump the blood around my body. This happens with anaemia, but I don't think I am anaemic at the moment.

The birds are really going for it this morning and I still haven't done anything about recording them. Must do that – it would be the perfect thing to die to.

Sue and Joe should be home today, but I don't suppose I shall see Sue until next week, by the time she has unpacked and sorted everything out. Looking forward to seeing her. I won't ask Sue C. to take Tess yet as I know one of her dogs is going to have puppies. I will wait until after that. At this rate I shall only just finish paying for my funeral before I die – what a thought!

I haven't spoken to the vicar recently or my doctor. Will wait until after Easter when my treatment has finished and apart from that the vicar will be really busy over the Easter period – it's Palm Sunday this Sunday and then services all over the Easter weekend. My doctor needs to know that the radiotherapy hasn't worked; he needs to be kept in the loop.

It's all doom and gloom, but I am determined to keep cheerful about this and I am looking forward to all these lunches I have been promised as soon as I feel up to it. Jane, Lesley, Carol, Sue C., Romy and even Barry and Michael have promised me a lunch – I shall be huge!

Friday, 4 a.m. – Can't sleep even with the help of two mega sleeping tablets. Once today is over I will just have six more days to go until 12th April – I have been having treatment for nine months and, although I am told that without this treatment I wouldn't be alive today, I really don't feel alive. I haven't lived for the last nine months at all. I haven't gained nine months, I have lost nine months and my hair – well, almost all of it! It wouldn't be so bad if at the end of it you could snap your fingers and immediately feel better. That won't happen because it takes months for your body to return to normal. Then what happens? Your body regains strength, the tumour has a new lease of life, your body starts to deteriorate, you become ill, then you die. Is that what happens? Actually – today I really don't think I have anything else to say. I'm tired, I still have a tennis ball in my gullet, swallowing is difficult, my hair is a mess, I'm depressed and I want it to end.

Saturday – Thank God I do not have to drive to that hospital today. Yesterday I had to have a blood test (one hour waiting), an X-ray (not too bad, half an hour waiting), and radiotherapy (pretty much on time). Nevertheless it still entailed being at the hospital from 1.30 p.m. until 4.15 p.m. and I didn't get home until 5.15 p.m. exhausted. Thought I was hungry – ate a large bowl of soup and promptly threw up! Wendy arrived between X-ray and radiotherapy.

I must admit that all the fight I had in me has gone since Tuesday when Dr Radio told me that ET (the tumour) had not responded to the radiotherapy – really disheartening and makes me wonder why I have to finish the course – six more days. I can almost guess what is going to happen. I'll finish the course, then (I believe) I will have 'a rest' before seeing Dr Radio again and having a scan just to see what's happening with ET, and then I feel sure that the next step will be an offer of – you guessed it – more fucking chemo. ABSOLUTELY NOT.

The radiographers were concerned yesterday because my blood count is low and I am still anaemic – did I have a support group at home? Yeah, right – I have a group at home that I support. They suggested I visit the Macmillan centre, but what would they do? I haven't got time to spend chatting to a 'support' group with dogs sitting at home waiting for me. Their lives have been turned upside down as well. Poor old Nymph and Rhea go off with Sam every day as I can't manage all six of them every day. Do you think Macmillan would send someone out to walk the dogs? Take the curtains down and wash them? Paint the kitchen? Clean the chickens out? Sam is working all the hours that God sends just to make a bit more money – he can't do any more.

It would be better all round if . . . No, perhaps not. Buck up, Judith – stop feeling sorry for yourself. Look on the bright side – Sue and Joe are home!

Felt like shit all day yesterday. It didn't help matters when the downstairs loo was blocked, but fortunately Ron was home next door and he ended up working on it all day! It was finally discovered (along with some of Ron's graphic descriptions, which turned my stomach each time he told me, but when I asked him not to go into too much detail he just carried on) that it was the roots from the hedge outside that had found a crack in the pipe and started growing inside the pipe! Ron and his rods ended up three manhole covers away down in the field, but I didn't care as, selfishly, my only concern was my downstairs loo.

Sue and Joe came over – very brown and healthy-looking. It was great to see them and they are both coming over on Friday (Good Friday), Joe to do the garden and Sue to help me clear the kitchen. Brilliant – some practical help.

Sometimes I think I am writing all this about someone else – it's purely fiction and I am going to publish this as a novel. It's going to be a huge success and I am going to make enough royalty money to live the rest of my life in luxury. Sadly, it is me and it will not go away. Every waking minute of every day death is on my mind and as the end of my treatment gets closer my thoughts increase because of the unknown. I try not to dwell on it, but it doesn't work – is it best that I don't know what is going to happen to me? Will it make me feel worse if I have a graphic description of what may happen to me? If I knew would

I constantly be looking for signs? What I would like to do is get this treatment over and then lead as normal a life as possible for as long as possible and put all thoughts of dying out of my mind. There are plenty of things to do in the summer and, even though in my heart I know I am never going to be strong enough to pick up on the shoot next year, I could stick at going to the trials. Plus I would so love to go to South Africa with Sue and Joe next year and then I really so want to go to Blenheim Game Fair in July 2008 with Paula and all the gang. That would be a great finale.

Palm Sunday – I really intended going to church, but I may not. I rested for most of yesterday and I think it did me good, so I think I may do the same today. Even getting changed and going to church for an hour is exhausting, but I feel guilty for even thinking about not going – how ridiculous is that? Next Sunday as it is Easter there is an Ascension service at 5.30 a.m. with lighting a bonfire, and bacon sandwiches in the church hall afterwards – I would like to go to that. Let's face it, I am always awake at that time anyway.

I don't know if my eating habits are ever going to get back to normal (well, normal for me). I still don't drink coffee although I have had a packet of cappuccino. I don't think I will ever drink black coffee again. Chocolate and ice cream are things of the past – forever, I wonder? Now it is always savoury cravings, such as cheese, more cheese, bacon (bacon?), toast and roast dinners(?). Basically I never plan my meals; I just eat what I want and when I want it – very strange.

Monday – I don't think I should write anything in this today as I am so bloody miserable. It was such a lovely day yesterday, but I didn't go mad. Walked the dogs as usual in the morning; didn't feel as strong in my legs as I have been, but just carried on. I did take the curtains down in the sitting room and wash them, but would not call that hard work. I put the valances back, but Bridget is going to iron them for me (the curtains), like she hasn't got enough to worry about with Pete deteriorating before her eyes. I just wish they could sell their house and Pete could leave work. He shouldn't be working. I don't really know how Parkinson's progresses, but Pete looks so frail and Bridget carries it all on her shoulders – not to mention me as well – bless her.

Back to yesterday. I really didn't do much – bit of cooking, and watched television most of the day. That's all I seem to do now. Decided to take the dogs for another walk in the afternoon, but got over into the field and my legs went to jelly. I cannot believe how weak I have become. I just pray that when this treatment finishes my health improves because like this I cannot function.

Went on line to Amazon yesterday and ordered a CD – what for? My funeral! Yep, that's right. I have asked for Aled Jones's 'You Raise Me Up' to be played in the church before and after the service. I know someone could have got it, but hey – who's organising this funeral? It's what I do best! Hugely tempted to sort out the catering and where they are going to have it. Village hall? Church hall? Pub? Don't know – wish I was organising this for someone else. It's rather sad that I will miss it. I need to speak to the vicar again and show him my proposed order of service and see what he thinks. Best leave it until after Holy Week as he will have a really busy schedule this week.

Sam came home yesterday and asked if any of my friends had been to see me. I told him I didn't want anyone here, I just wanted to be left on my own. They don't even phone me any more, frightened of what kind of reception they are going to get or whether I will even answer the phone. I do know though that if I picked up the phone any one of them would be here like a shot. Perhaps in a few weeks I will feel more like my old self, but at the moment I don't want anyone other than completely necessary to see me like this.

This is my comfort zone, my cocoon. I am even hesitating about going to have my hair done this morning – don't know what to do. I guess it will make me feel better – or will it?

Bridget is driving me to the hospital this afternoon. I have finally given in after five weeks of driving myself. Four days this week – I will drive every other day. Two days next week – Bridget perhaps can drive me on the last day.

Tuesday – Really counting down now – five more to go! Went to have my hair done yesterday and had my hair cut even shorter! See – once I am actually out I am OK. Hair really short and spiky. Amy gave me some special lotion (cost-a-fortune type) that you put on your hair daily (from a dropper) and it is especially formulated for people whose hair has suffered through illness, trauma, stress etc., so I am keeping my fingers crossed that it works for me and I will be able to grow my hair again.

So – in a hair-cutting mood – I came home and gave Gary (the guinea pig) a haircut then set about Katy and Fletcher, so they are all looking quite smart now! Rhea needs doing, but I will have to get the clippers out on her, so perhaps in a few weeks.

Apparently (as one of the radiographers told me yesterday) it will take six to twelve months for my body to recover from the battering of chemo then radiotherapy – another six months? Then you go through all that, never really feel better, get a chest infection and die? Great. Well, that's something to look forward to!

Bridget drove me down there yesterday. It was her first time. Hard to believe now that I have driven myself every day for five weeks up until now. I'm going to drive myself again today – I will be fine – then four days off this weekend – then two more treatments and apparently I get six whole weeks before I have to come back to see the consultant. Brilliant.

Wednesday – Four days to go. At 4 a.m. the terrier (Cracker), having consumed Sam's car seat yesterday, threw up everywhere and managed to get me up even earlier than usual, so in addition I have let all the other dogs out and given them breakfast and I shall try and get back to sleep once I have drunk my cup of tea.

Also – yesterday – saw Dr Radio again and much to the annoyance of all the other patients waiting at his Tuesday clinic with proper appointments (mine was just a text message saying he wanted to see me). He saw me first. I did attempt not to look smug – hope it worked. What a roller-coaster ride this disease is – this week he was pleased with the latest X-ray and said that sometimes it takes twenty treatments before any change is noted.

This week he was terribly excited and told me that ET had shrunk and to keep my fingers crossed. Fingers crossed? The man is a lunatic – actually he isn't, but I honestly think that he is looking at my case as a study challenge and I think he may have some kind of wager on with Captain Chemo, who initially thought that radiotherapy was not an option. Whatever, I don't care. I only have four days to go although on Tuesday he wants me to have an X-ray a.m., see him about 1.30 then go for my treatment – I call that pushing his luck!

Saw my friend Sandi yesterday, who was in complete agony. She had breast cancer and where she has had her radiotherapy it has burnt and split the skin and, poor thing, she looked in great pain. They do warn you that towards the end of your treatment the skin can start to burn and they advise you to use very simple soap and aqueous cream – not body lotion. This is OK, but if the skin splits you can't put anything like that on. Poor girl – it didn't stop her chatting though. I would like to keep in touch with Sandi. We are going for a lunch in April before her surgery in May. She still has to have a mastectomy yet. I feel so sorry for her. All the time I was having my treatment at BUPA I didn't get to meet other cancer patients, or at least very rarely and just in passing in the corridor. Coming to radiotherapy every day at St Mary's you are touched by so many other lives and so many different people with this disease in so many different places. Sandi is the only one that I have met that I would really like to stay in touch with and if she wants me to I will try and support her through this next phase of her illness. Like me, she probably has masses of support from friends and family, but there really isn't anything like talking to a fellow sufferer, someone who has been there and knows what you are going through.

Thursday – three more! Today, then four days off for Easter, and two more after that, and I know that is it! There is a maximum dose of radiotherapy that you are allowed to have and by next Wednesday I will have had it, so there definitely won't be a case of 'just another week'. It won't happen.

Bridget took me down yesterday, but I am driving myself

today and I have also made my mind up that I will be driving myself next Tuesday and Wednesday – may as well finish the job. I am much better off driving myself anyway, especially if I am in a bad mood! I really can begin to feel my spirit lifting with the prospect of no more treatment. What shall I do with myself? No field trials or Game Fair to organise! Although I do think that would be a tad overambitious!

The highlight of my day yesterday? I bought a bottle of juice from one of these machines dotted around the hospital. You know the kind – put a £1 coin in, press the corresponding numbers and letters for which juice you want and eventually the thing comes clattering down and you can retrieve it through some kind of cat flap at the bottom. Fine – I had my juice and then on our way to the oncology unit I tried (unsuccessfully) to open the damn thing. To my rescue came two strapping men with a hospital trolley, complete with an oxygen cylinder – which I was fast approaching needing. A small crowd formed (well, in truth it was a queue as we were blocking the thoroughfare), purple rubber gloves were put on (this is honestly the truth) and both men also failed miserably to open the aforementioned bottle. Pliers were found and by this time I was so dehydrated and breathing into a paper bag that the trolley and oxygen were looking more and more tempting. *Eventually*, with the tailback of people almost reaching the exit, the whole top was prized off the bottle – finally exposing the juice. So, with grateful thanks and my drink now available, Bridget and I then made our way to oncology with me taking a huge slurp of my juice en route only to discover – I didn't like it! So typical of me at the moment, my taste buds are still non-existent and the smell or taste of some foods makes me gag. Hopefully, this will improve when treatment has finished.

I feel very guilty at not having contacted Sue C. all week. She has been brilliant all the way through this and always keeps in touch, but it has just been one of those miserable weeks and it did depress me last week when Dr Radio said that the radiotherapy wasn't working so I haven't really wanted to chat. I will call her today though, as I am feeling a bit more positive and I am also a bit more cheerful about my hair. Having had it cut even shorter, it's looking much better.

Good Friday – Four days without driving to Portsmouth! I was going to have four days without driving at all and instead of taking the dogs to Butser I was going to walk them round Bereleigh. However, that has changed because I have all the dogs for the whole weekend! Sam's truck went in for its MOT yesterday. (Yes, the Thursday before the long Easter weekend – who in their right mind books a car in then? It's obvious that if it needs anything doing it won't be done until Tuesday, so why didn't they book it in for Tuesday?) So, because of this (lack of forethought and planning), I will have to take all the dogs to Butser every day as it is so much easier to keep an eye on them there. So I'm not too happy about that as I was looking forward to a fairly quiet time and catching up with things and not having too many dogs to worry about.

I arrived at the radiotherapy department yesterday in good time for my 3.50 appointment. There are noticeboards there informing patients if there are any delays on any of the machines. There are three linear alignment machines, LA1, LA2 and LA3, which are booked solidly every ten minutes every day. Sometimes there has been fifteen or thirty minutes' delay, but I have to say in six weeks my appointments have been pretty much on time. Yesterday the information being displayed was 'LA2 BREAKDOWN' (I was booked on LA2) with sixty minutes' delay on LA1 and LA3. The nurses were really great and extremely apologetic. They brought round Quality Streets, and then the tea trolley arrived with cups of tea. It was a stark contrast to the hours I spent on my own at BUPA with the machines breaking down and not enough nursing staff to cover the patients. The NHS is a national treasure and the treatment I have received from them has been far superior to the private treatment I had at BUPA. That still goes down in my book as a huge contributing factor to the stress I felt when having chemo at BUPA.

Back to yesterday, in fact it wasn't too bad at all. Wendy came and then Sandi turned up for her treatment, so we had a bit of a laugh and I got my treatment at 4.40, home by 5.30 – traffic wasn't too bad, dogs were fine.

Got a couple of sore patches, like blisters really, where I am being zapped. Could be worse. Sandi is still suffering with all her skin split and sore. I'm using aqueous cream on mine and they are OK. Must be careful not to get in the sun this weekend – apparently that is a definite no-no for anyone having radiotherapy.

Sue and Joe are coming today to do the garden – excellent. I'm looking forward to seeing it all nice and tidy! Baskets? Shall I do some baskets this year? All that watering? I will – could be the last time. I keep forgetting I am ill. I don't bracket myself as ill – it's like it is happening to someone else. It's not like having flu; this is ill, terminally ill – yeah, right! Bollocks to it.

Saturday, 5 a.m. – Really not feeling well this morning. Feel sick, head and heart pounding. I really think I overdid things yesterday.

I had all the dogs to contend with, so that resulted in Butser Hill early a.m., but then Sue and Joe arrived to help me. The garden really does look much better and Joe is going to put bark all up the side of the drive next time. Sue helped me with a couple of cupboards, but it was all I could manage; so because they were with me all day I really didn't have any rest. Plus, when they went, Tony brought a dog-food delivery, which I wasn't expecting on Good Friday. When I eventually managed to sit down with a cup of tea it was late afternoon and I was exhausted, shivery and cold – yes, cold, and it was one of the warmest days we have had. So I ended up wrapping myself in a blanket and curling up in a chair. I am so worn out. The bathroom needs cleaning, towels need washing, sheets need changing and I can't do any of it. I am so, so fed up with feeling ill. Every joint in my body aches and I am tired. Apart from that I'm fine!

No quiet day today either. Terry and Baz are coming to take the kennels down and take them away. Haven't told Sam they are coming – he will know when he gets home. Plus Jan (who used to work for me) is coming to see me this afternoon. She

230

is over from France for a week. It will be good to see her, but I don't suppose she will do all the cleaning while she is here! Half the kitchen contents are in boxes in the dining room and it's beginning to really get on my nerves. Suppose it will be done eventually – hopefully before I die. At least we have cleared some of the clutter. Sue took a huge box to the charity shop!

Easter Sunday, 5 a.m. – I am just having a cup of tea and considering going to the 5.30 a.m. Ascension Service at the Church (followed by bacon sandwiches in the Church Hall). I said considering – will let you know.

Yesterday was the end of yet another era when Terry came and dismantled the kennels and took them away. It was pointless leaving them there and I hope he gets some use out of them. He is young enough to enjoy them for a good many years, but I shall never see them again. Looks really strange out there without them and if I had longer we could probably re-landscape that back paddock, have somewhere to sit and barbeque plus a vegetable garden, but that won't happen. In the short term it will make a really great venue for the Buddies picnic later in the year!

After all the dismantling Jan came – it was great, we had a good old chat. I had forgotten how much I missed her and how I wish she had been here all through my chemo. What a blessing that would have been.

7.10 a.m. – Just got back from church – went to the 5.30-a.m. service and amazingly the church was full – loads of children there too. Long service, bonfire lighting, candles, lighting the Easter candle, renewing of baptism vows, Communion. It was a good service and I enjoyed it. Now going to see to the dogs, let the chickens out etc. Don't think Sam is even aware that I have been out! Just taken him a cup of tea – oblivious! He left me an Easter egg – shame I'm not eating chocolate (not since last July) – did he forget? Or didn't he know? Going to Sue's for lunch later.

Monday – We went to Sue's, Sam drove and didn't speak all the way. I tried to speak to him and he just said it always ends in an argument! When we got to Sue's he was still not speaking, or to Sue really, and it wasn't until Ian came back from 'getting a paper' (pint in the pub) that Sam started talking to him. What a nightmare, tiptoeing round him all the time. I know, I just know, that in his head he blames me for any upset at all, but it is so frustrating (even under normal circumstances) to have someone deliberately walk away from you and deliberately avert their whole head not to look you in the eye.

We had a super lunch at Sue's and I laughed more than I had in months. It was great talking to Ian. He really wanted to know about my illness, treatments etc. and I was completely open with him and it was really good – kind of gets it off your chest. He even asked the question "How long?" No one, but no one, has actually asked me that before. Sadly I can't answer the question; it is the one I ask the consultants and the one question that never gets answered. It must be difficult for people because I don't really look any different (especially if I have made an effort – washed my hair and put a bit of slap on – the thinning hair always looks a bit better when it has just been washed). I haven't lost weight, I look quite healthy (fresh air and fake tan), so it is almost like having an out-of-body experience and I am not talking about myself but some other poor person who is really ill.

ONLY TWO MORE TREATMENTS – TOMORROW AND WEDNESDAY. Knowing my luck I will probably start to feel better for a while and drop dead from a heart attack or something totally obscure and unrelated to lung cancer. Now there's a thought – best finalise all preparations just in case!

Tuesday, 10th April – Instead of being elated as it is my penultimate treatment, I have worked myself up into a real state of panic. Couldn't sleep, my heart is pounding and constantly have a rushing sound in my ears as I have so much to do today. Apart from seeing to the dogs and making sure they have a really good run this morning, as I have to leave them all afternoon, I am stressed because normally I would have something prepared for Sam's meal tonight and I haven't. Also I normally prepare all the rolls etc. for his lunch boxes in advance, but I haven't so I'm panicking. Sounds crazy, I know, but everything is a major issue at the moment – plus I am convinced I have another tumour somewhere. I keep getting these stabbing pains in my head, just over my eye. Also my appetite has once again gone to pot; I just can't be bothered any more and find myself living off toast. I just don't fancy anything, although I enjoyed the meal at Sue's on Sunday – perhaps it's just that I have to cook so much for Sam and all through this illness I have prepared his meals, that I have just sickened myself and can't eat it any more.

I have to be at the hospital early for an X-ray, then I have to upset everyone again by interrupting everyone's routine and asking for Dr Radio because he wants to see me, then I have to go for my radiotherapy, then I can come home and see to the dogs and I feel as though my head is going to explode as I am so anxious. Ridiculous, isn't it? This time tomorrow I will have done it all and this time tomorrow it will be my last day.

I'm not coping very well at the moment. I am concerned about Sam and seriously think he could do with some help. If I have ages to wait today (please, God, I don't) between seeing Dr Radio and my radiotherapy I may go up to the Macmillan centre and see if I can find someone to talk to. I think Sam needs a support group. I think he needs to know what to do and what to say. Everything is such a mess and at times when I feel like this I just wish it was all over and I was dead. I should be looking forward to some treatment-free time, but I just wish everything was sorted out and that I was dead. I feel sometimes as though I am doing this on my own, but that is my fault as I have pushed everyone away until I feel better although the funny thing is sometimes I wish the opposite. I was curled up in the chair yesterday afternoon, covered with a blanket (always cold), and I just wished for someone to bring me something to eat on a tray and make me a cup of tea. I know I would only have to pick up the phone for someone to come, but I fight against it all the time as I have my routine and don't want anyone fussing over me (but

I suppose there are always exceptions to the rule).

Let's get today and tomorrow over and see what the next few weeks bring. Hopefully I shall begin to feel slightly more human again and start to see people, but for the moment I AM TOTALLY PISSED OFF, STRESSED, AGITATED, MISERABLE, PESSIMISTIC, LETHARGIC – can't think of any more, but as NEGATIVE as you can get really!

I did actually *try* and cheer myself up yesterday by putting a red rinse on my hair! Shampooed it in (supposed to leave it for five minutes), looked in the mirror, lost my nerve and washed it out! All I achieved was a messy bath, a red towel and my fingernails were red. Thought it might brighten me up, but by the time I had finished cleaning the bath etc. I wished I had never started.

Wednesday – Feel a bit shell-shocked today! Having really stressed myself out with my impending multiple appointments yesterday and the thought of being at the hospital for hours and hours, it all went rather swimmingly really. Apart from the initial 'minor' blip when, having trudged from the car park to X-ray and sat down to wait for my appointment, I realised I had forgotten to put my car-park pass in my car window; it was only the thought of being clamped that gave me the energy to trudge all the way back again! Arrived at X-ray at 11.30 a.m., out of there by 12, went round to oncology to see Dr Radio, and saw him and the X-ray. Then my appointment for radiotherapy wasn't until 3.30, but the girls squeezed me in and I was back in the car, on my way home, by 1.15, so that was absolutely brilliant.

The X-ray? Well, Dr Radio who was full of doom and gloom a few weeks ago, was seriously pleased with himself when he showed me the X-ray (and, believe me, I can read an X-ray now) and there was absolutely no sight of ET. I couldn't believe it and queried the fact that it was still there right up until last week and he (Dr Radio) explained that this is how it sometimes happens – not much movement for weeks then suddenly zapped. Now, call me sceptical if you like, but I'm not about to start opening champagne or jumping through hoops. But where has it suddenly gone? There were no 'black holes' where it used to be. I believe that, for the moment, the radiotherapy has successfully 'killed off' the remaining cancer that was there after the chemotherapy. I do not believe that it won't come back or that it hasn't migrated somewhere else in my body. I do believe that I have longer than six months to live. I do not believe that I have longer than two years.

I haven't told Sam or anyone else that there is no sign of ET because it would just raise all their expectations too much. What I have told them is that the radiotherapy has been a success and has extended my life by twelve to eighteen months, which is what Dr Radio said. I see him again in six weeks, and then a full body scan in six months which will show up any cancer in any of my other organs.

So – my last treatment today and then steadily back to normal (normal?). Apparently it will take at least six months for my body to recover, so I've been advised not to start rushing around like a lunatic.

My next big hurdle with Sam (and my emotions) is Fletcher because I still intend letting Nigel and Mo have him, even if I have another couple of years. I still want Fletcher to be settled and happy and have the right home while he is still young enough for Nigel and Mo to enjoy him. I also seriously hope I outlive Nymph, Rhea and Gary the guinea pig. There have been times over the past nine months when I thought I wouldn't, but fingers crossed I can be around when the old girls have to go.

Was talking to Paula last night and when I told her I had been having treatment for nine months she said, "Hasn't it gone quickly?" Bless her; it has been the longest, most horrendous experience of my life! In six months, when I have my body scan, if they find any more cancer I won't have chemotherapy; I'll just take my chances.

Thursday, 12th April 2007 – Nine months since on 12th July 2006 I started on this roller coaster. Not one week has passed since then without treatment, scans, X-rays, blood transfusions, chemotherapy or radiotherapy and today the treatment has finished! Can I get back to a normal life? I still have cancer; it isn't cured and I don't know how long I shall feel well for, but for the next few weeks I shall just hopefully get some strength and a bit of normality back in my life and the lives of others around me.

I have to see Dr Radio in four weeks (8th May) and I have now been put on to the NHS system, so no more special treatment for me and I guess after I have seen him I will be referred back to Queen Alexandra Respiratory Centre. Not sure where I shall have the full body scan, but that won't be for six months.

This journal started as a diary of my treatment to leave for my family and friends, but it has become rather more than that. It is almost a friend to me, a crutch, and until I have written in it every day I feel that something is missing. Now, having reached the crossroads with the treatment, do I continue with this or perhaps just stop here because I have reached a turning point? Having said that, it is not a conclusion and there is no ending yet so I may just carry on. At least for a few weeks to see how I am and whether I am getting stronger. I don't know – at this point I just don't know. I may not be able to give it up as this is a very important part of my life with my early morning cup of tea.

Who knows, in years to come William might want to read it just to see what GAJ (Great-Aunt Judith) was really like! Talking of William, the poor little chap was in hospital again yesterday with suspected meningitis (actually it wasn't and he is home now – he has tonsillitis and a stomach infection). I went up to see him on the children's ward with Wendy after radiotherapy – poor little chap, he was really hot and bothered, but he will be fine. Do they take tonsils out these days? Don't know – I know I had mine out at a very early age, but I'm not sure if they still do that.

Just realised I didn't see Sandi before I left radiotherapy. Would like to keep in touch with her. She did write me a card with her phone number on it, so I will give her a ring.

So – what have I got to look forward to? The summer – the shooting season (never thought I would make another one). I don't think I shall be able to pick up normally, but I may do at least one day a week and it really won't matter if I don't have

Fletcher as I can take Flinn, Katy and Tess (Rhea and Nymph? One drive possibly.) Blenheim Game Fair 2008 – all of us – bit of a party. I will look forward to that. South Africa? Don't know – may not be able to afford it, but let's wait and see! Going out – seeing people – having a social life again? One step at a time, I reckon, and this is only the first day!

Friday, 13th – I think it is going to be difficult for me to give this up – it has become part of my life and what else am I going to do while I am having a cup of tea at 5 a.m.? I wish I could sleep until at least 6.30 a.m., but it is the same every morning; the dogs are so used to me going to make a cup of tea now that they are already awake and waiting for me, so I suppose I shall carry on. I don't really want it to turn into *Mrs Dale's Diary* as it is supposed to be a log of my illness, but then although I don't have any more treatment, I still very much have the illness. But I don't feel ill – exhausted, but not ill.

Had to really press on with the kitchen cupboards yesterday as John phoned and they are starting on Monday, but that's fine, I can cope with it now and I am hoping that everything doesn't continue to be a major issue and that I get back to my normal (bossy) self.

I seem to have put dying to the back of my mind (at least temporarily). Time will tell and the full body scan in six months' time will tell. It would be a miracle if the cancer had gone, but I'm afraid that is not very likely.

I actually never cease to amaze myself as yesterday, instead of Butser (and all the baby lambs being terrified of the Black Pack) I did one of my 'normal' long route marches round Bereleigh Estate and I was fine and when I came back I didn't collapse in a chair for two hours – I carried on, so things are looking up. I'm beginning to think that despite all the odds (etc., etc., etc.), I'm going to make it and go past eighteen months – that's how I feel today.

On my dog walk yesterday I met more people in an hour than I have been seeing in a month! I met Sarah and dogs first – stopped and had a chat with Ron on his tractor, then the new gardener and his wife, then Phillipa's mother, who doesn't know what day of the week it is. She was convinced she had been speaking to me the day before, but in truth it is over a year since I saw her last! Then Dangerous came round and removed the remaining tree stump from the garden, and finally Jacqui and Kate came round later in the afternoon. Blimey – all a bit much when I have been avoiding people for weeks because I looked and felt so dreadful.

Saturday – Everyone is really thrilled about the latest info. I'm sure they think that I am cured, but I haven't managed to get caught up in their excitement because I know that I still have cancer and it won't just go away!

Went to S and R's for supper and we had a really lovely meal. We sat out! Lit 'big mouth' and I sat in front of it, so I was really warm! G made fruit kebabs with marshmallows, which we toasted, and she informed me that she wasn't in the least concerned about her GCSEs – they were going to be easy! M was in great form and he is pleased that I am still going to be around for his graduation. It was a lovely evening. Told them all my decision with Fletcher and they all thought is would be for the best.

Spent most of yesterday packing up the kitchen ready for Monday! Exhausted and fed up with the dogs waking me up every morning – no one else in their right mind would get up and feed their dogs at 5 a.m. every morning. There are times when I wish I didn't have any dogs – or just one. It would be nice to have just one that would lie in bed until at least 9 a.m. and then be happy just to lie around all day.

Lucy came yesterday and chatted for a couple of hours. She seems to think I should help others get through what I have just been through, but I'm not sure that I am ready to be some kind of counsellor just yet.

I will just say that I wouldn't wish this illness and any of the available treatments on anyone, especially those I love. If me having it means that no one I care about gets it then I am happy to bear it, but the thought of anyone else having to go through it really depresses me. I wonder if I am now expected to just carry on and return to normal. Is this what people expect? Because it won't happen – I will never be normal again.

Monday – Kitchen day – I hope they don't let me down as I have completely cleared everything. I'm actually not dreading them doing the kitchen, but I am completely dreading cleaning up afterwards and putting everything back. I really find I cannot do a great deal without getting completely exhausted and wonder if I shall ever have real energy again.

Although Dr Radio said ET had shrunk, my chest feels really tight at the moment but I think that is because the radiotherapy has killed healthy tissue also. I presume that takes some time to recover.

I hate being lazy and that is what I feel I am when I find myself constantly sitting down for a rest. Everything takes twice as long. I have been thinking about changing the winter duvets for days, but still haven't got round to doing it. No one really wants to listen to how I feel; they just want to think I am OK and that I am looking OK and functioning OK, but there are times when I just want to let it all out. Sometimes when I phone someone for a chat I end up listening to their problems, so I tend not to say anything. The pheasants in the laying pens are waking up and all the birds are singing. I still haven't recorded that sound – should have asked M.

It's going to be a very busy day: kitchen (I hope), Amy coming to do my hair (I think), Sue and Joe p.m. to cut the grass (possibly). I'm knackered already just thinking about it.

Tuesday, 4 a.m. – Can't sleep. Bloody kitchen nowhere near finished. Thought they would arrive early, so I got up, walked the dogs etc. and expected an arrival by 8 a.m. Then had hoped for hard work and plenty of kitchen building and the job to be finished in one day. NO CHANCE. They arrived at 9.30, had a fag break and a chat, removed the old cupboards and left me to sweep up all the mess while they had another fag break and sandwiches. Then they did manage to build a couple of cabinets, discovered loads of things they needed for the job – plus one set of drawers was missing. Left me at 3.30 in virtually the same state as when they arrived, apart from now I was even without the dishwasher as they had disconnected that! So the upshot is that they are coming back today, but I have my doubts that they will finish the job today; so this could go on and on and I really don't need it. By the time they left I felt really ill.

PLUS Pauline – the new field-trial secretary – once again is not returning my calls and once again I am having serious doubts about her really doing this job properly. She is supposed to be meeting with me on Thursday for a proper handover and a trip to Exbury to sort out the judges' accommodation etc. I am so stressed about it and I really thought by this time I would not have any more responsibility for the field trials! It cannot go on – I'm going to die. I don't need all this hassle and yet I cannot just let go until I know that everything is in order. I built this up and no one is going to just let things slip, at least not while I am still alive.

Kitchen all day again today, so I can't rest while they are here, and then, once they have gone, what have I to look forward to? Putting all the bloody stuff away again! They will take the sink out today – God give me strength! Right, that's it, no more moaning. It will look nice and be much cleaner once they have finished. I might even celebrate and buy a new smaller microwave!

Wednesday, 4 a.m. – Sleep impossible. Chest feels really tight and I think it may have something to do with fumes from the Rayburn, which I lit again yesterday. I didn't plan on lighting it again until they had finished the kitchen, but as they only worked for four hours yesterday – and three of those were tea and fag breaks – obviously they still haven't finished!

In the midst of the kitchen mayhem, Pam phoned from New Zealand. Really great to hear her voice and also to hear she may be planning a trip here in November. She's never been in the winter before, so she'll have to bring clothes with her! I didn't like to tell her that her bed has gone from the spare bedroom! Not worried – can always get a blow-up mattress. In fact, I think Sue may have one. Cross that bridge and all that.

Have now left Pauline four messages and she still hasn't got back to me. I won't call her again and Paula and I will go to Exbury on our own and see if we can sort out the judges' accommodation.

Bought a new microwave on line and Sue is picking it up for me. Sorted – new kitchen, new microwave!

Thursday – Kitchen still not sorted. Yesterday was another nightmare – very shabby, rushed job and a mess left behind like I've never seen before. Just biding my time before I really complain and let Bill know what's going on and suggest he doesn't pay them. Made a long list of unacceptable things they have done.

The burns from radiotherapy are getting bigger, and especially the one on my back. I'm supposed to put cream on them, but the one on my back, which is the size of a saucer, is really difficult to reach so I had to get Sam to do it. It is so sore and obviously aggravated by clothing. I may have to cover it with a dressing.

Pauline finally rang yesterday, so she is coming to Exbury with us – I'm really glad and hope I can finally tie up some loose ends and hand over properly to her. Paula is coming at 10.30 and, to be honest, I shall be quite glad to get away from here for a couple of hours, especially as Sid is coming to sort the Rayburn out, so Sam can deal with him for a change!

Sue is dropping off the new microwave today, so that's good. I am finding the kitchen situation really depressing at the moment. I was so looking forward to having it done and now I am really disappointed with the result. Does nothing ever go to plan?

Friday – Had a really good day (apart from before I left and as soon as I got back!). Paula picked me up (and Pauline) and we went to Exbury. It was great to see Kev and Caroline and Kerry had the day off school especially because we were coming – bless her. Sorted out the accommodation for the field trial (that put my mind at rest) and then had a nice meal at the pub on the roundabout. Much happier about Pauline being field-trial secretary now and I think I can relax a bit, but I don't think it is going to be a long-term thing so we should look out for someone else.

The kitchen on the other hand is a nightmare. John came (John's the boss) and I showed him some of my complaints, which resulted in them having to take the sink that was put in on Wednesday back out and refit it. Thankfully, while that was going on, I left with Paula! On my return, nothing had improved and I have now suggested to Bill that he doesn't pay. It is a shabby, unprofessional job and I feel very let down by John, who up until this I had complete faith in. However, I am going to write it all down and e-mail it to Bill and try not to get upset any more.

Sid came to see the Rayburn and was just leaving, having lit the Rayburn. It was just as well I got home when I did as the kitchen was full of smoke and fumes. The Rayburn now has to have the flue swept and lengthened, so it is out again and I have organised a chimney sweep for Monday – no cooking!

Good news – well, I think so – one of my bantams is broody and sitting on seven eggs. Pathetic really, but I am quite excited – I love babies! I have moved her into her own little environment. I got the idea from Caroline, who puts her broodies in a little hutch until the eggs hatch and it just so happened that I had a brand-new hutch perfect for the job – brilliant, can't wait.

Just not going to worry about the state of the kitchen or the filthy house or the washing that is piling up or the fact that I can't cook on the Rayburn – bollocks to it all. I'm going to the seaside with Sue C. and the dogs.

Not thinking about dying at the moment and, although the burns on my back are very uncomfortable, I generally feel OK. Sam is being very supportive at the moment and trying to keep me calm through the kitchen situation.

Saturday – Had a great time at Hayling Island with the dogs and Sue C. and then lunch – did me good and Fletch had a great 'surf' as there were some big rollers coming in!

No builders in the kitchen yesterday. It's still nowhere near finished, but I have managed to start clearing some of the stuff away. I know they will come back and make more mess, but I can't live like that any more. Bill came and had a look at it and agreed it is a 'bad job', so he can take over the complaints now. I'll leave it to him and try not to get stressed!

I seem to be getting more and more energy, so that is good and it is so great not to have to drive to Portsmouth every day for treatment. Seems strange – no more treatment – and I am so adamant that I won't have any more, but on the other hand I can't help wondering if, as a bad experience, the chemo horrors gradually fade as does any illness, childbirth etc. Then when the time comes round again perhaps you think, 'That wasn't so bad' and agree to have more so that you can cling on to your little life for longer. I don't think so! I still maintain that if they find any more cancer in my body and offer me more chemo I would never ever have it again. Don't let's go there. At the moment, apart from the burns on my back (which are very sore and inflamed), I'm feeling pretty OK. Not quite back to full speed, but actually not far off it. I still get pretty exhausted, but I suppose that is to be expected after just over one week without treatment. *Plus*, I have been out twice this week on two consecutive days – pretty good going. Bridget is coming today – bringing my curtains that she has ironed for me – bless her.

Sunday, 22nd April – Definitely going to church this morning – I think I have angered the gods as nothing seems to be going terribly well, or am I still character building? I think my character has been built – thank you very much.

Bridget and Wendy came and helped me put the curtains up – that was fine apart from the fact that I shouted at Wendy – sorry Wendy! I seem to need to do everything myself at the moment. I also think it stems from not being able to do anything much during chemo and not having enough energy during radiotherapy, but I seem to have plenty of energy at the moment. I also think I want to do as much as I can, while I can. It's almost like preparing for a holiday really, trying to leave everything in order so that you can relax when you get there. Once I get 'there' I shall be thoroughly 'chilled'. Why don't I go away for a holiday now? Several reasons, the main one being I can't really afford it.

Another, I have too much to do – perhaps one day.

Having been really busy all day painting, cleaning etc., I decided to put myself through the torture of setting up my broadband connection. Got all the equipment out of the box, undid all the wires, rushed round the house putting the adaptors on all outside phone lines, put in the CD and followed the instructions, which I have to say were very clear and you could follow them if you were brain dead! Did all 'they' told me to do – wires and plugs everywhere, confirmed new e-mail and password – all done perfectly. AND THEN IT WOULDN'T BLOODY WORK – KEPT TELLING ME IT COULDN'T FIND THE USB CONNECTION! BOLLOCKS! Phoned M – he's coming over this morning and I am going to church!

Just heard the first cuckoo. Always look forward to hearing it, but give me a couple of weeks and it will drive me mad. Huge dog fox staring at me from the field – the bastard had better not even think about getting my chucks!

Monday – M was here by 8.30 a.m. yesterday, bless him, and I was still out dog walking, but he discovered I hadn't done anything wrong with the broadband connection and we spent quite a while trying to work out the e-mail connection, but I think we have sorted it now. He has grown up into a really nice person and I love him to bits.

Went to church and enjoyed it, but I do find these new hymns difficult to cope with. Hardly any of them I recognise – what was wrong with all the old ones? I have chosen the hymns for my funeral and I insist on the old music for them. Well, I insist in my head – I had better let the vicar know what I want.

Actually didn't feel too brilliant yesterday afternoon. I think the week had just caught up with me. Felt very sick, tired and shivery, but still didn't rest for very long and this morning I shall have to be up really early (have been up, but came back to bed with my tea – still haven't got out of this sleep pattern and I think the dogs expect breakfast at 5 a.m. now). The man is coming to sweep the Rayburn flue and also put a new 'thing' on the top.

What I am dreading – and I am trying to keep calm about it – is the bloody workmen coming back to 'finish' this kitchen! By rights it should all be taken out and started again, but I really don't think I could bear that and hesitate to complain any further in case they abandon the job. Hopefully they will ring me first whatever happens (and don't just turn up) so that I am prepared and they don't catch me on my back foot. PLEASE KEEP ME CALM!

I wonder how ET is. Has it started fighting back yet? I've got that surreal, it's-not-happening-to-me feeling back again as I am beginning to feel a bit better. I do get extraordinarily weary and really struggle sometimes to do everything I want to do but because I am feeling more able I do push myself to my absolute limits. I don't know if that is a good or a bad thing, but unless I am totally, totally on my knees I constantly find other jobs that need doing. I think it is a good thing because the alternative is not attractive. I cannot just not do things that need doing and do not find the constant rest that people keep advising very appealing at all.

Tuesday – Yesterday was again 'one of those days'. The man came to sweep the Rayburn flue, which was obviously not straightforward – I say *obviously* because nothing I ever have done ever turns out to be a simple job. I won't go into any details as it would bore not only you but me as well. Suffice it to say that he was here for four hours – the whole thing had to be removed and an access window put in, and then it all had to be put back, but he did do a great job. Sue and Joe came to do the garden, then Neil came round to remeasure the kitchen worktops as they are going to be done again. Bill phoned John and complained, John phoned me and apologised, and now we have to start all over again and I can't bear it. I have just finished putting everything back in the cupboards!

This morning I really don't feel well. I had funny pains in my chest in bed last night and I have them again this morning. I think – well, actually I know – that I just do too much and don't eat properly, but what can I do with workmen around all the time? I rang Sandi (my friend with cancer that I met at radiotherapy). It was 10.30 a.m. and she was just getting out of the shower having just got up. I should be taking it easy like that, but I just can't. As soon as I wake up I start thinking about what I need to do today and the list is always endless.

I don't think my chuck is going to hatch those eggs. Her heart isn't in it and I don't think I should have moved her. She is not sitting 'tight' on the eggs and gets off every time I go in there, so I will give her another couple of days and bring her out, put her back with the others and throw the eggs away. Really disappointed.

I can't seem to stop writing this; it has become such a habit and such a part of my life. I did intend stopping on 12th April, but I obviously haven't. Well, it keeps me sane (I won't say happy) and at the end of the day these journals can just be burnt or thrown away. It's my support group.

When you get chest pains (this is my thought for the day), you don't think about dying from cancer any more – it pales into insignificance. My first thought with chest pains? "God, I'm going to have a heart attack now and I haven't finished paying for my funeral." Yes – that was my thought!

Wednesday – What is happening today? Am I going somewhere special to relax and enjoy myself? Going on a little 'cruisette' to the Med? Even just going out to lunch? No! THEY ARE COMING TO DO THE KITCHEN AGAIN! Stay calm, just ignore them, don't get agitated, let them get on with it and go away.

3.30 p.m. – They are still here, nowhere near finished. Plasterer coming at 8.30 a.m. tomorrow and I am feeling really emotional and don't think I can bear this much longer without cracking up. I am tired, hungry (can't get into the kitchen for anything to eat) and totally exhausted. I just want it to be over – the drilling, the mess. It is all so totally unnecessary having to do it all over again. I'm on the verge of collapse and even when they have gone I have to sort out something for supper. Why am I doing this? Why can't I just leave home and let them get on with it? Because I CAN'T, because the dogs are here, because I haven't got the energy!

Thursday – They are coming back today! I hope this is the last day, but I doubt it. There is just the wall to plaster, the tiles to be put up and the sink unit to be sorted out, but, being realistic, that could take a week! It's my mistake – I shouldn't have arranged for it so soon after treatment. Isn't stress supposed to trigger off cancer? The state I am in I have probably triggered off every cell in my body. Think positive – stop moaning about it – it will all be over soon.

Added frustration was the guy I called in to check out the television aerial, which is wobbling. 'No call-out fee', it said. He whizzed round the property with some kind of device and charged me £25 plus VAT – then gave me a written quote for almost £300, then thought he was going to do the job. I admit I was stupid enough to pay him £25 plus VAT, but I'm not stupid enough to give him the job. I went on the Internet and found someone else who has quoted me £159.99 and they are coming to do it on 4th May. I had to pay fifty per cent up front, so I hope they turn up! Meanwhile, I am on a mission to get my money back from the original firm. I phoned yesterday and was told someone would call me back – they didn't. I shall phone again today and if I don't get any joy I'm writing to *Watchdog*. What do you think my chances are? Old-age pensioner with terminal cancer embezzled – let's do it!

Can I afford a day at a health spa? That's what I need, a bit of 'me' time, a nice massage, nails, facial, Indian head massage – I'll check it out today.

Friday – THE KITCHEN IS FINISHED! Well, as near as. I have to paint it, but I don't mind that and today I am anticipating a builder-free day – brilliant. I can start tidying up and Louise is coming today, so she will hoover everywhere and I can get the house back to normal-ish.

Checked out the spa prices – I could have a week in Spain for the price of one night, so that is a definite no-no. I still have my pamper day from Sue, so I might do that.

Next project – that huge deep freeze – it's got to go! Looked on the Internet yesterday – should be able to get a smaller one for a couple of hundred pounds, so may do that. I just need to get rid of that one and then I shall feel I have definitely left my house in order.

It's difficult to believe I have cancer at the moment. Everyone tells me I look well and will defy all the odds and live for years. I feel stronger than I did, still very tired sometimes, but having had 'the kitchen experience' for nearly three weeks I think it's pretty amazing that I haven't collapsed yet! (Still haven't recorded these birds and they sound fantastic this morning.) Still, that's nothing to go on. They call cancer the silent killer and until I have had a full body scan in six months we won't know the full story. I haven't lost any weight – in fact, I have put on weight. Losing weight is one of the first signs that the cancer has got hold, so as I am putting on weight I guess ET has had such a hammering from chemo and radiotherapy it's gone into a decline.

I suppose Nigel and Mo will be back from Australia soon and I have told them they can have Fletcher any time they want him after that. Such a hard decision, but it is the right decision. I'm not doing this for me, I'm doing this for Fletcher. Got to be sensible. Neither Sam nor I can manage six dogs on our own any more and Fletcher is the one I most want to settle. Think I might take them all to Hayling Island on Monday – could be the last chance. You're not allowed to take dogs on the beach after 1st May.

A and D working test tomorrow. Looking forward to getting out of here (the prison) for a day and see some friends!

Saturday, 5 a.m. – I thought I might sleep a bit longer today. It took all day to clean this house from top to bottom. Louise did upstairs and I did down – even polished the dining-room floor. Absolutely exhausting, but so much better. Just have to wait until the plaster has dried before I can finish the painting and the kitchen will be done! It does look better and hopefully it will be easier to keep clean. Next project – getting rid of that huge freezer and whitewashing the utility room! Still can't understand why I am doing all this – why should I care? Anyway, it looks as though Terry and Louise might take the old freezer away and I'm going to look on the Internet to see if I can get a small cheap one from there. I'm dreading taking that freezer out – it will be disgusting, thick with gunge and dog hair! I think my hair has stopped falling out! Sarah is picking me up at 7.45 to go to A and D test, so best not fall asleep again!

I have just looked back at the start of this journal (number 2) and the contrast between my writing then and my writing now is amazing. When I was writing in January I had theoretically given up on the chemo, but obviously my hands were very shaky and a bit all over the place; it looks pretty much like my normal handwriting now, so I'm obviously getting back on form. Perhaps when I have got this house and garden straight I will be able to start painting again, you never know. I could leave a masterpiece or two behind!

Sunday – Had a good day at the A and D working test yesterday. Completely exhausted when I got home, but thoroughly enjoyed seeing everyone. Ezio and Ellie were in great form and I was on the go all day. When I got home I could hardly move and, believe it or not, my ankles had swollen up! Why? Thought that only happened when travelling, but it's probably because it was very hot. Don't know, but they are OK today. NO BUILDERS – NOT GOING ANYWHERE – HOPEFULLY PEACEFUL DAY just pottering. Not going to rush round doing the painting or anything. Michael didn't turn up yesterday and it looks as though he is going through a rough time. His mum is ill again and has been rushed back into hospital and his dad is still terminally ill with cancer. I knew there was something wrong. It's not like Michael not to turn up.

Monday – Last day of April. Spent yesterday cleaning, washing and cooking. Didn't see anyone all day and the only person that rang was Nigel about Fletcher. I think they will probably have him sometime in June. Scary really, but I still think it is the best thing to do.

Going to take the dogs to the beach today. Feel lousy at the moment. I keep getting these sharp pains in my head and have almost convinced myself that I have now got a brain tumour. Don't feel like writing any more in this today.

Tuesday – What a fabulous morning we had at the beach. It was absolutely perfect weather and the dogs had a great time. I wished I had taken my sketchbook and a picnic – could have stayed there all day.

Bridget has adopted an orang-utan for me for my birthday – bless. She is called Sogo Sogo (Sogo for short) and they sent photographs and a certificate plus details of a trip to go and visit them. I would so love to do that, but apart from the travel insurance details (still can't get travel insurance) I just couldn't raise the £2,050 that is needed. But if I win the lottery this week? Sell one of the cars? Have I got anything worth £2,050 that I could sell? Actually, no, I don't think I have, so I had best forget that.

If I did win the lottery at this stage of my illness I don't think it would really have that much effect on me. I wouldn't want to move, but could pay ten years' rent in advance; that would be OK for Sam. He could stay here until I die and then decide what to do. He could definitely give up work and retire properly (although personally I think it would be the worst thing he could do). I could then afford to go to a health spa for a week, cruise the Med, treat the Buddies to something special and set M up in business and G if that's what she wants. Pay off S and R's mortgage and give them enough to buy whatever property they wanted. Get Bridget and Pete out of that house and his job within a week and get their flat for them. Sort Wendy out! Buy Ian a place in London, so even if he goes off travelling he will have somewhere to come back to. Pay off Claire's mortgage. Buy Wendy's flat for Neil. Get Sue and Wendy a little sports car each (and me if I'm still capable). Buy a boat – the list goes on! It would be great though. I could give most of it away as Sam and I won't need it. Just dreaming, it would make what life I have left much easier, but it isn't going to happen so . . .

Wednesday – I seem to be on some kind of a mission to clean and paint this house to perfection! Have run out of paint for the kitchen, but I'm already planning to do the utility room (for the first time in twenty years), get rid of that huge rusting deep freeze and buy a new small one. Why? Why am I doing this? How much use am I going to get from a new fridge-freezer? I really don't know. I imagine other people in my circumstances would spend what little spare money they had in going out and enjoying themselves, but I suppose I have done enough of that in the past.

Sam came home with a stash of information on this new wonder-drink (herbal) from Australia which is supposed to cure all. I'll have a look at their website, but it probably costs a fortune and the guy that sent all the information to Sam is obviously an agent from the firm touting for outlets in the UK. I'm probably totally wrong, but that's how sceptical I am.

Feeling pretty energetic although I have a bad cough since the radiotherapy, also my chest feels very tight and sometimes I get strange chest pains. I also get stabbing pains in my head just above my left eye. Imagination running riot? I don't know. I think when you have got cancer the thought that it is spreading all over your body is never very far away. If, when I have this full body scan, there is no cancer anywhere else in my body (apart from where it is already) I will be totally amazed as I am convinced it's got me somewhere else.

This time last year it was the run-up to the Game Fair and I was inundated with e-mails, phone calls, site visits, keeping the committee happy. One thing's for sure, I won't be doing Broadlands in 2010. Strange how my life has changed in nine short months. I wonder what the next nine months will bring.

JOURNAL 3

2ND MAY 2007 – 30TH SEPTEMBER 2007

Includes:

- I was going to stop writing this, but what else am I going to do at 5 a.m. when sleep is impossible?
- Organising my own funeral.
- Getting all the dogs blessed at the Pets and Gardens service in the vicarage garden. Hilarious – the volunteer to play the old Yamaha organ is aged at least ninety and wearing a headscarf. Brilliant – the dogs and cats, including one huge elderly Labrador who pulled his elderly neighbour. A little girl had a clockwork rabbit as she wasn't allowed a pet, and Fletcher was riveted to it. It was an absolute joy, just like a sketch from *The Vicar of Dibley*. Terry (our vicar) was amazing and blessed each animal individually. Afterwards there was champagne and biscuits for the humans and Bonios for the dogs. It was brilliant. I loved it and wouldn't have missed it for the world.
- Meeting Sue and Jane to go to the seaside. Yeah! Hurrah – we took all the dogs and had fish and chips on the way home. Fan-tas-tic!
- Butser Hill at its most glorious – God's country.
- Avoiding the Teletubby who was painting the house – it took forever!
- Losing count of the chest infections and mouth ulcers.
- Watching the Race for Life with my name on Sue's back.

- Fletcher being rehomed.
- *Challenge Anneka*!
- God works in mysterious ways.
- Jumping out of an aeroplane and raising £9,500 – an amazing amount of money – from really generous friends.
- Going to Tom and Louise's wedding.

JOURNAL 4

1ST OCTOBER 2007 – 12TH FEBRUARY 2008

Includes:

- A new book – a new day – raining at the moment, but it is only 5 a.m.
- My diary room uncut.
- Will I be here next year?
- Missing William's first birthday.
- Letting go of the field trials.
- E-mails from Fletcher.
- Dinner with Lord and Lady Romsey.
- All the really privileged places I have been either competing, helping, judging or having dinner, including a cocktail party at Windsor Castle; dinner at Sandringham the Guards Club (Windsor), Bolton Abbey and Blenheim Palace (twice), and lunch at Queens. I can't remember all the dates – all distant memories now – I wish I had taken notes.
- Will Gary the guinea pig outlive me?
- Have I lost a little bit more of my heart, my optimism and my enthusiasm for getting on with my life?
- Don't want to write this any more.
- ITV 'surprise' for Bridget, who was totally underwhelmed.
- Drawing-office memories.
- Gordon Ramsey.
- Struggling all our lives about money and now struggling in death with funeral costs.

- It's official – it's a bean – baby-scan photo.
- What shall I do? Shall I stop now? There is never an ending – I can't write 'THE END'.

And the last paragraph:

But that's another story and this is the end of another chapter. What will the next one bring? Something to sort out the nerve endings in my legs, I hope. My mobility worsens by the day. I just want to go for a decent walk – without any pain.

JOURNAL 5

12TH FEBRUARY 2008 – 11TH JUNE 2008

Includes:

- Major disaster – my toaster blew up.
- Els breaking her foot.
- Valentine's Day and flowers from Fletchers Freesias, Guernsey – Sam? No. Cleaver Fletcher has a new business.
- The tale of the kitten and Sam's reaction – hilarious!
- The bone-scan story with a radioactive injection and having my feet tied together.
- George Melly.
- Volunteering at Westbury House every Friday.
- Lots of photographs.
- Bone cancer?
- Applying for a Disabled Parking Badge!
- Arthritis in my spine and hips.
- Feeling closer to heaven on the top of Butser Hill.

And the last paragraph:

So, on 4th August we shall know and it will just give me something else to worry about until then – Sam thinks I don't worry about him, but I watch him get out of that truck every day and wonder just how much longer he will be able to continue. I really thought I would be dead by now, but I am still here. I am glad if, for nothing else, I can at least help Sam make this decision. Another book finished – how many more can I get through?

JOURNAL 6

11TH JUNE 2008 – 13TH NOVEMBER 2008

Includes:

- Losing the will to live, my sense of humour, my appetite, my energy.
- Gary the guinea pig.
- Is this becoming a rather dreary 'Dear Diary'?
- Sophie Louise.
- I left my heart at Melbury Cottage.
- Many photographs and memoirs.
- Resting is a most boring thing to do.
- Being an honoured guest and judge at the Blenheim Game Fair in July 2008.
- Nymph.
- Some very funny (well, to me they are) stories.
- Some very sad stories.

And the last paragraph:

It is really strange how I tend to rush around cleaning, painting, buying new lampshades etc. I am sure it is because I want everything to be spotless when I die and there will be no sorting-out for anyone to do. Why don't I just leave it as it is?

PS: Must get some new knickers and sort the underwear drawer – again!

JOURNAL 7

13TH NOVEMBER 2008 – 21ST JUNE 2009

Includes:

- A surprise helicopter landing in my garden and Michael taking me for a flight and landing for lunch.
- Not so good PET scan results.
- Refusing more chemo in January 2009.
- Being offered a new drug – Tarceva. No way.
- Puppy party, Boxing Day.
- Sam's operation.
- My referral to the hospice as a day-care patient in palliative care.
- Where is the cuckoo this year?
- Pets and Gardens service at the vicarage – all my dogs were blessed.

And the last paragraph:

They say that life is a journey, but I believe you have a choice of two paths. For me it has been a long journey – I took the long path, not the short one.

THE LAST ONE

NON OMNIS MORIAR

21ST SEPTEMBER 2010 – 5TH JULY 2011

This journal covers a long period of time and, unlike the others, is not a daily diary – just a record of significant happenings.

Today's date – 21st September 2010 – is of no great significance, but 16th September last week marked a huge milestone in my life. Four years ago, on 16th September 2006, I had my first cycle of chemo. My journals, my counsellor, my therapy, were part of my coming to terms with everything and I wrote in them almost daily, but my last entry, on 24th August 2009 – for our twenty-fifth wedding anniversary – saw me in a good place. It really was a perfect day.

The year 2010 has so far been my annus horribilis – sometimes overwhelmed with grief for friends that have died and my darling Katy and Tess also. I do still also have no fear of my own death, but ask, "Why am I still here?"

There is now an almost completely new group on Tuesdays at day care, and my initial determination not to get too closely involved with anyone else has now completely gone out of the window. I find myself so emotionally involved with some of my group it is sometimes just too much to bear. In a purely selfish way, I want to die before them so that I don't have to watch them die and suffer and experience the grief when they do.

I have been through a period of actually not wanting to go to the hospice because I am becoming so terribly emotional, not with myself but because of myself, and have been advised to make sure the day at the hospice is for my benefit and not to surround myself with the problems of others. It's too late to even attempt to distance myself now, especially from Paul, who is now a very dear friend (even though we have nothing in common and he is an avid Portsmouth football fan!). He had good scan results today and rushed to tell us at the hospice with complete and utter joy glowing from his face. Once again a reprieve, but I have grown so sceptical I wonder for how long he can keep this evil disease from destroying his body.

I cannot rid myself of the overwhelming sadness I feel. I thank God for the support and love I have. Sometimes you can relate to flies constantly banging against the same old windowpanes. They buzz around, suffer, waste away, get depressed then wonder how they got caught up in this spiral that is taking them where they don't want to go. When illness enters a home, not only does it take hold of a body, it also weaves a dark web between hearts, a web where hope is trapped and each passing day the illness and grief overwhelms your lives.

Profound thought for the day: I actually need silence. I enjoy silence because it helps me to go inwards. Anyone who is interested in something more than just life outside actually needs silence.

14th October – CT scan today – something I need to get over and done with, neatly out of the way, and then I don't have to think about anything hospital-orientated until 5th November – Bonfire Night, Danny's birthday – a significant date in many ways.

We are all prisoners of our own destiny, must confront it with the knowledge that there is no way out, and in our epilogue we must be the person we have always been deep inside, regardless of any illusions we may have nurtured in our lifetime.

26th October – Bit of a milestone – or perhaps that is not quite the right word, but I'll use it for now. I made the decision to give day care at the hospice a miss for now, so 19th October was my last day. It was Bryan's last day. He has moved to a new care home in Nether Wallop to be nearer his family, so it seemed the right day for me to end on.

Janet and John's son Keith died on Thursday at the hospice after almost four weeks suffering with a brain tumour. Janet also has cancer and John has Parkinson's. I went to church on Sunday not for one minute expecting to see either of them just three days after Keith's death, but they were there. I sat with them. John rang the bells as usual then joined us; Janet held my hand. What faith they must have. Surely they must ask the question "Is there really a God?" And yet, perhaps it is the comforting, calm peace of the Church they seek for reassurance.

22nd November – Saw Captain Chemo. He had my notes – and my scan. It was our four-year chemo anniversary and he seemed pleased with that. One can only assume that he regards me as one of his success stories. He was the man who gave me six months to live without treatment and only a sixty per cent chance of the chemo working. It certainly did a twenty per cent better job, but Dr Radio with the radical six and a half weeks' radiotherapy increased my longevity even more. My 2008 and 2010 chest scans were up on the screens and, although there is a lot of damage in both lungs from radiotherapy, the tumour is still the same. The visible change is negligible.

I intend approaching the New Year as someone *without* cancer – I have been gradually trying to cut my medication down, but I will still have to use the fentanyl patches for nerve endings.

I feel good at the moment – still get tired, but don't we all? Still unable to drive any distance, but that is the nerve endings not the cancer.

13th December – My friend Bryan died today and I felt an overwhelming grief for the friendship we had. I have never been able to give him a hug or hold his hand. The only physical thing anyone could share with Bryan was a kiss. But we had a huge bond and I shall miss talking to him and listening to his stories (and his dirty jokes). I am grateful that our lives touched and will always have a place in my heart for him.

Roger sent me an extract from a book he is reading as he said it reminded him of me! I wonder if I would have done that if I had been born in the early 1900s – probably. I like to think had I been born earlier I would have been one of those lady pilots who delivered all the Spitfires and other planes used in the Second World War to the airbases. They are hardly mentioned, but I watched a fabulous documentary on them a few months ago. Some of them are still with us today in their eighties and nineties and the interviews were splendid – really articulate, red nails and lips, and they could all remember every detail. Yep – perhaps I would have done it.

30th December 2010 – Went to Bryan's funeral today and it was not as sad as I expected. His music was played throughout and hundreds of people attended. Most of the hospice staff were there, which was a huge tribute to Bryan. It was obvious that they all loved Bryan, for them all to attend. I would imagine they attend very few patients' funerals – they would be at one daily. I sat with Gary, Paul, June and John (June's husband). Gary deteriorates daily and June is looking and obviously feeling ill.

6th January 2011 – June's test results are bad. Cancer has spread everywhere and is seriously life-threatening. This is when I am glad in a way that I have no idea what is happening inside my body.

7th January 2011 – Actually went to the Bereleigh Field Trial – Paula came and collected me. She was delighted to have me as her protégée for the day. Debbi came too and we left Sam at home dog sitting with Dolly, Harry, Indie and Cracker. It was an appalling day weather-wise, but an absolute joy to see some of my mates, especially Graham (Grizzly Adams). I am glad I went. It was good to be with Paula and Debbi. We didn't manage (or should I say *I* didn't manage?) all day. Paula took me home around 2 p.m. and then took Sam out for the rest of the day. She was in her element and had a great time. I had quite forgotten how well she always looked after me and I admit to enjoying her fussing over me.

I was quite saddened really to see the club not quite the same as it was and it was clear for me to see what the committee members had been telling me. I really cannot worry about it any more and if all the hard work to gain the status slips away then sadly I am unable to repair it. Capitulation is a serious risk and falls from my thoughts until the recipients believe they are their own thoughts and the autosuggestion is complete.

12th January 2011 – It would appear that 2011 is not going to be the year without sadness that I had hoped for. Joss had his results yesterday and they are not good. The cancer has spread also to his lungs. I hope I am wrong, but I now believe that he will die before me. June is also gravely ill and I fear the same for her.

Myself? I have stopped (or at least I am attempting to stop) feeling guilty that I am still here – 'survivor guilt' it is called. I *must* be happy that I am. I never wanted to end up a weak person. I need to celebrate the fact I am still here, not beat myself up about it.

1st February – Having been confined to barracks with pain and sickness for the past thirteen days (who's counting?) I am today going back to the hospice and I am really looking forward to it. I think the pain was my own fault and I have been feeling so well for the last few weeks, done so much, triumphantly even, that the onslaught of the pain surprised and debilitated me so quickly. Increasing my medication was necessary; now I hate where it takes my head, but when the pain completely obsesses me I have no choice. Then, with the increase, the inevitable constipation – more medication.

All that aside, I think I am feeling somewhat better although that could perhaps be excitement, adrenalin even, at the prospect of actually leaving the premises!

14th February – A year since Helen died.

19th February – Having got the pain under control again the onslaught of a chest infection ten days ago knocked me sideways and I had no other option than to take to my bed. Having seen many others debilitated, not with the cancer but with an infection, and then going on from that to die from the infection, my latest malaise filled me with fear – my time had come.

Debbi had to come and take Indie away a week ago as I couldn't even manage to take care of her. But – here we are – ten days of radical antibiotics and, believe it or not, I think I am feeling better. Once again it looks as though I am going to reach a level of recovery. Obviously I am weakened and shaken, but if I am sensible and don't rush headlong into doing stuff I will live to see another spring (does that mean I have to do all those flowerpots and baskets again?).

My GP came yesterday and gave me a good going-over – he thinks my infection is on the way out, but because of the damage in my lung from treatment he doubts that I shall stop wheezing now. Obviously, every time I have an 'episode' it weakens me. Anyway, having sat and chatted for a good half-hour (which was really great) I had him all to myself. It was lovely to hear him say how 'amazing' I was, how well I have 'dealt with the situation', how he hoped I would 'probably outlive Sam'.

His parting comment to me was "YOU ARE A TOUGH OLD BIRD!"

Charming.

Tuesday, 22nd February – Back to the hospice today and picking Indie up on the way home. Feeling better!

Saturday, 26th February – Sue and Joe back

Monday, 28th February – Today is tinged (yet again) with sadness – Gary has been admitted to the hospice and is not expected to live. Siobhan (his girlfriend) spoke to me today. She has been there 24/7 since he arrived. Day care tomorrow is going to be difficult – it's possible that Paul and myself will be able to visit Gary – Siobhan will let us know. Bless him, I pray he stops fighting and dies peacefully!

3rd March – 'Because truly being here is so much; because everything here apparently needs us, this fleeting world, which in some strange way keeps calling to us, is the most fleeting of all.' I just put this on Gary's Facebook wall. It's a quotation from the Ninth Duino Elegy, translated by Stephen Mitchell.

He is so very ill, but fighting every inch of the way. I hope I don't fight when the crunch comes. All I wish for Gary is for him to go to sleep and not wake up, but that's not what he wishes for himself.

Monday 7th – Not looking forward to the hospice tomorrow. Gary is still there and fighting. June is gravely ill.

Sunday 13th – Gary is still ill and hoping to be going home. Continuous care 24/7, hoist, completely dependent – I wouldn't want to go home. June is gravely ill, but I'm not sure she knows. It's painful to see her skeletal frame, completely unable to support or fend for herself. Paul phoned me today – in great pain. Calling out emergency services – oh, God.

14th March – Can't sleep – took loads of tablets, but my nerve endings are completely taking over. I can hardly see to write this. With the amount of tablets I have thrown down my neck I should be dead.

I'm tired, Sam's tired. I can't even go to church any more – I can't get up the hill. Carol and Ron have offered to take me to Langrish one Sunday – I may take them up on that.

> Now I lay me down to sleep
> I pray the Lord my soul to keep.
> If I should die before I wake,
> I pray the Lord my soul to take.

I remember – way back in Journal 1 – I worried about my soul. I don't worry about it any more.

I've been in quite a lot of pain recently and have resorted to upping the opiate patches – this results in me hardly being able to string a sentence together, but I am sure my body (possibly not my brain) will get used to it.

Gary, June and Paul are still deteriorating. Gary has been at home for three weeks now with twenty-four-hour care and seemingly feeling better. I don't wish him the life he has now – one room and twenty-four-hour care – but he is alive. June is gravely ill, but amazingly optimistic. I am not. She continues with hospital appointments, radiotherapy, everything they throw at her, and she clings on to a very frail existence. Paul is still having treatment. Some days he is good, some days bad, but I am convinced that he will also die before me.

I am not prepared to continue with a depressing round of hospital appointments and debilitating treatments. I would not want to risk one of my 'good days' at the hospital, especially now the sun is shining.

My GP is coming on Thursday as I have requested a 'lilac form', which he has to fill in with me. Basically, although I have already written an advanced decision to refuse treatment it now has to have a backup of this new 'lilac form' because if I had a 'turn' away from home or anything the first thing anyone would do is try and resuscitate me. I thought I already had this covered, and I do to a certain extent, but this form backs it up completely and I don't want any hiccups.

Sunday, 10th April – June died this morning at 4.40 a.m. Bless her.

Tuesday, 19th April – Went to June's funeral today. I was wrecked as soon as they started playing the entrance music, 'You Are My Sunshine, My Only Sunshine'. Apparently this was June's party piece from a very young age standing on a chair! Tracy and Babs came with us from the hospice. I'm so glad they were there to support me and Paul. John (Superman) was so brave. He read a poem – Superman to the end.

Just me and Paul now. I hope that we go together to spare each other from going through the emotions of seeing another friend's funeral.

There are a lot of new people on Tuesdays at the hospice and we try not to get involved in their lives, but it's difficult. I'm quite fond of Maureen already, but determined not to exchange addresses.

Wednesday, 27th April – Thought for the day: Wherever you go, you take yourself with you.

6th May – A year since George died.

Sixty-seven – blimey!

Message I received from Anthony (Lesley's son): 'Here's wishing you a steady and gentle remission of your illness, my prayers for your happiness and safety and all who love you. May God hold you in the palm of His hand and when it is time welcome you into His eternity where we shall join you in the blink of an eye.'

Anthony is my first reserve for my funeral service if Terry is for any reason unable to conduct it.

I had the loveliest birthday. I didn't leave the house, but I can honestly say it was the most enjoyable day.

Debbi came for Indie in the morning to take her for a 'cut and blow-dry'. Flowers arrived from Linda and Joss. Sam sent a text to say 'Happy Birthday and Love You'. Carol arrived with flowers. Liz arrived with lunch – smoked-salmon salad, very simple but delicious – and a beautiful begonia for the garden. Annie walked round with a card. Literally dozens of 'happy birthday' messages. Joe sang down the phone. Debbi came back with Indie and brought a new screen for my computer and a cake.

I always knew that I had gained respect from a lot of people over the years, but truly until today I wasn't aware of how many people loved me.

16th May – Hospice tomorrow, but going early at 2 p.m. so we can visit Gary – not looking forward to that, but . . .

Had a really busy but brilliant weekend. Walked further than I have in over a year, cleared cupboards and did garden, but it has all come to a sudden end today – tired, all energy drained. I think Paul is deteriorating quicker than me – dread to think of it, but will support him whatever. I'm convinced I am going to be the last one standing.

Let's hope we find somewhere to live before I flag too much.

24th May – Really emotional day at the hospice

Gary is in Queen Alexandra's Hospital – still dying, but clinging on to every last breath and it's tearing me and Paul apart. Please, God, just let him die.

Paul is suffering again and is booked for blood transfusions next week to be followed by yet another course of chemotherapy.

Just the two of us now amongst all these strangers and yet I still seem to defy all statistics and keep going. The grief is overwhelming, but I shall be there for as long as Paul needs me. I guess we shall be going to Gary's funeral soon – I want it to be soon. Please, don't hang on any longer, Gary. His mum and dad are exhausted. He is too young and to watch him just wither away over the past twelve months is agonising and the worst part is he is not snuggled up in comfort, dying in peace. He is fighting for every last breath he takes. Who makes the laws that euthanasia is not an option? More than anything, apart from losing people you love, it strikes fear into your heart, fear that we will deteriorate the same way June and Gary have and that we will have to watch each other die. If we are truly honest, neither one of us wants to be the last one standing.

It's a strange love and strength we have, all of us sharing the terminal illness became another 'family'. Outside of that knowledge I doubt that any of us would have been friends.

31st May – Gary is back home. Went to visit him – amazingly chipper and glad to be back – in his own words: Gary 2 – Grim Reaper 0.

1st June – Paul was too weak to visit Gary with me yesterday. Today he phoned me to say the hospital rang with his scan results, which he didn't expect for a couple of weeks. He already has cancer in his liver and kidneys, but now it is in his bones, his hips and his spine. He told me before he told Michaela – she was still asleep. He had to go straight to the hospital today and in one day has seen his oncologist and been tattooed in a set-up for radiotherapy. He starts radiotherapy tomorrow. That's fast track for you. I already know that this may gain him a little time, but in my heart I don't think it will be much. God, I pray I can be strong for him. I let Gary know on Facebook today and, bless him, he texted Paul with words of encouragement (Gary doesn't usually send texts). I must still be here for a reason – that's what Sam said when I told him this evening. And the reason is?

5th June – Indie, Dolly and Harry were blessed today! At the Pets and Gardens service in the vicarage garden.

7th June – I picked this up as it usually helps. Today I find I have lost the ability to express how I am feeling. Time is not in any way a commodity of which anyone has an infinite supply.

16th June 2011 – Janet, my friend from church whose son Keith died last year, died yesterday – another funeral to go to next week.

June would have been seventy tomorrow.

Paul is gravely ill.

I have a cold which will inevitably go to my chest and the most scary thing is today I have been coughing up blood – and that's where it all began.

Gary is still with us.

Will I get frightened and grasp at straws? Accept palliative chemo? I like to think not, but the prospect of how long it will take me to die and in how much pain is daunting.

I watched a programme on Terry Pratchett about Dignitas – the society based in Switzerland that offers 'assisted death'. It was the sort of programme you get halfway through and only watch the rest out of morbid curiosity. It actually showed the whole process – an extremely well-to-do couple where the husband has a diagnosis of motor neurone disease and decided to organise his own death before he got to the debilitating state the disease leaves you in. In a little 'blue hut' on an industrial site with the mountains over the top as these buildings are not allowed (understandably) in a residential area. The 'hut' contains two apartments with single beds, a small dining table and chairs with a fruit bowl and chocolates (which apparently take away the taste of the poison you are required to swallow). You watch him do it and his wife – perfectly coiffured complete with pearls and earrings – strokes his hand, not even lying on the bed, sitting on the sofa. He swallows the poison, chews a chocolate, gasps for water – the German assistant tells him he can't have water – then he falls asleep, snores, then dies. It was positively ghastly – only the Germans could be that clinical.

As for assisted dying – that's a different thing and I can quite understand a loved one helping with an overdose, but I sincerely hope it never becomes legal in this country.

Monday, 27th – Gary died early this morning, peacefully.

6 p.m. – Paul has been taken into hospital.

Wednesday 29th – Paul has been given just weeks to live and is being transferred to the hospice.

When I come to the end of the road
And the sun has set for me
I want no tears in a gloom-filled room
Why cry for a soul set free?

Miss me a little – but not for long
And not with your head bowed low
Remember the love that we once shared
Miss me – but let me go.

For this is a journey we all must take
And each must go alone
It's all a part of the Master's plan
A step on the road to home.

When you are lonely and sick of heart
Go to your friends that we know
And bury your sorrows in doing good works
Miss me – but let me go.

Author unknown

Tuesday, 5th July – Paul died today at 4 p.m.

The events of today were so extraordinary that I cannot, without launching forth into insignificant rambles, find the right words to describe it. Suffice it to say that I was included in the family circle and it was a privilege. They were all convinced that Paul had been waiting to say goodbye to me before he let go. I did have a quiet ten minutes with him; I did tell him he could go now and how much we all loved him. He died just a couple of hours after.

8th July – I feel like a rock on the beach when the tide had gone out.

EPILOGUE

There is no end to this story – yet.